THE CLOSET

The
CLOSET

The Eighteenth-Century Architecture *of* Intimacy

DANIELLE BOBKER

PRINCETON UNIVERSITY PRESS
PRINCETON AND OXFORD

PUBLISHED BY PRINCETON UNIVERSITY PRESS
41 William Street, Princeton, New Jersey 08540
6 Oxford Street, Woodstock, Oxfordshire OX20 1TR

press.princeton.edu

ISBN 9780691198231
ISBN (e-book) 9780691201542

British Library Cataloging-in-Publication Data is available

Editorial: Anne Savarese and Jenny Tan
Production Editorial: Natalie Baan
Text and Jacket Design: Chris Ferrante
Production: Danielle Amatucci
Publicity: Katie Lewis and Alyssa Sanford
Copyeditor: Annalisa Zox-Weaver

Jacket image: James Stephanoff, *The Queen's Closet, Kensington Palace*, 1819.
From W.H. Pyne, *The History of the Royal Residences of Windsor Castle, St. James's Palace,
Carlton House, Kensington Palace, Hampton Court, Buckingham House, and Frogmore*, 1819.
The Miriam and Ira D. Wallach Division of Art, Prints, and Photographs:
Art & Architecture Collection, The New York Public Library

This book has been composed in Baskerville Pro

Printed on acid-free paper. ∞

PRINTED IN THE UNITED STATES OF AMERICA

1 3 5 7 9 10 8 6 4 2

CONTENTS

ILLUSTRATIONS

PREFACE

In the seventeenth and eighteenth centuries, *intimacy* was roughly inter-changeable with *conversation* and *intercourse*, words whose meanings have since narrowed considerably. Intercourse then defined a range of verbal, sexual, commercial, and spiritual transactions, and could also refer to an architectural space, a passageway or entrance. Conversation originally denoted what we might now call co-presence, the "action of ... having one's being *in* a place or *among* persons."[1] It was an embodied relation—hence *criminal conversation*, the legal term for adultery in the period. Con-tinuing to draw together many forms of physical, cognitive, and emo-tional proximity, intimacy holds the past in relation to the present much more fully than intercourse or conversation—or than *sexuality*, a category invented by psychologists in the nineteenth century that promises to strip us down, scientifically, to one central itch. For some academics and activists, the word *queer* has recently become a comprehensive qualifier for myriad historically underrecognized desires and experiences, espe-cially those at odds with social or legal norms.[2] The expansiveness of intimacy accommodates such queerness too.

Despite the promising resonance and reach of intimacy, however, our histories of interpersonal feeling have tended to visit and revisit the in-stitutionalized and conventionalized relationships and identities that we can most readily name, especially those linked to marriage and the fam-ily. Expressly seeking to explore some of the less familiar, less familial, and generally more fleeting attachments of the eighteenth century, *The Closet* approaches the category of intimacy from the outside in, as it were, by way of the period's most desirable rooms. Looking particularly, though not exclusively, at the long moment of the closet's proliferation in British households and British writing from around the time of the Restoration, when Samuel Pepys encountered the extravagant new culture of intimacy at Charles II's court, until just over a century later, when closets (and texts called closets) were everywhere, this book argues that these spaces framed and probed the shifting boundaries of social experience—not least of all, the strangely virtual relationships produced by the burgeoning market for printed books in this period.

In material culture, closets were remarkably resilient in the face of substantial changes to British social structure over more than two hundred years. The English closet had important origins in sixteenth-century palace apartments designed in enfilade. The lockable room at the end of a series of adjoining chambers provided a secluded place for reading, writing, and storing valuables. It was therefore private in the general intuitive sense of the word. Because it accommodated the shifting alliances on which absolutist politics depended, however, the closet was a channel of traditional public power as well. Admission to the closet, unlike most other parts of the court, depended only on the approval of the royal owner or her proxy, and the criteria for admission were necessarily opaque. Courtiers who had already been appointed special roles could be invited in, but so too might random petitioners from remote regions of the city or beyond. A breeding ground of secrecy, the closet gave a distinctive charge to the experience of proximity. Architecturally speaking, it was a marginal space. Yet the room itself and the bonds it afforded were crucial to early modern politics and culture.

Minimally requiring nothing more than four walls and a door, closets thrived for the next two centuries. As the power and influence of the monarchy gradually fell away, closets proved temptingly simple to redesign and reconceive. In the houses of the nobility and gentry and, increasingly, of merchants and traders, corner rooms and antechambers were styled as studies, prayer closets, curiosity cabinets, dressing rooms, libraries, galleries, impromptu bedrooms, or several of these at once. Merging with the bath or the privy, such rooms also gave rise to bathing closets, water closets, and earth closets or outhouses. In these new iterations, as in their courtly ones, closets remained potentially interactive spaces where physical closeness, or the exchange of knowledge, or both, heightened a sense of connection between occupants.

At the same time, closets multiplied in all kinds of writing. The detailed representation of everyday interiors would not become a literary convention until the nineteenth century, but closets were the settings that writers wrote about before they wrote about settings as such.[3] With royal roots yet endlessly reworkable, they appealed to authors of all stripes grappling with a changing social and political landscape, not least the changes to their own relationships with readers, as the commercial trade in publishing grew. On the one hand, the erosion of divine right and of scribal tradition—the practice of copying texts by hand—led authors to question, or long for, patronage or favoritism, the established bonds of the closet. On the other hand, the proliferation of closets far beyond the court gave rise to new kinds of connections, including those now known as voyeurism and stranger relations, which were intriguing in themselves, and as models for the anonymous bonds between authors and readers of print. Thus the eighteenth century saw the development of a wide-ranging rhetoric of closet intimacy that at once looked back to elitist social arrangements and forward to a democratic paradigm that presumed people could and should feel connected to one another, regardless of the socioeconomic differences or geographical distances between them.

The Closet builds this argument most directly through close readings of fictional and historical intimate encounters as informed by early modern and eighteenth-century histories of architecture and material culture, politics and sociability, genre and media. Chapter 1 lays the broad historical and conceptual foundations for the focused explorations to follow. While scholarly interest in domestic privacy and modern selfhood has overshadowed the closet's origins as a site of politicized intimacy and its flexibility as a locus of interpersonal relations in eighteenth-century Britain, scholarly interest in the emergence of democratic social feelings has generally directed attention away from the closet altogether, toward more obviously heterogeneous scenes of sociability like the coffee house. Exposing and preparing to fill these gaps, the introductory chapter considers the closet's peculiar aptness as a setting and symbol of social transition. Widely recognized as a place where reciprocal feelings could flourish against a backdrop of rigid status distinctions, the closet revealed not only how exhilarating, but also just how uncomfortable the new processes and prospects of inclusion could be.

The four following chapters trace a loose chronology. Chapters 2 and 3 take up texts from the first half of the eighteenth century explicitly written for manuscript circulation. Chapter 2 looks at the courtly closet alliances in *Memoirs of Count Grammont* by the Anglo-Irish nobleman Anthony Hamilton, with particular attention to a seduction scene set in the Duchess of York's bathing closet. In many respects, the setting of Hamilton's longest intrigue shores up the elitism of his retrospective secret history by situating homoerotic desire within a tradition of competitive favoritism at Charles II's court that he clearly admires. At the same time, evoking despotic excess, the bathing closet stands as Hamilton's reluctant acknowledgment that English absolutism, manuscript culture, and their unique modes of power-soaked intimacy are in fact on the decline. Indeed, as the memoir itself soon made its way into print, Hamilton inadvertently helped to launch a model of author-reader relations as a kind of inclusive virtual favoritism.

Chapter 3 offers a new view of Jonathan Swift's much-discussed "excremental vision" by approaching it not as a personal quirk or neurotic symptom so much as a prescient critique of the excretory autonomy that flushable water closets would soon come to embody. Country-house poets had traditionally celebrated abundant fields and communal feasts in the great hall as signs of the patron's generosity. In his mock country-house poem "Panegyric on the Dean," Swift imagines the pair of his-and-hers privies that he himself had built on Lord and Lady Acheson's country estate as the antitype of such places. At odds with natural cycles of regeneration and feudal hospitality, they send the mind in and down, away from the earth, the cosmos, and other people, in a burlesque of closet prayer. Intertwined with this material-cultural satire is an act of resistance to the print market that had by then already made Swift famous. By casting Lady Acheson as the speaker in his first scatological poem, Swift tries to preempt his patroness's desire to circulate the poem-gift made exclusively for her and thereby to situate the poem, and their relationship, more squarely within older paradigms of literary patronage and literary exchange.

Whereas, for Hamilton and Swift, closets can still represent the highly circumscribed sociability associated with the face-to-face exchange of handwritten manuscripts, chapter 4 shows that, far more often in the period, closets served efforts to establish the value of printed knowledge and to justify its wide commercial distribution. The book's appendix, "Closets without Walls," lists the more than two hundred books designated as closets or cabinets, and often qualified as broken open or unlocked, that had been published in Britain by the end of the eighteenth century. As the authors and editors of these printed closets and cabinets nervously underscored their own close connections to courtly closets, prayer closets, and elite cabinets of curiosity, they implicitly positioned their readers as illegitimate intruders or spies. These complex dynamics of partial inclusion are directly addressed in a particularly self-reflexive instance of the form called *Miss C——y's Cabinet of Curiosities; or, the Green Room Broke Open*. While literary historians have already considered closet voyeurism in relation to aesthetics, philosophy, and the new science, this chapter emphasizes that this one-way mode of visual intimacy also channeled the excitement and the social disorientation accompanying the increasing accessibility of knowledge in the eighteenth century.

A radical strand of eighteenth-century print-cultural rhetoric rejected the personal room, picturing it as the twisted heart of a stagnant manuscript culture, a site of solipsism and secrecy that could only inhibit the modern drive toward sharing feelings and ideas. Chapter 5 considers the original spin that Laurence Sterne put on this trope in *A Sentimental Journey*, the semifictional travelogue that he wrote in a flush of pleasure from the international success of his first novel *Tristram Shandy*. Since the seventeenth century, coaches had sometimes been characterized as "moving closets." As the carriage trade and infrastructures grew rapidly throughout the eighteenth century, more and more strangers now found themselves sitting face-to-face for hours, or even days, at a time, as they traveled together. Whereas previous writers of the period had tended to represent enforced mingling in carriages as a source of social anxiety, in *A Sentimental Journey* Sterne layers closet and carriage symbolism to celebrate a small post-chaise called the vis-à-vis as the ideal vehicle of intimacy between strangers, both in person and on the printed page, and as the ideal emblem of the unprecedented social potentials of mass communication.

Together the four central chapters provide an account of closets and closet rhetoric spreading, from manuscript to print, from the court to the streets, fueling fantasies of universal access along the way. The owners of the spaces featured in the chapters—a duchess, a lady, an actress, and a parson, respectively—chart a movement down the social ladder that encapsulates this central arc. As the architecture of intimacy became increasingly desirable and increasingly available across the social spectrum, questions about whom to get close to, and how, intensified, and the answers inevitably changed. Throughout *The Closet*, the secret history, the original genre of exposure of courtly closet affairs, proves as resilient as the room itself. Yet many of the featured texts adapt the conventions of secret history to signal not only the benefits but also the risks associated with alliances formed at the borders of family life. Thus despite its broadly progressive momentum, *The Closet* also demonstrates that the eighteenth-century architecture of intimacy continually routed a good deal of psychic resistance to the very possibilities of letting go of or redistributing *noblesse oblige*, of virtual access—of democratic feeling—that it helped to manifest. Change is complicated.

Moreover, the structure of this book aims to make room for many other historical and narrative patterns, relationships, voices, and anecdotes. In this respect, it is less a developmental story than a set of collections.

The featured literary texts in the four central chapters have been selected both for their similarities and continuities, and for their distinctiveness from one another. Each one brings into view a different kind of closet, a different kind of intimate bond, a different literary form, and different engagements with the medium of print. By reading a featured text along-side many other texts, obscure and canonical, visual and verbal alike, each chapter considers many histories that intersect with and inform that of the eighteenth-century closet: that of the Turkish hammam, the water closet, the camera obscura, and the museum, among others. These multiple strands make it possible to assemble a lexicon of intimacy that encompasses the evolving connotations and denotations of the word *closet* along with those of many related terms, such as *cabinet, green room, peeping Tom, privy, secretary, seraglio,* and *vis-à-vis,* to name just a few.

Minor threads produce further points of tension and convergence between the chapters. The juxtaposition of chapters 2 and 3 reveals that the histories of the bathing closet and the water closet, though both concerned with cleanliness and plumbing, unfurl—and often loiter—across very different time lines and may evoke very different social milieus (the court or the country) and cultural associations (orientalism or pastoralism). Closet prayer's extensive hold over the intimate imagination is revealed through its depiction as a form of erotic favoritism in chapter 2, as a practice for the privy in chapter 3, and as a source of spiritual insights to be immortalized in print in chapter 4. Recurring international perspectives situate the rise of British closet culture within larger political dynamics. Reflecting Britain's colonial rule of Ireland throughout the eighteenth century, the strong Anglo-Irish presence in the book—Hamilton, Swift, the Achesons, Sterne—suggests that this liminal national identity fostered an acute awareness of the vagaries of power in the closet as elsewhere. The book also repeatedly looks to France and its enduring status as the object of what we might call British closet envy. King Charles's redesign of the Whitehall Palace bathrooms, discussed in chapter 2, the influence of the boudoir, discussed in chapter 4, and Sterne's alter ego's daydreams about the closets at Versailles, discussed in chapter 5, evince a long-standing British fascination with Bourbon etiquette and the baroque architecture that elaborated it. (Parson Yorick is so *enchanté* that he forgets that England is at war with France when he travels there.)

Given Laurence Sterne's pointed formal engagement with physical spaces, and the thoughts, feelings, and real and virtual relationships to which they give rise, it's fitting that not only Sterne but also an imitator who called himself "Tristram Shandy," after the protagonist and narrator of Sterne's first novel, occupy prominent places near the end of this study. Other recurring authors suggest different through lines. Feminist satirist Delarivier Manley attends to the sexual politics of proximity just as sharply in her *Stagecoach Journey to Exeter*, a domestic travelogue, as in her *New Atalantis*, an allegorical secret history of the English court brimming with scenes of closet decadence. The Elizabethan gentleman of letters Sir John Harington may have been the early modern period's greatest closet enthusiast. Composer of an early poem set in a lady's cabinet, disciplined practitioner of private prayer, inventor of England's first flushable privy, he is one of *The Closet*'s primary representatives of the discourse of privacy inherited by eighteenth-century British writers.

The author who appears at the most regular intervals is the renowned English diarist Samuel Pepys. Writing in his journal almost daily, generally in one of his closets, between 1660 and 1669 as his administrative career in the Royal Navy was taking off, Pepys composes something like a secret history of his own everyday life, in which events, people, places, and things become noteworthy to the extent that they have become objects of or obstacles to his desires, his ambitions, or—in the case of sex—his predatory addiction. Five preludes, appearing before each of the main chapters, showcase Pepys as the period's most vociferous and prolific known recorder of closet conversations. Each prelude introduces a facet of closet culture that the chapter to follow examines in another context and across a longer historical span. Thus the first prelude about Pepys's obsessions with closet connections leads into chapter 1's argument concerning the historical and theoretical significance of closet intimacy, the second prelude about Pepys's mixed feelings with regard to giving and receiving favor leads to chapter 2 on the decline of court favoritism, the third prelude about how Pepys negotiates waste removal with his neighbors leads to the more substantial exploration of privy intimacy in chapter 3, and so on. As Pepys discriminates, sometimes consciously, often not, between those courtly manners that he wants to emulate and those that he does not or, as the son of a tailor, fears he cannot, his journal registers fault lines in closet relations, especially vis-à-vis status, that would be further fractured or inventively bridged as the culture and rhetoric of the closet became more widely dispersed in the century to follow. Some of these fault lines are directly addressed in the subsequent chapters, while others remain implicit. Pepys's diary represents the only text in *The Closet* that eluded mass mediation throughout the entire eighteenth century. It is "mighty pretty," as Pepys might say, to ponder how Pepys's own entanglements in and with intimate architecture were nevertheless helping to create the social conditions that would propel the journal's journey from manuscript to print more than a hundred years (and some of it not until well over two hundred years) after his death.

As the five preludes find eighteenth-century closet culture and closet rhetoric foreshadowed in the mid-seventeenth century, so the book's coda contemplates their aftereffects within the latest coming-out narratives, bringing together two topical undercurrents of *The Closet* as whole. The first undercurrent has to do with sexual minorities. The fact that closet relations were often queer in the broadest contemporary sense, insofar as they were homoerotic, fetishistic, intense, hyper-self-conscious, or virtual, is simply a thrum throughout most of the book, which deliberately holds a space between past modes of relating and our own. (Indeed, chapter 2 proposes that, given our current metaphor for queer and trans shame, it takes a special effort to notice just how socially and politically empowering the homoeroticism of the eighteenth-century courtly closet could be.) The second undercurrent has to do with twenty-first-century media shift. Though the parallels between current and past forms of mass mediation are only briefly discussed when print and digital voyeurism are compared near the end of chapter 4, the social wishes and worries of our own hypermediated age also run as a pulse throughout the book. The coda traces a genealogy of the closeted/out opposition from its origins in early print culture through the Stonewall Riots and on to twenty-first-century coming-out stories, arguing that eighteenth-century aspirations to mediated intimacy, though largely dormant in the language of the closet for two centuries, have acquired new relevance in the now widely accepted view that queer and trans recognition in fact depends on mass mediation. Whereas queer theorists have already shown the closet's limitations and liabilities as a metaphor for the privacy and invisibility of sexual minorities, the eighteenth-century rhetoric of closet intimacy illuminates the central role sexual minorities have come to play in current commercial aspirations to virtual public feeling.

It's hard to name an eighteenth-century text that doesn't make reference to an intimate space of one sort or another. Although this book surveys a range of genres of seventeenth- and eighteenth-century British writing, it is by no means exhaustive. Novels by Eliza Haywood, John Cleland, Henry Fielding, and Ann Radcliffe might well have made significant appearances. *Clarissa* and *Pamela* could have shown up much more often. And though chapter 5 pursues coach sociability across more than a dozen works, there are a great many other eighteenth-century narratives whose plots turn on close encounters in moving closets. In *The Expedition of Humphrey Clinker*, for instance, Tobias Smollett envisions the Bramble family as a diverse group of strangers who can nevertheless learn to get along in part thanks to their time spent together in a carriage. In Frances Burney's *Evelina*, the young heroine and her gauche grandmother continually depend on the kindness of men with carriages, a combination of properties that is apparently all too hard to come by. Closets appear as seemingly circumstantial details in all kinds of poetry, drama, and essays as well, such as when in *The Way of the World* Millimant demands "to have my closet inviolate" as a proviso of her marriage contract, or when a reader from York hand delivers a letter to Mr. Spectator's closet.[4] In such instances, too, closets should draw our attention to the shifting conditions under which knowledge, power, and writing are exchanged, as the court and manuscript culture lose their hold over the British social imaginary. Furthermore, as the chapters' multiple epigraphs intend to suggest, the issues raised by the eighteenth-century architecture of intimacy continue to reach across the disciplines and beyond academic discourse altogether. The book's layered and serial structure stands, finally, as both an acknowledgment of its own partiality as well as an invitation: here and elsewhere, there are still so many doors to be opened, connections to be made.

Rooms for improvement

Samuel Pepys's father was a tailor, but his cousin Edward Montagu, named Earl of Sandwich after the Restoration, had used his influence at court to get Pepys a clerkship in the Royal Navy. As his administrative career advanced throughout the 1660s, Pepys increasingly had the desire and the means to renovate and redecorate, and his closets were often singled out.[1] That the navy owned Pepys's office on Seething Lane in the City of London as well as the house across its courtyard that he shared with his wife, Elizabeth, and their few servants did not curb his appetite for improvements in both places, especially not after he learned that navy carpenters, known as joiners, would take care of structural changes, and the costs would be covered by the king.[2]

At first, Pepys's main closet was on the second story of the house. After an extra story was added, at navy expense, in the summer of 1662, there was another closet off the couple's new third-floor bedroom that officially belonged to his wife, though Pepys sometimes used it as well. A third closet adjoined his office. These rooms were always on his mind, and with the help of numerous tradespeople, they were always changing. As the house's extra floor was being built, Pepys arranged for a door opening to the roof to be added to Elizabeth's closet, working hard to convince his neighbor, who was already angry about the extra space that the additional floor was taking up, that he and his family would not make "a through-faire" of the new terrace.[3] Joiners laid moldings in the office closet in August 1663.[4] The upper closet was refreshed that autumn: a chimneypiece was installed, walls were painted. To the "great content" of her budget-conscious husband, Elizabeth put up the hangings herself.[5] A joiner returned to the office closet the next spring to move the door and alter "several other things," and then again the following summer to mount some "neat" decorative plates Pepys had commissioned.[6]

In the summer of 1666, Pepys set up his principal closet in the former music room and hired upholsterers to cover the walls in a dark fabric. He had picked out the color himself but soon doubted his choice: "I ... fear my purple will be too sad for that melancholy room."[7] After the serge was up and everything was in order, he still wasn't sure: "I think that it will be as noble a closet as any man hath ...," he writes, "though, indeed, it would be better to have had a little more light."[8] He immediately set out to "break open a window to the leads-side" in the old closet, "which will enlighten the room mightily."[9] Nine months later, he went to the New Exchange "to consult about covering the wall in my closet over my chimney, which is darkish, with looking-glasses," but he must have decided against the idea since he doesn't mention it again.[10] However, he did hire glaziers in the winter of 1667 to enlarge the window in his office closet.[11] Notwithstanding his pleasure at her original DIY attempt, Elizabeth's closet was professionally reupholstered in the winter of 1668, perhaps with the "fine counterfeit damasks to hang my wife's closett," whose expensive "uselessness" had preoccupied Pepys one evening a couple of years before.[12]

Pepys knew how obsessed he could become. "With my head full of the business of the closet, home to bed. And strange it is to think how building doth fill my mind and put out all other things out of my thoughts," he reflects in the middle of one of the renovations, and in the middle of another, "So to the office, and then home about one thing or other about my new closet, for my mind is full of nothing but that."[13] Sometimes he projects the concern onto Elizabeth: "my poor wife, who works all day at home like a horse."[14] But Pepys's investment of time, money, and emotional energy is not really "strange," as he puts it, given the very evident value of closets in the elite circles he moves in.

He noticed how this space heightened the experience of contact during his frequent visits to Whitehall Palace. Before weekly meetings with the Duke of York, who was lord high admiral of the Royal Navy, Pepys and his colleagues would wait in one of the outer chambers of his apartment while the duke dressed or finished prior business. Then the duke would greet them and escort them back to his personal room.[15] Pepys recognized the importance of his performance in this setting—was pleased when his meticulous record-keeping and managerial insights allowed him to shine, and only occasionally disappointed when the topic of conversation moved beyond his areas of expertise.[16] He registered the distinctive informality of some of these conversations, noting in his journal when he observed that "in his night habitt [the duke] is a very plain man" or when the duke dropped the planned agenda to tease him about his love of fashion or inquire about his eyes.[17] Even when the navy meetings were held in noble closets outside of Whitehall, the small talk might be worth mentioning.[18] After some "discourse of business" in the closet of the administrator Sir Robert Long, the "large, and pleasant" conversation turns to "the plenty of partridges in France," and how Louis XIV and his company at Versailles "killed with their guns, 300 and odd ... at one bout."[19]

Especially as his career advanced and the navy came under increased scrutiny, Pepys was sometimes called before the King's Cabinet, the group of Charles's most trusted advisers named for the room, from the French word for closet, where they most often met.[20] Before the cabinet, Pepys took special care to read signs of the ebbs and flows of favor, knowing that those closest to Charles could determine the security of his own position. The stakes of his performance were even higher here than in the duke's closet, and on at least one occasion the king's summons took him by surprise and Pepys found himself scrambling to organize his thoughts.[21]

By 1663—the same year that he overhauled Elizabeth's closet, added moldings to the office space, and bought himself a wig—Pepys began receiving guests in his own private rooms. As among the royalty and aristocracy, alliances were forged and sealed in his closets too, sometimes by way of elevated conversation, sometimes by way of riskier exchanges.[22] It was during a meeting in his closet at home that Pepys was first assured of his good reputation: "This morning Mr. Cutter came and sat in my closet half an hour with me; his discourse very excellent, being a wise man, and I do perceive by him ... that my diligence is taken notice of in the world, for which I bless God and hope to continue doing so."[23] After Pepys helped a former rival secure a post in the navy, he received the anticipated kickback in his closet: "Thence home and Creed with me, and there he took occasion to owne his obligations to me, and did lay down twenty pieces in gold upon my shelf in my closet, which I did not refuse, but wish and expected should have been more."[24]

Just as Pepys recognized that his appearances in elite closets were especially subject to evaluation, he assessed his guests' merits on their performances in his. Of his reception of John Spong, who had recently begun making and selling optical instruments, Pepys writes, for example, "After dinner, to my closet, where abundance of mighty pretty discourse; wherein, in a word, I find him the man of the world that hath of his own ingenuity obtained the most in most things, being withal no scholler."[25] Similarly, when entertaining the actor John Harris, he writes, "Harris I first took to my closet; and I find him a very curious and understanding person in all pictures and other things—and a man of fine conversation."[26] Even as host, Pepys often felt he needed to prove himself too, such as when Sir William Warren, a timber merchant, visited his closet to talk about measuring wood for shipbuilding: "I made him see that I could understand the matter well, and did both learn of and teach him something."[27] When Sir William Coventry dropped by unexpectedly, Pepys was "not displease[d]" with the opportunity to show off his newly reorganized closet.[28]

The things people kept in their closets were nearly as telling to Pepys as what they said in them. Whatever the state of the house, whatever the rank of the owner, there might be something worth looking at in the most private rooms. A closet tour by a spouse or servant wasn't quite as much an honor as having been invited in by the owner, but it was often very interesting in a different way. Sometimes Pepys praises the overall impression of the room: the Queen Mother's chamber and closet at Somerset House are "most beautiful places for furniture and pictures," and the whole of Lady Smith's closet is "very fine."[29] More often, he exercises a discerning eye, commenting only on striking objects. In Lady Batten's closet he finds that in particular the execution chair, in which "he that sits down is catched with two irons, that come round about him," "makes good sport."[30] In January 1663, the perspective painting in Thomas Povey's closet is at the top of Pepys's list of the admirable features of his colleague's house, and he makes a point of looking at Povey's art again and again on subsequent visits (figure 1).[31] On his fourth visit to the closet belonging to Mrs. Pierce, wife of the royal surgeon, Pepys takes note of a shoddy portrait of the duke.[32] Pepys brought to closet viewings a set of assumptions about what he was likely to see, based on the owner's rank and character. Except for the "fine modells of ships in it," Commissioner Pett's closet "came short of what [he] expected."[33] In Sir Philip Carteret's closet, on the other hand, Pepys observes, "beyond expectation, I do find many pretty things," including "ingenious" paintings, drawings, and watches made by Carteret, which are themselves "above my expectation."[34]

At times Pepys is tempted to correlate a collection with the owner's other personal qualities. His changing impressions of Charles's closet, for example, at first reflect Pepys's declining estimation of the king. During an initial visit, when his clerkship in the navy is still very new, Pepys is awed by the lifelike pictures he sees there: "Among the rest, a book open

FIG. 1. Pepys admired the perspective paintings in Thomas Povey's closet, like this one by the Dutch painter Samuel van Hoogstraten, and kept going back to look at them. (Samuel van Hoogstraten, *A View through a House*, 1662. Oil on canvas. Dyrham, Gloucestershire. © National Trust. Reproduced by permission.)

upon a deske which I durst have sworn was a reall book."[35] In 1663, Pepys records gossip that the king had procured for his closet a stillborn fetus that had been "dropped at the ball at Court," which he later dissected, as well as two or three stones—"very heavy, and in the middle of each of them either a piece of iron or wood"—that had been voided by one of the royal horses.[36] Upon visiting the king's private room during this same year, the multitude of "pictures, and other things of value and rarity" overwhelms Pepys: "I was properly confounded and enjoyed no pleasure in the sight of them—which is the only time in my life that ever I was so at a loss for pleasure, in the greatest plenty of objects to give it me."[37] The chaos seems to encapsulate the king's self-indulgence that Pepys decries elsewhere in the diary. Yet, in his record of a visit four years later, Pepys sees more "brave pictures" by "the best hands," and calls the closet a "very noble place" despite the fact that he is otherwise quite critical of Charles.[38] Ultimately, style was separate from other qualities, and could be evaluated on its own terms. After not having seen Mrs. Pierce for "many months," Pepys notes that she "holds her complexion still; but in everything else, even in this her new house and the best rooms in it and her closet, which her husband with some vainglory took me to show me, she continues the veriest slattern that ever I knew in my life."[39] Pepys grew confident enough in his own preferences to resist the pressure of others' judgments. He had admired the unusual round desk Sir Coventry had invented for his closet, whose central opening allowed him and his secretary to work together surrounded by papers and books. After Coventry was suspected of corruption and briefly fell from royal favor, he and his table were mocked in a play, but Pepys thought the satire was foolish.[40]

Closet intimacies were not always easy or pleasant, particularly not when the relative status of the parties involved was unclear, as Pepys's fraught relationship with Abigail Williams demonstrates. Abigail Williams was the mistress of Lord Brouncker, a nobleman and Pepys's close colleague. Like others in his navy circle, Pepys disapproved of their arrangement, of how she dared to "fallow him ... wherever he goes and kiss and use him publicly," and secretly called her a whore.[41] But Pepys regularly socialized with Lord Brouncker, and thus went to Williams's lodgings quite often over a two-year period. He had no trouble separating his assessments of her taste and her worth when she first showed him her closet: "Endeed a great many fine things there are, but the woman I hate."[42] He refused to offer Williams the hospitality that would have been expected of him had she and Lord Brouncker been married, and Williams noticed and took issue with Pepys's unwillingness to reciprocate. By August 1666, the tension had become outright antagonism. Pepys heard rumors that "Mrs Williams ... doth speak mighty hardly of me for my not treating them and not giving her something to her closet."[43]

Williams's awareness of Pepys's own transgressions made things worse for him. Following an afternoon at the theater, Pepys had planned to spend the evening in the company of the actress Elizabeth Knepp, who had called to him at the end of the play, but found himself "forced to step to" Mrs. Williams's lodgings with Lord Brouncker. Pepys soon left "for fear of [Williams] shewing me her closet, and thereby forcing me to give her something." Disgust at the prospect of further intimacies with and obligations to his colleague's mistress was compounded by "fear of my wife's coming home before me," so, Pepys writes, "I was forced to go straight home, which troubled me."[44] Three times in this entry Pepys feels himself "forced" to do things, as though Williams and his wife have conspired to foreclose the possibility of his date with Knepp. Nine months later, he was still running into Williams from time to time, and still worried about what she might ask him for. After dining with Lord Brouncker at her lodgings, he found no way to refuse her offer to chat in private: "She did show me her closet; which I was very sorry to see, for fear of her expecting something from me; and here she took notice of my wife's not once coming to see her; which I am glad of, for she shall not."[45] Perhaps realizing that she was never going to get anything from him anyway, Williams scolded him again.

Pepys was aware of how prominent a place these rooms played in the gift economy of the uppermost echelons of society as well as among his colleagues, some of whom were, like him, not of high birth. An invitation into a closet was itself understood to be a privilege, and so, like the other generous gestures that might accompany such invitations, it was often commemorated and reciprocated by a present from the invitee to the closet owner—something that, ideally, the owner would then display in her closet as a pleasing reminder of their time alone together and the mutual benefits of their alliance. On Pepys's first visit to the king's closet, he had witnessed the delivery of a gift from his cousin: a "great iron chest" that Lord Sandwich gave in recognition of many obligations to Charles, including his own title and the new post for Pepys.[46] At an early meeting in the Duke of York's closet, he observed "two very fine chests, covered with gold and Indian varnish, given him by the East India Company of Holland."[47] In his capacity as a navy accounts man, Pepys and his wife received objects ideal for closet display, including a "very fine" alabaster bust of St. George from Elizabeth Russell, a widowed ship's chandler, and "a pretty Cabinet" from John Shales, who supplied food to navy ships.[48] As his confidence in his own taste developed, Pepys also bought things for their closets, among them: another wooden cabinet, a silver snuff-dish, a copying instrument known as a parallelogram, two iron chests for storing valuables, maps, decorative plates, and many pictures for the walls, including a perspective painting like those he had admired at Thomas Povey's house.[49] Pepys also exhibited, in a custom-made storage case, the tennis-ball-sized stone that he had had surgically removed from his own bladder.[50] As textual collectibles, books were in a category of their own. Pepys admired the many "handsome books" in Sir Coventry's closet at St James's Palace and became an avid collector himself.[51] The evolution and style of his library in particular, which was housed in his personal closet, kept pace with the overall closet improvements during the years he kept his diary. He had Thomas Simpson, the navy's master-joiner, build special glass-fronted "presses"—the first-known purpose-built bookcases—then had the books themselves bound and gilded "to make them handsome." Pepys spent countless hours with his books: cataloging them, showing them off, and sometimes reading them.[52]

The growth of Pepys's collections brought more opportunities to deepen and expand his social network by way of their display. Sir John Winter asked expressly to see Pepys's bladder stone, measured it, then proposed to come back with the Earl of Southampton, the lord treasurer, so that he could have a look too.[53] The closet tour could lead into or flow from other conversations. After hosting a dinner for fifteen—"eight of them strangers of quality"—Pepys and his cousin's daughter Betty Turner "fell one to one talk, and another to another, and looking over my house, and closet, and things."[54] After showing his closet to a large party of visitors, he lingers alone with Lady Hitchingbroke, Lord Sandwich's daughter-in-law, in particular, finding her to be "a very sweet-natured and well-disposed lady, a lover of books and pictures, and of good understanding."[55] In 1669, Pepys reports on a visit from the architect Hugh May, member of Parliament Sir Henry Capell, and barrister and architect Philip Packer: "a pretty dinner" is followed by "excellent discourse" then guided tours of both his office and his personal closet to show off their order and organization—"to their great content." Pepys reflects: "More extraordinary manly discourse, and opportunity of showing myself and learning from others, I have not in ordinary discourse had in my life, they being all persons of worth."[56] Referring to the group of men as "persons of worth," Pepys signals his appreciation for their

personal integrity and their social status in a characteristic blend of hyperbole and contradiction: their conversation is at once "ordinary," in
the sense that no official business is being done, and "extraordinary" in
its quality, in how it stimulates and intellectually challenges him while
affirming his talents, hard work, and authority—his manliness. Among
many things that perturb Pepys as the Great Fire rages across the City of
London is how the conflagration is spoiling his plans to show off his
closet to a recent acquaintance. Mr. Moone, the secretary of the governor
of Tangier, comes for lunch as scheduled, but the closet tour feels inap-
propriate now: "Mr. Moone's design and mine, which was to look over
my closett and please him with the sight thereof, which he hath long
desired, was wholly disappointed; for we were in great trouble and dis-
turbance at this fire, not knowing what to think of it."[57]

Because closets were known to hold valuable and secretive papers,
they were prime targets for intruders. Pepys records several stories about
closet thefts. The Anglo-Irish diplomat Sir George Downing boasts to
him about spies he employed in Holland, who took keys from the pocket
of a powerful Dutch politician while he slept, removed papers from his
closet, brought them to Downing for an hour, then returned the papers
and keys unnoticed.[58] The Duke of York's secretary, Matthew Wren, tells
Pepys a secret about a recent closet break-in that the Duke himself does
not yet know about. That rare plates and a watch have not been taken
is a worrying sign that the thieves must have stolen official papers.[59] Like
courtiers and other nobility, Pepys locked his closets and entrusted loyal
servants with their care. Unlike the king and most noblemen, he didn't
have a secretary devoted exclusively to the management of his closet affairs, so he relied on servants with clerical skills for help in preparing complex documents and, when leaving town, entrusted them with the key to
his closets "in case of fire or other accident."[60] Afraid that he would be
found guilty of misusing navy resources, before leaving for the trial Pepys
gave his servant Thomas Hayter "my closet-key and directions where to
find 500l and more in silver and gold, and my tallies, to remove in case
of any misfortune to me."[61] After every closet renovation or cleaning,
Pepys spent an evening or more reordering the papers and books, sometimes requiring the assistance of a servant or family member—a compulsive process he apparently found very satisfying.[62] During the Great Fire,
Pepys had had to clear out much of his home closet. Upon restoring it
with the help of a housemaid—"very late up with Jane setting my books
in perfect order in my closet"—he was "mighty troubled" at missing some
of his "great books," but the next day they were found again.[63]

Throughout the diary, closets often become sites of sexual liaisons and sexual coersion. Povey gives Pepys a lengthy account of how the Duke of York arranged for his mistresses to be escorted through the long gallery leading to his closet.[64] Drunk on horseback, the Lord Chamberlain's secretary, Richard Cooling, takes pleasure in disclosing to Pepys a new low in the king's relationship with Lady Castlemaine, who has recently taken up with Henry Jermyn, the Duke of York's Master of the Horse: "The King had like to have taken him a-bed with her, but that he was fain to creep under the bed into her closet."[65] Pepys used his closets for sex too—generally with the young and nonnoble women he most often targeted, among them his colleague's daughter Pegg Penn, a widowed shopkeeper called Mrs. Burrows, and Nell Peyne, the family's cookmaid. Though there is none of the aura of plotting and jockeying that he enjoys and scorns when describing the debauchery at court, Pepys's sexual cipher, and here the verb *suffer*, signal a degree of awareness of the scandal of his own affairs: "Pegg with me in my closet a good while, and did suffer me a la besar mucho et tocar ses cosas upon her breast"; "after dinner to the office, where yo had Mrs. Burrows all sola a my closet, and did there besar and tocar su mamelles as much as yo quisere hasta a hazer me hazer, but ella would not suffer that yo should poner mi mano abaxo ses jupes." With his mix of Romance languages, Pepys tries to package his predation as playfulness while also conveying some of the remorse that he mentions in passing in the Nell incident: "And then I into my closet and there slept a little ... and then after dallying a little with Nell, which I am ashamed to think of, I away to the office."[66] The fallout of these clandestine encounters and assaults might be faced in the closet as well. Pepys is surprised one evening to find his wife "in her closet, alone, in the dark, in a hot fit of railing against me." Having dismissed a servant named Deb Willet after discovering Samuel's ongoing affair with her, Elizabeth had just heard new rumors that her once-beloved former maid is now behaving like a kept woman: "living very fine, and with black spots" and "speaking ill words" of Elizabeth. Pepys concedes that these rumors sound bad, and "with good reason might vex" his wife. But he also expresses hopes to resume his pursuit, admitting in the diary, "I know nothing of her, nor what she do, nor what becomes of her, though God knows that my devil that is within me do wish that I could." Even Pepys is skeptical of the vow of fidelity that he has sworn to Elizabeth, again.[67]

The closet also becomes a potential site of sexual voyeurism in the diary. After an early-morning rush of lust at the sight of "Griffen's girl," the housekeeper's servant, cleaning the shared part of the navy office, Pepys immediately "fell upon boring holes for me to see from my closet into the great office, without going forth." Small wall openings like this may have facilitated official surveillance, providing a view of the comings and goings into the shared office space so that advance decisions could be made about whether and how visitors would be received. But it's telling that Pepys begins drilling after watching the maid and claims to "please himself much" in the task. He finished making the closet holes just over a week later, while his wife chatted with him about her summer plans. If Elizabeth asked what he was doing—or how he answered if she did—Pepys does not say.[68]

Like the royal and noble closet owners whom he emulated, Pepys also spends time by himself in his closets, balancing accounts, writing letters, organizing his books and papers, or "perfecting" his journal.[69] On at least one occasion, he mentions "read[ing] solemne vows"—praying—in a closet.[70] Yet, on the whole, the diary suggests that it was the unusual interpersonal intimacy of the closet, not the opportunities it offered for time alone, that he found especially compelling. Consider that, on the morning of the Great Fire, after dutifully surveying the extent of the damage to the city out of a second-floor window, Pepys goes straight "to [his] closett to set things to rights after yesterday's cleaning" in anticipation of the tête-à-tête with Mr. Moone in the afternoon.[71] Even when no one else was actually there, the closet held out the promise of contact.

I

The Way In

The closet was to have a long and honourable history
before descending to final ignominy as a large cupboard
or a room for the housemaid's sink and mops.

—MARK GIROUARD[1]

After dinner, to my closet, where abundance of mighty
pretty discourse.

—SAMUEL PEPYS[2]

intimate, adj.
when two people are within each other[']s minds, without
boundaries

—URBAN DICTIONARY[3]

How, and where, does social change become imaginable? In eighteenth-
century Britain, one answer lay in the closet. *The Closet* argues that these
marginal spaces were channels for some of the period's greatest ideological tensions and most complicated feelings, both immediately, in the
practical issues owners faced everyday about whom to invite in and what
sorts of obligations these invitations brought with them, and abstractly,
as symbols both of traditional hierarchical relations, and of the possibility of leaving them behind. Liberal theories of modernity sometimes
give the impression that notions of social equality and universal access
to knowledge flourished alongside independent wealth in eighteenth-
century Britain as an almost inevitable triumph of reason and democratic goodness. The eighteenth-century closet insists on a messier story.

This chapter sets out the terms and stakes of the book's new view of
the closet as a fundamental vehicle of the shifting social imaginary. Cur-
rently, the dominant image of the eighteenth-century closet is that of a
person alone, in the process of finding out that life is more than a set of
duties to fulfill, that he—or perhaps she—has depths and limits to dis-

cover, values to uphold, tastes to refine. Thus the first move here is to survey the interdisciplinary terrain that has given us this composite image. In recent decades, literary and cultural historians have studied a wide variety of closet discourses and practices, generally in isolation, tending to highlight the rise of personal identity and psychological interiority in the context of increasing bourgeois domestic privacy. Though separately and together these studies have beautifully illuminated the contours and depths of the modern individual and the poetics of personal architecture, they have minimized the closet's social dimensions, its residual elitism, as well as the many continuities in closet uses and discourses. Preparing to fill these gaps throughout the book, the chapter's second section proposes that the intimacy of eighteenth-century closets comes into sharp focus only when we take their courtly public origins into account. The Restoration and eighteenth-century literature and language of the closet often pointed to the prospects of connection across status difference that had long been at the emotional core of this traditional public space: the original elitist protocols of alliance continued to send out a charge even as they were increasingly intercepted or outright rejected by actual closet occupants and the authors imagining them, making the interpersonal relations of the closet especially fraught. The third and final section of the chapter provides a conceptual frame for this affective complexity by considering how closet alliances both reinforce and challenge liberal accounts of social change. At a glance, the proliferation of intimate closets evinces the gradual emergence of horizontal social relations that liberal theorists emphasize. On closer inspection, however, eighteenth-century closets and closet rhetoric also become touchstones for the queer and feminist critique of this utopian master narrative, calling attention to many visceral obstacles to apparently inclusive models of access and connection.

THE MODERN PRIVATE CLOSET

Seventeenth-century transformations in domestic architecture and the growing value of privacy are implicitly or explicitly the ground zero of most studies of seventeenth- and eighteenth-century closets. Medieval and early modern house designs had ensured that people had space to practice their trades or, in the case of the royalty and peerage, ample room for hosting visitors. Architectural privacy was then defined negatively as withdrawal from the fundamental publicness of the household as a whole, particularly withdrawal from elaborate communal dining rituals. Indeed, as Michael McKeon suggests, the mid-seventeenth-century coinage *drawing room* for "a private chamber attached to a more public room" illustrates the overlapping conceptual and architectural changes that eventually produced privacy as a distinctive and desirable experience: "The development of domestic architecture ... may be imaginatively encapsulated in the transformation of the withdrawing room from a negative into a positive space, from a public absence to a private sort of presence, a process that was marked by idiomatic usage in the positivizing shift from 'withdrawing room' to 'drawing room.'"[4] In other words, beginning in the seventeenth century, homeowners began to enjoy relaxing by themselves without thinking of this experience simply as a break from or preparation for the truly vital experiences of entertaining guests, conducting business, or managing servants in some larger space on the other side of the wall.

Formal enfilade apartments, in which all rooms but the closet had other rooms leading off them, were giving way to double pile plans, in which hallways now made it possible to keep almost all of the rooms separate from one another and to minimize the intrusions of visitors or servants (figures 2 and 3). Lawrence Stone calls the advent of the separate hallway one of the "most significant physical symbols of ... profound shifts in psychological attitudes among the elite."[5] Yet, despite the overall trend of separating rooms, corner rooms, side rooms, or antechambers designated for personal use remained in high demand. In the seventeenth and eighteenth centuries, such rooms had a variety of other names, including *study*, *office*, *library*, *dressing-room*, *gallery*, or *oratory*. But most common was *closet*, the period's generic term for a private space. In a mid-eighteenth-century treatise, English architect Isaac Ware urged, "In the planning out of the several rooms, the architect must not forget, on any occasion, to make the best use of all natural recesses for closets, and he must contrive for them where the disposition of the plan does not readily throw them in his way."[6] As Pepys's journal makes clear, the appeal of closets had already begun filtering down from the top of the social spectrum by the mid-seventeenth century. By the mid-eighteenth century, even designs for tiny country cottages included closets (figure 4).

Thus far, the most prevalent theme in the history of the closet has been collecting. At least since the sixteenth century, midwives, cooks, alchemists, and apothecaries had stocked closets with the obscure ingredients, documents, and equipment needed for their arts and trades. In the seventeenth century, other closets began to house a greater range of things, including beautifully bound books and manuscripts, preserved

FIG. 2. In the late sixteenth century, many rooms in the enfilade wings of the ground floor of Longleat House, Wiltshire, could be accessed only via other rooms. (Architectural plan of Longleat House, 1570. Reprinted from Colen Campbell, *Vitrivius Britannicus* [London: Bell, Taylor, Clements, and Smith, 1715]. Courtesy of Marquand Library of Art and Archeology, Princeton University.)

FIG. 3. By the early nineteenth century, the rooms on the ground floor of Longleat House were both better separated from and better connected to one another, thanks to the addition of corridors and doorways. (Architectural plan of Longleat House, 1809. Reprinted from John Britton, *The Architectural Antiquities of Great Britain* [London: Longmans, Hurst, Rees, and Orme, 1807]. Courtesy of Marquand Library of Art and Archeology, Princeton University.)

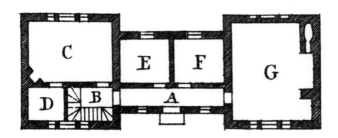

FIG. 4. The closet (D) on the ground floor of this small farmhouse links to the parlor (C). (Architectural plan of cottage with closet. Reprinted from William Halfpenny, *Useful Architecture* [London: Robert Sayer, 1760]. Courtesy of University of Wisconsin-Madison Library.)

animals and plant specimens, coins, medals, shells, gems, and all kinds of works of art—things deemed special, explicitly not for everyday use—as collecting was increasingly deemed a requisite feature of the fashionable lifestyle. The sons and, occasionally, the daughters of English merchants and traders were following in noble footsteps on their own Grand Tours of Europe, and from spectacular continental closets such as that of Ferrante Imperato, they cultivated desires for cosmopolitan collections of their own (figure 5).

John Tradescant and his son, both travellers and gardeners, created one of the most famous English curiosity collections of the century, known as the Ark (figure 6). In 1656 it contained:

1. Birds with their eggs, beaks, feathers, clawes, spurres.
2. Fourfooted beasts with some of their hides, hornes, and hoofs.
3. Divers sorts of strange Fishes.
4. Shell-creatures ...
5. Severall sorts of Insects, terrestriall.
6. Mineralls, and those of neare nature with them.... Outlandish Fruits from both the Indies, with Seeds, Gemmes, Roots, Woods, and divers Ingredients Medicinall, and for the Art of Dying.
7. Mechanicks, choice pieces in Carvings, Turnings, Paintings.
8. Other Variety of Rarities.
9. Warlike Instruments, European, Indian, etc.
10. Garments, Habits, Vest s, Ornaments.
11. Utensils, and Housholdstuffe.
12. Numismata, Coynes antient and modern, both gold, silver and copper, Hebrew, Greeke, Roman both Imperiall and Consular[.]
13. Medalls, gold, silver, copper, and lead.[7]

FIG. 5. The son of a wealthy apothecary in Naples welcomes visitors to his father's renowned cabinet of curiosities. (Engraving from Ferrante Imperato, *Dell'Historia Naturale* [Naples 1599].)

To *John Tradescant* the younger, furviving.

Anagr:
JOHN TRADESCANT.
Cannot hide Arts.

HEire of thy Fathers goods, and his good parts,
Which both preferveft, & augment'ft his ftore,
Tracing th' ingenuous fteps he trod before :
Proceed as thou begin'ft, and win thofe hearts,
With gentle curt'fie, which admir'd his Arts.
Whilft thou conceal'ft thine own, & do'ft deplore
Thy want, compar'd with his, thou fhew'ft them
Modefty clouds not worth; but hate diverts, (more.
And fhames bafe envy, ARTS he CANNOT
(HIDE
That has them. Light through every chink is
fpy'd.

Nugas has ego, peffimus Poëta,
Plantarum tamen, optimique amici
Nufquam peffimus aftimator, egi.

GUALTERUS STONEHOUSUS
Theologus fervus natus.

Iohannes Tradefcantius Filius, genij ingenuiq,
paterni verus heres, relichum fibi rerum vndiq,
congeftarum thefaurum, ipfe plurimum adauxit
et in Mufeo Lambethiano amicis vifendum exhibet,
W. Hollar ad vivum delin: et fculp:

FIG. 6. The poem that opens the Ark's catalogue plays on an anagram of the collectors' name: John Tradescant CANNOT HIDE his ARTS. (Frontispiece reprinted from John Tradescant, *Musaeum Tradescantianum; or, A Collection of Rarities* [London: Grismond and Brooke, 1656]. Courtesy of the Smithsonian Libraries, Washington, DC.)

The Royal Society of London for Improving Natural Knowledge, England's earliest scientific institution, founded in 1660, aimed to generate formal universal rules for analyzing collections like the Ark. Tradescant's inventory reflects a commitment to thinking systematically about the range of objects in the collection. Suggesting the hierarchy of nature over art, natural specimens come first, grouped into separate animal and mineral categories, followed by human-made objects, grouped into discrete aesthetic and cultural categories, which include antiquities from around the world. However, whimsy is given its due in the inventory too, in catchall qualifiers like "Divers sorts" and "choice." The vague "Other Variety of Rarities" is even granted a line of its own. Charles II and Pepys were in good company as collectors of things like fetuses and gallstones. Sometimes just the impulse to look at something and think about it a little bit longer was enough to make it closet-worthy.

The first English use of closet for a private room dates to the late fourteenth century. Cabinet, which initially evolved as the diminutive of the

English word *cabin*, came into use as a close synonym of closet in the mid-sixteenth century.[8] But its meaning was also colored by the French word *cabinet*, which could refer either to a private room or a chest of drawers. Mark Girouard explains: "As collections grew the owner's personal closet or cabinet [room] was likely to prove inadequate to house them.... Little extra cabinets [mobile storage] appeared, devoted entirely to precious objects."[9] Throughout the long eighteenth century, cabinet continued to be used interchangeably with closet to refer to a private room, especially in political contexts. However, as these rooms filled with collectibles, the cabinet was increasingly distinguished as a moveable wooden storage unit, one that might be housed in the closet. By the middle of the seventeenth century, makers of freestanding wooden furniture had a distinct and busy enough trade to form a guild apart from the joiners: like joiners, cabinetmakers were carpenters, but they did finer, more detailed woodwork (figure 7).

By Krystof Pomian's definition, a collection is "a set of natural or artificial objects, kept temporarily or permanently out of the economic circuit, afforded special protection in enclosed spaces adapted specifically for

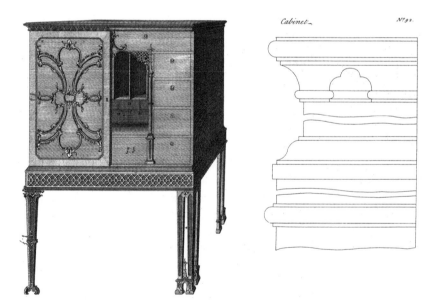

FIG. 7. By the mid-eighteenth century, intricate designs, like this one for an elegant freestanding cabinet, had made Thomas Chippendale a household name. (Engraving reprinted from Thomas Chippendale, *Gentleman and Cabinet Maker's Director* [London: Osborne, Piers, Sayer, and Swan, 1754]. Courtesy of The William Ready Division of Archives and Research Collections, McMaster University Library.)

that purpose."[10] Studies of collecting suggest that the physical isolation of the closet brought a feeling of stillness and timelessness that served the pursuit not just of knowledge but of self-knowledge, and of personal, even existential autonomy. Susan Stewart envisions the closet as a place emptied of "any relevance other than that of the [collecting] subject," where the collector satisfies a yearning to stop the relentless flow of history, of labor and industry.[11] "The ultimate term in the series that marks the collection is the 'self,'" Stewart proposes, "the articulation of the collector's own 'identity.'"[12] Patrick Mauriès reiterates, "It is possible to define the 'collector' as ... a man with a mania for completeness. By taking objects out of the flux of time he in a sense 'mastered' reality."[13] Barbara Benedict points out that even as universal systems of classification became more widely known in the eighteenth century, collectors' awareness of their unique interests and perspectives also stood to gain to the extent that they consciously rejected or refined such shared systems: "Curious people—virtuosi, collectors, people with private cabinets—take valuable objects out of the sphere of public meaning and use them in their individual construction of a mirroring but independent field of power."[14] As John Brewer notes, illustrations of seventeenth-century cabinets and collections often included a figure of Venus, reinforcing the idea that collectors were *amateurs*, indulging their own fanciful pleasures.[15]

A humbler version of modern self-making comes to light in the scholarship on closet prayer. In a large English household in the seventeenth and eighteenth centuries, the closet could refer to an oratory where the whole family and any guests could pray together, perhaps under the guidance of a private chaplain. Notably, the recessed closet from which Pepys watches the king take communion in Whitehall Chapel is big enough to accommodate him along with "a great many others."[16] However, far more often, the closets used for prayer were smaller, and closet prayer was solitary. In the early seventeenth century, the King James Bible lent new concreteness to a passage from chapter 6, verse 6 in the Book of Matthew: "But when thou prayest enter into thy Closet; and when thou hast shut thy Door, Pray to thy Father which is in secret, and thy Father which seeth in secret shall reward thee openly." Previously the passage had been loosely translated from the original ancient Greek as a call to look inward. Now a specific setting was named. Some Protestant theologians insisted that such solo prayer was more important than going to church because the practice entirely dispensed with the hierarchical mediations, not least the clergy, that in their view had corrupted Catholicism (figures 8, 9, and 10).

to front the Duties of the Closet?

Gen. 24 V.12

J. Pine del. & Sculp: Gen. 22 V.13

FIG. 8. Dozens of manuals, like *Duties of the Closet*, printed and reprinted throughout the period, elaborate the procedures and rewards of developing a personal relationship with God. (Frontispiece from William Dawes, *Duties of the Closet* (London: J. Wilford, 1735). Reproduced by permission of the British Library, London, UK © British Library Board. All Rights Reserved/Bridgeman Images.)

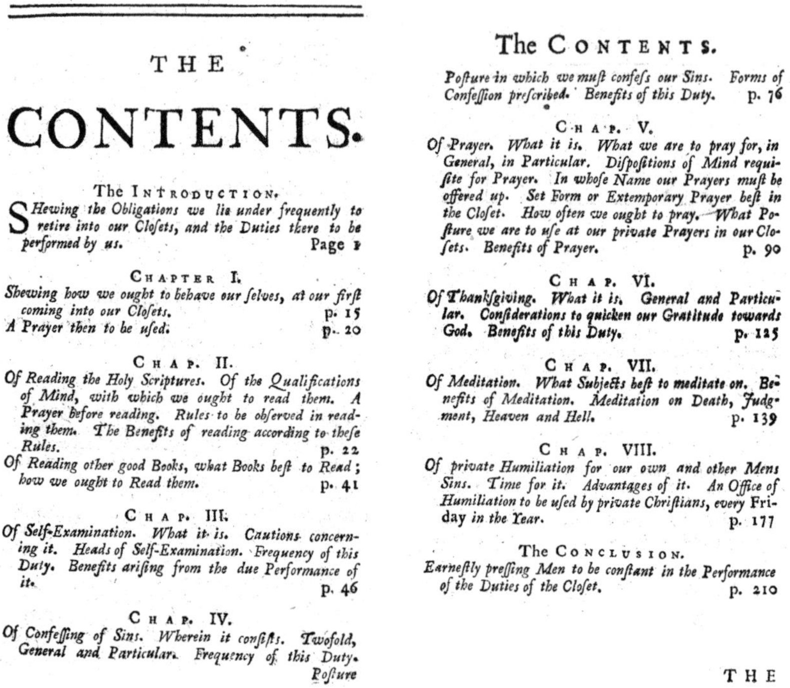

THE
CONTENTS.

THE

FIGS. 9 AND 10. The carefully choreographed program of self-reflection prescribed in *Duties of the Closet* is typical of private prayer manuals. (Table of contents from Dawes, *Duties of the Closet*. Reproduced by permission of the British Library, London, UK © British Library Board. All Rights Reserved/Bridgeman Images.)

Studies of closet prayer have especially considered how spiritual self-reflection shored up modern psychological interiority. Michael Edson calls closet prayer "a tool" for "diverting attention" inward, away from "the sensual and practical concerns that dominate everyday life."[17] Richard Rambuss calls it "the technology by which the soul becomes a subject," finding in seventeenth-century men's private confessions to God and Jesus the beginnings of the view that our most hidden desires and passions determine our personal identity.[18] E. J. Clery notes that the rooms where Pamela and Clarissa write and meditate on escape in Samuel Richardson's novels also serve as prayer closets: both heroines can surmount the values, if not the violence, of their persecutors by way of sustained solitary attention to their own Christian virtue. Clarissa is "rarely deprived of closet and key," Clery observes, and Pamela's "distinctive and autonomous female mind . . . is cultivated in the closet."[19] In a reversal of this logic, Effie Botonaki also considers the patriarchal limits of the apparent autonomy of women's prayer closets, proposing that, for a married woman, this private room, like the diary she was instructed to keep there, was "at once a prison cell and a space of freedom," since the same Christian doctrine that invited her self-reflection also demanded that she share these thoughts with her husband.

Many women and men, not least Pepys, read and wrote religiously in their private rooms less in the spiritual sense than in the idiomatic sense. Diaries, commonplace books, and all kinds of other documents and papers shared drawer and shelf space with other objects in closets. However, as collections grew in scale and variety among the wealthiest English people, the number of closets devoted exclusively to the storage of books increased.[20] Private libraries were mostly a male prerogative, but Heidi Brayman Hackel has shown that already by the mid-sixteenth century at least a few elite English women also had them.[21] As the closet came to be known as the best place to engage quietly with texts, plays written to be read rather than per-formed were first called *closet dramas* in the late eighteenth century. Scholarship on closet drama highlights how noble female authors came to define this genre and, by extension, the closet itself in opposition to the theater's unpredictable, embodied, and distinctly eroticized sociability.[22] Yet, as Thomas Laqueur points out, women absorbed by books in private were negatively associated with sexual autonomy and caricatured as one-handed readers (figure 11).[23]

In the second half of the seventeenth century, some his-and-hers closets were first designated as *dressing rooms*, underlining the common use of the space for putting on and taking off clothes (figure 12).[24] In theory the term was as gender-neutral as *closet*. However, because for at least two centuries

LUXURY,
or the Comforts of a Rumpford.

FIG. 11. Without recourse to books, the cat has already found the pleasure her mistress seeks. (Engraving from Charles Williams, *Luxury, or the Comforts of a Rumpford*, 1801. Reproduced by permission. © The Trustees of the British Museum. All rights reserved.)

NORTH.

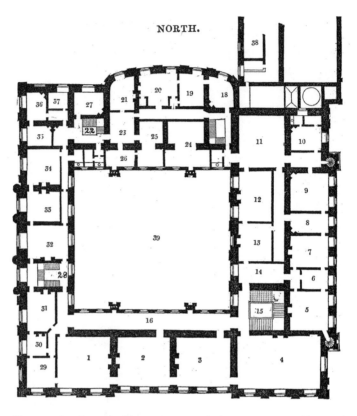

FIG. 12. The state dressing room is a corner room on the upper story at Chatworth House (29), which attaches to another dressing room (30), which in turn attaches to a large bedroom (31): his, hers, theirs. (Architectural plan of Chatsworth House, state room story. Reprinted from Stephen Glover, *The Peak Guide* [Derby: Mozley and Son, 1830]. Courtesy of Widener Library, Harvard University.)

the English closet had cultivated a reputation, alongside that of the Italian *studiolo*, as a site of "thinking, writing, and masculinity," as Mary Poovey puts it, women's closets were far more likely than men's to be associated specifically with dressing and undressing.[25] Tita Chico has uncovered the layers of misogyny surrounding the gendered opposition of closets and dressing rooms: "Women's privacy in the eighteenth-century dressing room ... threatened to imitate the paternalistic order that the gentleman's closet had embodied for over three centuries."[26] By reductively associating the dressing room with increasingly polarized and essentialized views of femininity and female sexuality, male writers of the period were trying to minimize this threat, Chico argues. At first, women's private dressing rooms called to mind the reputed sexual accessibility of Restoration actresses by way of association with the period's theatrical *green rooms* or *tiring rooms*, where playgoers, ostensibly passing through to their theater seats, might see female players getting ready for the performance. Later, as domestic ideologies were more sharply articulated, the dressing room came to emblematize the introspection and modesty of the ideal wife and mother.[27] Chico's readings of *Pamela*, *Clarissa*, and *Sir Charles Grandison* demonstrate Richardson's pivotal role in redefining the dressing room as "an architectural analogue for the production of virtue, epistolarity, and interiority."[28]

Chico and others have explored how the visual sense helped to cohere the gendered subjects forming in and around historical closets. On the one hand, as Barbara Benedict points out, as the emerging scientific discourse of the period legitimated curiosity as the affective engine of the intellectual drive, the desire to closely examine the world and everything and everyone in it was increasingly recast in positive terms. On the other hand, the limits of this voracious visual desire were signaled by those who fixed their gaze. *Peeping Toms*, who looked through the key holes of ladies' closets or hid in closets to peer into adjoining chambers, personified the selfish, excessive extreme of this way of looking.[29] Given how quickly examples like Pepys with his peep holes or Mr. B spying on Pamela spring to mind, it's not hard to see why, via the name Tom, this aggressive form of voyeurism was usually attributed to men and male characters.[30] Yet Benedict, McKeon, and Diane Berrett Brown show how experiences of private erotic spectatorship precipitate the psychological and intellectual development of young women and of female characters of the period too. Brown finds that in French erotic literature the closet setting serves "the auto-enlightenment of a young girl through voyeuristic experiments."[31] Similarly, McKeon argues that, in John Cleland's pornographic novel, the experience of secret looking teaches Fanny Hill to distinguish between sexual and more refined aesthetic pleasures.[32]

The closet and the visual sense also converge in one of the period's most flexible philosophical symbols of intellectual autonomy and of the cognitive processes by which we come to know anything at all. From the Latin for dark chamber, the camera obscura, sometimes known in England as a dark closet, is entirely enclosed except for a small opening or lens. As light passes through the aperture, a detailed image of whatever is outside is projected onto the inner wall. Jonathan Crary explains that in the early modern period this ancient technology was "a widely used means of observing the visible world, an instrument of popular entertainment, of scientific inquiry, and of artistic practice" as well as "a model, in both rationalist and empiricist thought, of how observation leads to truthful inferences about the world."[33] John Lyons explores how, for the rationalist René Descartes, the camera obscura provides an abstract metaphorical image of the inner light of reason separating clear and distinct ideas from less certain types of knowledge.[34] Later in the century, the new empirical epistemology that evolved in and around England's Royal Society drew on both the dark closet and the collectors' cabinet as interrelated material models or metonyms for how we acquire ideas via experience and then retain them. In John Locke's *Essay Concerning Human Understanding*, the mind, like the camera obscura, begins as a blank space of visual possibility: "Methinks, the understanding is not much unlike a closet wholly shut from light, with only some little openings left, to let in external visible resemblances, or ideas of things without."[35] Yet our ideas endure because the mind also has a storage capacity: "The senses at first let in particular ideas, and furnish the yet empty cabinet: and the mind by degrees growing familiar with some of them, they are lodged in the memory, and names got to them."[36] Though Locke's *Essay* has the best known mental closets in late seventeenth-century England, as Brad Pasanek and Sean Silver have demonstrated, such figures were quite common and varied widely.[37]

Technological autonomy merges with architectural and bodily autonomy in the prehistory of the modern toilet, in which the separate historical trajectories of the dressing room, privy chamber, *garde de robe*, close stool, water closet, and bath intersect. As Girouard and Lawrence Wright point out, much of the necessary plumbing and engineering had been available for two centuries when flushable toilets first regularly appeared in select English homes at the end of the eighteenth century. Both the equipment and the private room in which it was housed reflected a new desire to have human waste disappear immediately—the substance, but also smell of it—without further human intervention. The many uneven efforts at distancing bodies from waste that constitute the history of the English bathroom are reflected in the language of toilet, which, Wright observes, is "an etymologists's nightmare":

> *chamber* comes by way of *chamber pot* to mean the pot itself; the adjective *privy* (private) comes by way of *privy chamber* to mean the chamber or room itself. *Closet* (small room) comes by way of *water-closet* to mean the apparatus, not the room. *Lavatory* (washing place) comes to mean the water-closet, and to some dainty-minded manufacturers

even means the apparatus. *Apparatus* is used here only for want of one accurate word for it. Luckily for confused foreigners, W.C. is one of England's three great contributions to universal speech.[38]

Significantly, the broad association in eighteenth-century Britain between the word *closet* and the increasing desire for personal privacy has a lasting legacy in the term *water closet*, which to this day is the euphemism of choice in many languages for both the flushing toilet and the room for a single occupant that holds it.

THE TRADITIONAL PUBLIC CLOSET

Drawing substantially on an older and more overtly political history of architecture, *The Closet* unsettles the dominant image of the solitary, autonomous, and specialized closet. It stresses that the closet's various functions and associations overlapped, that these overlapping functions often brought people together, both actually and virtually, and that, in closet encounters, status, power, and publicness—not just privacy—were always at issue. The proposition that eighteenth-century closets, both at court and beyond it, were always in some way public spaces rests most simply on the question of numbers and semantics. As Lawrence Klein points out, "What people in the eighteenth century most often meant by 'public' was sociable as opposed to solitary (which was 'private')."[39] More centrally, however, the proposition rests on the question of how sociability was inflected in the context of the eighteenth-century closet. In this regard, it's worth noting our modern intuitive association of intimate relationships, especially romantic or conjugal couples, with privacy. As Patricia Spacks observes, if we now readily understand privacy to potentially include another person in "a union of two against the world," that's a reflection of how the modern value of privacy has been established in connection to the idea of loving freely.[40] Indeed, many twentieth-century philosophers have claimed that privacy must be prized precisely because it is a means to the end of intimacy: "Without the possibility of privacy, the argument goes, intimate relationships would prove impossible."[41] Or, as Spacks puts it elsewhere: "The difference between relationships chosen and those inflicted involves the playing out of a dynamic of privacy."[42] To approach the closet as a site of public intimacy is, therefore, to deliberately take a step back from—to register the historical contingency of—this modern investment in affective choice. When the king invited you to his closet and to say no would be treason, had you really chosen that intimacy? While making visible many of the ways that affect, ambition, and obligation inevitably intermingled in eighteenth-century interpersonal relations, approaching the closet as a site of public intimacy also uncovers its important role as a conceptual bridge between the traditional publicness of the centralized and hierarchical court and the new form of mediated, inclusive publicness that, in Jürgen Habermas's influential argument, would become the lifeblood of modern liberal democracies.

Whereas under the feudal system, court duties and the privileges that went along with them had generally been passed down through generations of estate holders, the Tudor kings and queens discovered that continually assigning and reassigning key positions gave them many more opportunities to exercise their supposedly God-given prerogative. Floor plans at court were adjusted accordingly. Under Henry VII, the primary chamber where the monarch sat in state surrounded by his courtiers had been split into a presence chamber, accessible to all suitors, and a more remote privy chamber, for informal receptions and meals. The division represented "at once an architectural and an administrative innovation," as Curtis Perry puts it. Henry VIII later finessed the use of this frontier by dividing the privy chamber into separate withdrawing and bedchambers and furthermore by choosing "to staff [his private rooms] with men of sufficient status to capitalize on the unique access made possible by their intimate service."[43] Thus the king established a buffer zone between himself and the court, in the form of a special class of courtiers who had the privilege of serving his two bodies: not only the divinely ordained sovereign, but also the mortal man, who retreated to remote rooms for food and rest. Elizabeth I took even greater advantage of this new strategy of withdrawal from the most frequented, central spaces of the palace by sometimes dining quietly in the privy chamber while important guests banqueted in state in her presence chamber, with the "full ceremony" extended also "to an imaginary queen at an empty table."[44] These transformations of court interiors and their uses ensured that the majority of courtiers could make contact with the monarch only in formal settings, while the elite servants on the intimate side of the buffer zone, such as gentlemen or ladies of the bedchamber and the master or mistress of the robes, had many more and markedly different opportunities to communicate with the king or queen.

Influenced by French palace architecture, the Stuart monarchs further refined the Tudor strategy of withdrawal. The closet in particular became central to the English court after 1660, when the newly restored Charles II began adapting the European etiquette he had admired during his exile. In previous English courts, the closets attached to bedchambers were used for private study or prayer, or as privies or sleeping quarters for close servants, and were considered, in Girouard's words, "useful but not essential."[45] After the Restoration, however, the king's withdrawing chamber and bedchamber were turned into sumptuous reception rooms, in which large groups of visitors might be received either at a *levée* in the morning or at a *couchée* in the evening, and thus the privacy of the closet was increasingly singled out, assuming the same secretive role as the *cabinet* in French *appartements*.[46] As Girouard explains, French courtly *cabinets*, "small rooms but very richly decorated," were "like little shrines at the end of a series of initiatory vestibules."[47] Likewise, access to the English royal closet came to indicate or bestow a greater degree of respect and prestige than had been possible anywhere in the Tudor or previous Stuart courts when the privy chamber, withdrawing chamber, and bedchamber were all intimate spaces in their own right.

Emulating Louis XIV, Charles appointed a senior page of the back-stairs and keeper of his closet to ensure his control over those who could penetrate his inner sanctum. This eclectic group of visitors included family members and prominent courtiers as well as courtesans and lower-status petitioners—anyone that he didn't want to receive in the view of the whole court. The ritual that Pepys describes, of waiting for the Duke of York in the outermost room of his apartment at Whitehall then being led back to his closet—the innermost room—reflects the way elite architecture shaped the performance of intimacy and access. As Girouard puts it, "Since each room in the sequence of an apartment was more exclusive than the last, compliments to or from a visitor could be nicely gauged not only by how far he penetrated along the sequence, but also by how far the occupant of the apartment came along it—and even beyond it—to welcome him" (figure 13). Alternately, the keeper of the closet could mediate access to the royal master or mistress via the successive rooms in the apartment or via a private back staircase that led directly into the intimate room: "While the crowd was hopefully approaching the king by the official path—through the saloon and along the axis of honour—the person or persons to whom he really wanted to talk could bypass them entirely, and be quietly introduced at the inner end of the sequence by being brought up the backstairs."[48]

People honored with extended private time with royalty or top courtiers were called favorites. Offices like groom of the stole, master of the robes, or secretary entailed regular and very close proximity to the master's or

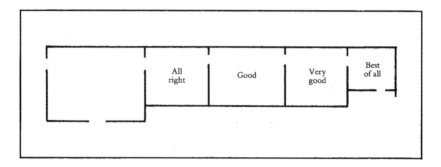

FIG. 13. The incremental status of rooms in a state apartment accounts for the special charge of the closet at the end. (Mark Girouard, "The Axis of Honour in the Formal House." Reproduced from *Life in the English Country House* [New Haven, CT: Yale University Press, 1994], 144, by permission of Yale Representation Limited through PLS Clear.)

mistress's body, often in various sorts of closets. Especially where such offices were concerned, both men and women tended to select favorites of their own sex. Magnanimously suspending the codes of deference that typically distanced them from social inferiors, royal and noble patrons exchanged this basic hierarchical difference for a state of intense mutual dependency for as long as they wished. Whereas affairs between men and women could threaten lines of dynastic succession, the predominantly same-sex alliances of the closet acquired their charge in relation to other tenuous networks of power at court and shared secrets of state. More so than other relationships, favoritism acquired its meaning relative to the whole social complex of the court from which the patron and favorite were physically but never fully psychically withdrawn: others needed to know what they were missing. In Thomas King's words, "Courtiers, male and female, flaunted their subordination as the mark of their favor. They displayed, proudly, their proximity to sovereign spectacle as the sign of their preferment."[49] This form of relationship posed greater risks than simply remaining, undistinguished, among the crowd of courtiers, but the potential for rewards, including but by no means limited to the emotional ones, was also far greater. On the other hand, although power very clearly flowed from the top down prior to admission to the closet, the unusual intimacy of closet relationships made kings and queens feel vulnerable too. They needed loyal allies and had reason to fear when their special attentions were received with indifference, or worse. With respect to the hierarchical conditions of admission, the protocols of alliance were continuous with those of the rest of the court. However, with respect to the special informality and state of temporary equality with which the favorite was honored, they were utterly unique and circumscribed by their distinctive architecture.

Though husbands, wives, and other family members sometimes had occasion to meet in these rooms, closets were designed above all to bring together people not already bound by blood, marriage, or a formal courtship—not adhering to protocols of family or romance. Unlike family ties, preference could be taken away as quickly as it was given. The closet's historical role in continually consolidating and asserting royal prerogative meant that the interpersonal relationships of the closet were unstable as a rule: their form was impermanence no matter how long they actually lasted. Moreover, as chapter 2 will especially show, throughout the long eighteenth century the fundamental precariousness of closet sociability was amplified by growing uncertainty about the nature and source of closet relations. The political and cultural power of the court and aristocracy was unraveling, private cabinets of curiosity were increasingly widely displayed, and many more nonelite people—including some who were less well-connected and less wealthy than Pepys in his prime—visited, coveted, and acquired private rooms. It was not always obvious how the former models of formalized informality and absolutist interdependence, for which closets had been designed, could or should apply.

Mark Girouard points out in passing that the spatial dynamics of the early modern formal apartment would be reversed if the quality of the visitor superseded that of the host: in this case, the "grander visitor was pressed to penetrate to the inner sanctuary, but could not always be tempted."[50] In the diary, Pepys describes this sort of inverted absolutist dance with men like Sir William Warren, Sir William Coventry, and Sir Henry Capell, whose visits to his closet appear to honor him more than them. However, the diary also reveals that a growing uncertainty and disagreement regarding the traditional importance of good blood could make the social dance of the closet more intricate than the simple reversal that Girouard describes. Pepys was on close terms with the future king, and the value of closet encounters had to do in part with the other people to whom each party was allied. As Pepys's wealth and administrative responsibilities grew, his mediocre birth came to seem to him less relevant as a measure of his social position, and his reputation and connections more so. Hyperaware and thus, at times, duly wary of the potent interplay of power and proximity in this space, Pepys might defer to hierarchical codes of closet decorum, but he also sometimes resisted or reinterpreted them. His efforts to stay out of Abigail Williams's closet after his initial curiosity had been satisfied, without insulting his colleague Lord

Brouncker, show how complex the social calculations could become. If the key question for closet solitude was "Who am I?," proximity to other people in closets led occupants to ask, "Who am I in relation to you?" Pepys understood—though surely not half so well as his maids—how uncomfortable the answers could be, and moreover that merely to entertain the question was to begin to create a bond, however unwelcome.

Though literary and cultural historians have predominantly focused on closets as sites of self-knowledge and self-development, the sociability of the space has attracted interest from scholars of collecting. Collectors knew that opening up the closet and explaining its contents to others were crucial stages in the collecting process.[51] Evidence from Pepys certainly suggests that the roles of closet guest and closet guide could be equally pleasing, whether the tour happened spontaneously or was orchestrated in advance. Recognizing the residual public intimacy of the closet serves to amplify the attention to social capital already present in the scholarship on closet display and the prehistory of the museum. Kate Loveman argues that the closet where Pepys stored his growing collection of books—and later his private library—served not only as "reflections of the self, sites of learning, repositories of wealth," but also as "claims to status" and "manifestations of social ties."[52] Similarly, in her account of female art collectors, Sheila Ffolliott explains that royal and noblewomen filled their closets with portraits "not just of their immediate families, but their enlarged kin network" in order to exhibit the superiority of their lineage as well as their wide circle of influence.[53] Daniela Bleichmar considers how collectors determined the meanings of collected items anew in the context of impromtu descriptions to guests: "The collection functioned not only as an accumultion of objects but also as a narrated social experience."[54] John Brewer discusses how British collectors also gathered select acquaintances into another kind of collection, a club of *amateurs* and *aficianados,* that could ensure that cherished antiquities and curios would elicit just the right kind of appreciation from just the right sort of people.[55] Throughout this book, remembering courtly origins helps to contextualize and flesh out the closet's intricate social dynamics while considering how such dynamics were both reiterated and refashioned by way of their many textual representations. Chapter 4 in particular examines dozens of the closet collections that were displayed virtually, in print. Thus, for example, when the British Museum briefly appears in this chapter—in a printed catalog—its origins in an elite cabinet of curiosities help to explain the vast discrepancy between the museum's purportedly inclusive yet practically exclusive models of access and education that the catalog explicitly aims to bridge.[56]

The Closet and the Shifting Social Imaginary

If the closets proliferating in seventeenth- and eighteenth-century literary and material culture were interiority and autonomy machines, turning owners into themselves, they were also, at least as crucially, intimacy machines, turning occupants toward one another. The chapters to follow tackle closet connections between royals and favorites (chapter 2), patrons and artists (chapter 3), owners and intruders (chapter 4), and strangers (chapter 5), showing how the uncertain potential for temporarily suspending differences of social rank—as compounded or complicated by differences of wealth, culture, sex, religion, and nation—often made closet connections feel uneasy. The chapters will also demonstrate the closet's value as a conceptual tool for navigating social change and media shift in eighteenth-century Britain. Though highly influential, social theorists Charles Taylor and especially Jürgen Habermas have been criticized, among other things, for understating the extent to which a new ideal of equality emerging in the eighteenth century covered over the inequity and violence that persisted, and persist to this day, under its guise. As figures of politicized intimacy in process, eighteenth-century closets provide a fresh vantage for this sort of critique, uncovering, alongside pleasure and enthusiasm, the confusion and uncertainty cast over the potential of relating as equals, whether face-to-face or virtually in print, even as its value was first positively articulated.

The social imaginary is Charles Taylor's term for the mental plans by which people find their place in relation to others in a given society. Taylor points out that such mental plans may be conscious but generally remain largely unconscious. That is, a given social imaginary may be shaped and reflected in explicit theories, like Taylor's own, that offer comprehensive explanations of how and why members of particular social groups interact with one another as they do or how and why these patterns should or could be altered. But for the most part, members of a given sector of society learn about their social reality simply by existing within it, imitating others and following or subtly deviating from shared practices and codes of etiquette. Our "'repertory' of collective actions" includes all the things we know how to do together, "all the way from the general election, involving the whole society, to knowing how to strike up a polite but uninvolved conversation with a casual group in the reception hall," Taylor proposes, emphasizing the social understanding this process entails: "The discriminations we have to make to carry these off, knowing whom to speak to and when and how, carry an implicit map of social space, of what kinds of people we can associate with in what ways and in what circumstances."[57] As they multiplied in English households, closet protocols were gradually absorbed into the common repertory and assimilated into a shared practical map of social space. At the same time, increasing numbers of written representations of closet conversations served as scripts that readers might consciously or unconsciously draw on if they entered or imagined entering such spaces. By occasioning and distributing a deeper awareness of social patterns, the multiple representations of closets also cohered into an explicit map, an imaginative form of social theory.

The closet's efficacy as an orienting structure for the eighteenth-century British social imaginary is in fact suggested in the spatializing language that Taylor and others commonly use to describe the social changes taking place in the period. In Taylor's formulation, from fixed vertical networks, in which those at the top, by virtue of their royal or aristocratic blood, naturally protected and disciplined those below, a horizontally oriented social imaginary gradually emerged, in which an abstract equality between autonomous individuals was ascribed, and birth—innate status—lost its orienting force in social interaction. To a large extent, Britain's new horizontal social imaginary was a way of reckoning social connection on a much grander scale than ever before: most ambitiously, by picturing all of humanity as one inclusive group in which traditional hierarchical differences could simply fade away. On the theoretical side of things, the social change was announced in radically anti-absolutist political philosophies, like Locke's *Two Treatises of Government*, which famously declares all men to be "by Nature, all free, equal, and independent."[58] With respect to social practices, this change has previously been linked to new places where British people from all levels of society began to enjoy mingling with one another across differences. Pleasure gardens, like Vauxhall and Ranelagh in London; circulating libraries, which supported new groups of readers all over England; masquerade balls, where music, gambling, and disguise temporarily overturned everyday social strictures; and especially coffee houses, busy hubs of business, news, and conversation, have all been represented as quintessential scenes of modern equalizing sociability.[59] Since the closet's horizonal social orientation initially developed as a strategy for buttressing the vertical orientation of the court and the absolutist state as a whole, to allow that the closet too was one of the "spaces of modernity," to borrow Miles Ogborn's phrase, puts a provocative spin on that category, underscoring the sometimes muddled, often surprising course of social progress.

Taylor argues that the development of the modern social imaginary came hand-in-hand with three intersecting "forms of self-understanding" that penetrated and altered eighteenth-century British society: the economy, the public sphere, and popular sovereignty, correlated respectively to the rise of capitalism, of the print market, and of democratic political models. Though the closet arguably participated in all three areas of change, its association with reading and writing as well as sharing and storing knowledge made it peculiarly resonant in relation to the uneven emergence of print culture. William Caxton had brought the printing press to England in the late fifteenth century, but the handwritten manuscript had remained the dominant medium of textual transmission for the next two hundred years. In 1695, Parliament allowed the Printing and Licensing Act to lapse, and the Stationers' Company, the royally appointed printers' and publishers' guild, lost its official jurisdiction over not only which books were made and sold, but also where, how, and by whom. Then, in 1710, the Statute of Anne specified that a publisher's right to print a new text would not last in perpetuity, as previously, but only for a limited term, and that, for the first time, authors could hold the copyright to their own works. The eighteenth century therefore saw both quantitative changes in textual production, including the conspicuous increase in the numbers of printers and authors, books and broadsides, and in the range of opportunities for people to gain access to them, and qualitative changes, like the commercialization of the publishing industry and the professionalization of authorship, that followed from the new legal conditions of publication. The importance of the newer medium was not always evident or uncontested, however. As book historian Harold Love puts it, "Cultures of communication progress by supplementation as much as by replacement.... While we tend to think of early modern scribal culture as a survival of pre-print practices, we should remember that it was a triumphant survival, in that many times more handwritten texts were circulating in Britain in 1700 than was the case in 1600 or 1500."[60] The scribal tradition had reflected and reinforced the elitist assumption that authorship and erudition were, and naturally should be, the prerogative of gentlemen and clergymen who had the requisite leisure for classical learning and for accruing comprehensive knowledge. Commercial booksellers and commercial authors still had to defend and promote their less reputable, profit-driven trade. Only very gradually did they articulate a coherent position of their own.

Jürgen Habermas was the first to extensively theorize how the rise of print culture helped to transform the eighteenth-century social imaginary.

However, not much of the cultural hesitation that Love emphasizes is reflected in his *Structural Transformation of the Public Sphere*. Habermas has played a major role in drawing scholarly attention to the rise of bourgeois domestic privacy. Of particular significance to *The Closet*, Habermas argues that it was new horizontal relationships at home that laid the foundation for new horizontal connections via print throughout this period.[61] He notes in particular that the replacement of the great hall, which had served for centuries as the ceremonial center of royal and noble households, by smaller, single-story rooms occurred alongside an emotional turn inward in family life, as represented especially by the rise of companionate marriage and the nuclear family. Though Habermas highlights interpersonal relationships between bourgeois spouses, and family-centric spaces like living rooms and dining rooms, his description of the value of the psychological freedom afforded by the new domestic privacy is much like that found throughout the body of scholarship on closet solitude: domestic privacy leads to a widespread "emancipation ... of an inner realm, following its own laws, from extrinsic purposes of any sort."[62] He proposes that new kinds of broadly social—or, in his terms, modern public—feelings were bred from these deepening family connections by way of new feeling-ful literary genres, like the domestic novel, which generated endlessly self-fulfilling feedback loops, but which also, due to their popular appeal, connected readers emotionally and imaginatively with other family-loving readers:[63]

> The sphere of the public arose in the broader strata of the bourgeoisie as an expansion and at the same time completion of the intimate sphere of the conjugal family.... On the one hand, the empathetic reader repeated within himself the private relationships displayed before him in literature; from his experience of real familiarity, he gave life to the fictional one, and in the latter he prepared himself for the former. On the other hand, from the outset the familiarity whose vehicle was the written word, the subjectivity that had become fit to print, had in fact become the literature appealing to a wide public of readers.... They formed the public sphere of a rational-critical debate in the world of letters within which the subjectivity originating in the interiority of the conjugal family, by communicating with itself, attained clarity about itself.[64]

Thus, as Habermas explains it, people who, on the basis of birth alone may previously have been at the margins of political and intellectual life, were empowered by their shared appreciation of family intimacies to represent and value themselves, and one another, in a new way. By making use in turn of the increasing accessibility of print, the very medium that had represented them, they came to assert, both as writers and as readers, a new kind of mediated collective agency that competed with, and ultimately surpassed, that of the court.

As an exploration of the shift from a vertical to a horizontal social imaginary and more particularly of the interrelations of lived experiences of intimacy, literary representations of intimacy, and the imagined attachments between readers and writers of print, this book both leans on and pulls away from these well-known accounts of social change. As Clifford Siskin and William Warner point out, Habermas's "liberal-Marxist agenda" and that of many subsequent public sphere studies have emphasized human agency at the expense of the "wide range of objects, forms, technologies, and interactions" that also contributed to eighteenth-century media shift: "By separating the human from the tool and the group from its informing structures, public sphere studies makes the business of mediating meaning something that rests with strictly human agency."[65] In Jonathan Sterne's words, "To study technologies in any meaningful sense ... requires attention to the fields of combined cultural, social, and physical activity—what other authors have called networks or assemblages—from which technologies emerge and of which they are part." Attending to the specificities of various closets as architectural, material cultural, social, and textual spaces, and to the particular protocols of exchange that came along with them, helps to situate the new sensibility of print within a complex network of interpersonal and nonhuman elements.[66] It especially complicates the democratic impetus of public feelings that is often assumed in liberal social theory. Though Habermas apparently offers *public sphere* as a neutral or descriptive term for a new kind of horizontal collective agency made possible by print, it also serves a prescriptive function for him, standing as "a model for rational negotiation through communication that we ... have fallen away from (through the ... 'decay' of the public sphere) but to which we should return," as Warner and Siskin put it.[67] For his part, Taylor notes that the universal human equality that was (and still is) central to the horizontal orientation has always been an ideal, demanding "a high degree of virtue" in the people with the most to lose.[68] However, considering that even for Locke there was little inconsistency between the natural state of human equality and either the British colonial policies justifying the displacement, enslavement, and massacre of millions of African and

Indigenous peoples or the laws of coverture that deemed wives male property, the new horizontal social imaginary in eighteenth-century Britain now seems not naive so much as tragically insincere. By revealing that of one of the most powerful blueprints for social change and media shift came from the deepest recesses of the absolutist court, the intimate closet unsettles the too-neat oppositions between antiquated (aristocratic/ elitist) and modern (progressive/democratic) values, and between modern liberal (truly democratic) and degraded (hypercapitalist, empty) values on which the nostalgia of these narratives rests. Underscoring the intricate continuities between the traditional hierarchical publicness embodied by the monarch, court, and nobility, and the modern egalitarian publicness encapsulated by the virtual collective experience of print, the closet proffers an oddly pragmatic and performative prototype of social leveling.

Standing almost as a parody of Habermas's idealized domestic sphere, the eighteenth-century intimate closet also disrupts the sexism and heteronormativity of classic liberal theories of social change, in which confident bourgeois husbands are often explicitly or otherwise tacitly the protagonists. In Habermas's account, men's deep emotional connections to their wives shore up their desire and ability to actively engage in both commerce and critical discussions of state affairs beyond the home. Habermas suggests that stronger bonds with their husbands gave eighteenth-century literate women at least as much authority as men as readers of the popular literary genres that represented these feelings and as consumers in the new world of manufactured goods. But he also acknowledges the very real constraints for women when it came to taking up public space. Wives had long been and were still legally bound to a state of dependence. Loving or not, husbands were masters. Moveover, the new sexual division of labor was compounding the effects of traditional patriarchal ownership to further limit wives' participation in business and public discussion. Habermas notes that the many obstacles to actualizing emotional reciprocity between spouses were common themes of eighteenth-century writing and conversation.[69] Nevertheless, there is no necessary inconsistency for him between the radical promise of modern print publics as sites of universal communion and the ongoing political and economic supremacy of men over women, and of wealthy over poor men, in eighteenth-century Britain. The disembodied neutrality of published discourse, he supposes, created a terrain on which people could bracket their differences and meet and exchange ideas as equals.

The eighteenth-century closet lights up anew the contradictions in liberal discourse that have been exposed by feminist and queer critique.[70]
The emotional structure of eighteenth-century closet bonds resembles
that of Habermas's formative conjugal "community of love" insofar as,
like in the newly private drawing or dining room, the hierarchical differences acknowledged elsewhere could dissolve into mutual feelings of
concern. Yet the model of emotional parity established in the closet—
a calculated strategy for repeatedly consolidating or acquiring power,
largely, though not exclusively, under the control of the closet owner—is
decidedly more instrumental and provisional than the model that Habermas attributes to psychologically autonomous spouses at home. Indeed,
ironically, the reciprocity of the closet, even of the courtly closet, more
closely resembles the sort of temporary bracketing of difference that
Habermas attributes to participants in the modern public sphere.

Notwithstanding the essential precariousness of closet intimacies and
women's disproportionate vulnerability to abuses of power, women often
stand to gain when closet relationships take the place of conjugal cou-
pledom as the imagined wellspring of modern public feelings. At court
and in traditional ideology, birth trumped gender (and wealth): a queen
ranked above a duke, and her closet would be bigger than his, or in any
case more charged, because of it. This lingering aura of queenly entitlement may help to explain why women across the social spectrum desired
and acquired closets or cabinets of their own throughout the eighteenth
century. As closet guests, women benefited materially and emotionally
from temporary reciprocity with other women (and sometimes men); as
closet owners, women were in control of these benefits, exercising a
widely recognized mode of social and political authority. By the same
token, the precariousness of closet relations throws the men a bit off balance, undermining some of the lord-of-the-manor self-assuredness that
Locke and Habermas implicitly celebrate. As the eighteenth-century fetish for voyeurism especially evinces, men's desires for closet intimacy
could become excessive and disorienting. The heteronormativity of
classic liberal social theory is especially destabilized. Centering modest
companionate marriages as the basis for abstract emotional connections,
Habermas privileges domestic novels in his account of the rise of the
modern public feelings. The closet calls attention to literary texts, especially secret histories, in which all kinds of embodied extrafamilial relationships are prominent. Moreover, since the courtly closet had been designed for elite men and women to forge intense, potentially erotic bonds
primarily with people of their own sex, it generates a more libidinal and

sexually fluid model of imagined sociability. Closet encounters are also much more suggestive than conjugal companionship of the overt and sometimes volatile negotiations of social status that characterized relations between strangers in the period and also, by extension, between authors and their anonymous readers.

Favor

Knowing about secret closet affairs, and being known as someone in the know about them, was necessary for Pepys's career. From the start, he uses the diary to collect everything he hears about private courtly alliances, whether or not these rumors concern him directly. Several months in, Pepys sketches an account that his patron and cousin Edward Montagu, the Earl of Sandwich, has shared with him, as a bit of dinnertime entertainment, about the backroom negotiations around the Duke of York's relationship to Anne Hyde, daughter of Sir Edward Hyde, the Earl of Clarendon, who was King Charles's Lord Chancellor and primary advisor at the time. Speaking in French so that the servants probably won't understand, Sandwich tells Pepys that the court is lately full of talk about how the duke "hath got my Lord Chancellors daughter with child, and that she doth lay it to him, and that for certain he did promise her marriage and had signed it with his blood, but that he by stealth had got the paper out of her Cabinett. And that the King would have him to marry her, but that he will not."[1] Pepys's concise record interweaves several strands of gossip: the sexual scandal of the duke's affair with Clarendon's daughter, the potential legal scandals of the duke's alleged contract and its alleged theft from her cabinet, the political secret of the king's patriarchal directive to his younger brother to marry Anne Hyde—which is obviously motivated by Charles's dependence on Clarendon—as well as the private conversation that has brought Pepys into the loop in the first place. Later, Pepys tracks anecdotes about how Sir William Coventry helps to orchestrate Clarendon's fall from the king's favor. Of one story about Coventry kneeling before the Duke of York in his closet, to beg pardon "for what he hath done" to his father-in-law, Pepys writes that he "dare[s] not soon believe" it.[2] Gossip about closet affairs has social capital and is therefore worth recording even when it's unlikely to be true.

Yet, however much Pepys apparently enjoyed and valued this sort of gossip, he did not wholeheartedly embrace favoritism, the fundamental mechanism of social and political advancement that this space had been designed to nurture and reinforce. Pepys is by turns fascinated and disgusted by how quickly elite attachments can dissolve. When Sir George Carteret, on a downward spiral, seeks to confer with him privately, Pepys muses: "Herein I first learn an iminent instance how great a man this day, that nobody could think could be shaken, is the next overthrow[n], dashed out of countenance, and every small thing of irregularity in his business taken notice of, where nobody the other day darst cast an eye upon them. And next, I see that he that the other day nobody durst come near, is now as supple as a spaniel, and sent and speaks to me with great submission, and readily hears to advice."[3] This capricious way of the world is of general interest to Pepys, but he is also acknowledging here that he stands to gain personally: his own distance from the nobleman is decreasing as Carteret becomes "supple as a spaniel"—desperate for allies. When Lord Sandwich falls from royal favor and is sent to serve as ambassador in Spain, Pepys observes: "My Lord very meanly spoken of, and endeed, his miscarriage about the prize-goods is not to be excused."[4] For Pepys, Sandwich's removal from court may not have been undeserved, though, significantly, he sets his own judgment apart—"and endeed"—from that of the implied larger group responsible for "meanly speaking" of his patron.

During a stroll around Westminster one spring morning in 1667, Pepys and his friend, the diarist and collector John Evelyn, compare King Charles's and Lord Arlington's approaches to taking favorites. Evelyn is impressed that Lord Arlington has passed over socially superior candidates in selecting Thomas Clifford as his right-hand man. Though Clifford's family and education are unexceptional, he is "a man of virtue, and comely, and good parts enough." Evelyn likes too that Arlington commits fully to his choices: "Of all the great men of England there is none that endeavours more to raise those that he takes into favour then my Lord Arlington, and on that score he is much more to made one's patron then my Lord Chancellor, who never did nor will do anything but for money."[5] Both Pepys and Evelyn are wary of the king's reckless way of bringing people close. Because "it is not in his nature to gainsay any thing that relates to his pleasures," Charles has let into his inner circle a band of "wicked men and women" who are largely responsible not just for his excessive expenses but also for what Pepys and Evelyn call "the badness of the Government" as a whole. Recording gossip about a debauched royal hunting party, Pepys concedes that the king at least has the wherewithal to rein in discussion of his indiscretions the morning after.[6]

Anxiety over the misuse of royal or noble prerogative seems to go hand-in-hand with Pepys's political fears of absolutist tyranny and exploitation as well as his more immediate fears of career barriers for hard-working nonnoble people like himself. Though he realizes that the same clientage system responsible for the undue influence of Charles's so-called merry men had launched his own career, the sense of enduring obligation made him uncomfortable. It was thanks to Sandwich that he had been in the right place at the right time, among the entourage on the boat bringing Charles II back to England in 1660. And Pepys records an exchange on that trip with the Duke of York, "who called me Pepys by name, and upon my desire did promise me his future favour." Pepys acknowledges here, somewhat indirectly, that he has asked for and received special treatment on the basis of his connections.[7] But as the years pass, he rewrites that story. In 1665, he complains to his close friend Thomas Hill about "how little merit do prevail in the world, but only favour" and avoids the latter category when narrating to him his own trajectory, remarking instead that while "chance without merit brought me in" to the navy, "diligence only keeps me so, and will, living as I do among so many lazy people that the diligent man becomes necessary, that they cannot do anything without him." In this version, the good fortune of his extended family ties to his patron ("chance"), not royal favor as such, has led to his position, while his own hard work ("diligence"—and implicitly "merit") has assured his rise. Pepys is now in a position to write of the king and the duke, "God forgive me! though I admire them with all the duty possible, yet the more a man considers and observes them, the less he finds of difference between them and other men" and to insist that his own advancement has depended on the good opinion of many others rather than the arbitrary affections of these particular men.[8] He's proud, too, of how well he meets this diplomatic challenge, telling his friend about the "cares I am in to keepe myself having to do with people of so different factions at Court, and yet must be fair with them all."[9] Recognizing that favorites incur considerable social and emotional debts, Pepys prefers to disperse rather than concentrate his commitments and, wherever possible, to earn his perquisites and privileges.

At the same time, as his wealth and position improve he is increasingly aware of his own capacity to bestow favors, and calculates the potential return of any favor, big or small, before committing to it. His uncle Thomas Pepys—"a sorry dull fellow" whose own wealth Samuel estimates in the tens of thousands of pounds—is ridiculous for asking him to "help him to some imployment" as there is not "a turd of kindness or service to be had from him." Pepys plans to "neglect" his father's elder brother as soon as an immediate obligation has been settled.[10] On the other hand, when an acquaintance called Mrs. Daniel visits to "pray me to speak for her husband to be a Lieutenant," he readily indicates his willingness, knowing that this promise improves his chances of "kissing her again and again."[11] She comes back the next day, and again they "were alone a great while, and I had the pleasure of her lips."[12] The pattern continues for nearly three years. Samuel Daniel does eventually become a naval officer (and Pepys is godfather to their child), so Mrs. Daniel's efforts are not for naught. However, beyond noting after the second encounter that "I do ... mean to do what kindness I can to her husband," Pepys does not mention him in relation to their affair, and his narration of their last meeting suggests that, for Pepys at least, the pretense of anything but an immediate quid pro quo exchange has entirely slipped away: "So home to the Office, where Mrs. Daniel come and staid talking to little purpose with me to borrow money, but I did not lend her any, having not opportunity para hater allo thing mit her."[13] "Talking to little purpose," Mrs. Daniel's mission is doomed from the start since Pepys's schedule leaves him no time to exact from her the usual advance payments in kind.

Following a Valentine's Day caper in a coach near the end of their affair, Pepys buys Mrs. Daniel eight pairs of gloves, "and so dismissed her."[14] From very early on in his career, he has gathered that the exchange of small gifts, also commonly known as favors, may facilitate and enhance relationships of all kinds. En route back to England with the king, Pepys accepts wine and a barrel of pickled oysters as "a very great favour" from the ship's captain, and a few months later Sandwich sends Pepys to the goldsmith's "to look out a piece of plate to give Mr. Fox," who has loaned him money.[15] Though much less vexing overall than court favoritism, participating as giver, receiver, and go-between in these more circumscribed material exchanges is not without its own risks and stresses for Pepys, such as when Abigail Williams persists in obliging him to enter her closet on the expectation of some return, or when his aunt and uncle Wight send his wife "a new scarfe, laced, as a token for her many givings to [them]."[16] Pepys initially says he is "glad enough of" the gift. But after a day's reflection, he admits that his "aime" had been "to get myself something more from my uncle's favour than this."[17] Even when the stakes are relatively low, recipients may misinterpret, underestimate, or fail adequately to reciprocate; thus favor is for him at best a speculative form of social and economic investment.

2

The Duchess of York's Bathing Closet

The Historian considers almost ever Men in Publick, whereas the Anecdotographer only examines 'em in private. Th'one thinks he has perform'd his duty, when he draws them such as they were in the Army, or in the tumult of Cities, and th'other endeavours by all means to get open their Closet-door; th'one sees them in Ceremony, and th'other in Conversation.

—Antoine Varillas[1]

a long improving moral lecture delivered to a naked woman, by a Lesbian: what a period

—Northrop Frye[2]

Omg I didn't realize #TheFavourite was so gay

—Bridget McAuliffe[3]

Absolute Ambivalence

Closets had initially become important features of court architecture as a means to foster favoritism. Royals and nobles, exercising their prerogative, singled out social inferiors of their own sex for special access to their bodies, secrets, and private rooms, and these favorites sometimes singled out others in turn for similar, lesser privileges. This elite form of intimacy became and remained a common theme of English writing from the sixteenth through the eighteenth centuries. Though in eighteenth-century scholarship favoritism has largely been eclipsed by categories associated more directly with modern domesticity and privacy, such as the conjugal couple, the sovereign self, and emergent sexual identities, the courtly closet demands a closer look. This chapter begins with a brief overview of the political and social history of favoritism in the seventeenth and eighteenth centuries, then focuses on Anthony Hamilton's witty secret history of the Restoration court. Written just after the turn of the eighteenth century, *Memoirs of Count Grammont* registers complex feelings about this mode of courtly intimacy at a time when the Stuart dynasty and absolutism as such were on the decline. "Where, speaking quite literally, does love between women take place?" Terry Castle asks in the introduction to *Literature of Lesbianism*, before remarking that fictional representations of intimacy between women have "conventionally depended on what might be called the 'islanding' or physical and social isolation of women: their segregation or seclusion in some location or institution relatively apart from the world of men" and "opposite-sex competition."[4] The *Memoirs'* most intricate intrigue, centered around two noblewomen in a Whitehall Palace bathing closet, poses a distinct challenge to that supposition.

The most famous and infamous favorites of the Stuart monarchs include Robert Carr, whom James I named the Earl of Somerset; George Villiers, who, having been given the title of Duke of Buckingham by James I, later competed for the affections of James's son, Charles I, and was eventually murdered; Villiers's son, the second Duke of Buckingham, who was in the cabal that superseded Lord Clarendon as Charles II's primary advisors; Hans William Bentinck, named Earl of Portland, and Arnold Joost van Keppel, named Earl of Albemarle by William III; and Sarah Churchill, Duchess of Marlborough, who was later ousted by her cousin Abigail Masham as Queen Anne's bedchamber mistress and primary advisor. Marriage and reproduction were the major mechanisms for building alliances between elite families and kingdoms. Yet clientage, or the taking of favorites, because of the less binding social ties it produced, gave kings and queens opportunities for more spectacular and more idiosyncratic displays of savvy than in their other, generally more enduring, relationships. When the monarch's capacity to provide a legitimate heir was in question, as was the case for both Charles II and Anne, the need for this provisional means of extending dynastic power was especially urgent. Favorites rose from disparate backgrounds and could play many different roles: servant, counselor, manager, advisor, apprentice, secretary, spokesperson, confidant, spy, or lover. Whatever the particulars, whatever the specific quality of the intimacy that emerged, the favorite's function was understood to be thoroughly political.[5]

Competing terms for this category of attachment came into England in the early seventeenth century from the Spanish and French courts that then exemplified absolutism: *privado*, *valido*, and *favori*. All three words stressed the privilege of private contact with the monarch. Bodily proximity was assumed to shape and reflect a reciprocal emotional connection. *Privado* and *valido*, both from fifteenth-century Spanish, were first "used of someone who ... enjoyed the royal ... *privanza* [favor], or was valued and protected by the monarch, whose *valimento* [high estimation] he enjoyed." *Favori* had originated in sixteenth-century France.[6] Though the Anglicization of the French *favori* eventually won out, as Antonio Feros points out, in early seventeenth-century England all three terms, along with more specific designations such as *prime minister*, "referred to the same court character—a person who enjoyed the monarch's favour and confidence and who as a result played a key role in court policy, the distribution of royal patronage, the appointment of royal officials and other activities associated with the monarch's craft."[7]

Social historians have argued that all same-sex friendship was essentially political in nature in the early modern period. That is, not unlike marriages of alliance, the bonds between two close friends held the potential for both of them to elevate or strengthen their respective positions and those of their families within the hierarchical power structures that organized society at large. As Alan Bray notes, "Friendship was ultimately inalienable from the particular loyalties in which it was begun."[8] In fact, because the social and political dominance of the patron over the favorite was explicit, it seemed, to some, the least complicated form of friendship. David Wootton observes for instance that, while ancient philosophers had promoted the idea that social equals of the same sex could cultivate the purest, most soulful connections, this notion lost traction among the early modern elite: "It is astonishing to what extent they treat friendship as a focus of anxiety, as the most difficult of all social negotiations."[9] It was not just that the finely stratified social order made the possibility of identifying an equal difficult, but rather social equality in itself was perceived as an obstacle to attachment. Thus in the late sixteenth century, the natural philosopher and statesman Francis Bacon could argue, "There is little friendship in the world, and least of all between equals.... That that is, is between superior and inferior, whose fortunes may comprehend the one the other."[10] "Equality provided the perfect environment for competition and rivalry to flourish," Wootton explains.[11] Especially from the courtier's perspective, intimacy thrived when differences in social position were as transparent and as frankly acknowledged as possible: only if each person knew who was on top and what each stood to gain from the other could they both let down their guard and enjoy one another. Naomi Tadmor finds that, still in the mid-eighteenth century, "if there was a sense in which the term 'friend' acquired … a sweeping meaning, it was the political sense."[12]

If the foundations of favoritism seemed especially firm to Bacon, many others saw cracks. Court historians note that the overpowerful royal favorite, whose manipulative hold on the monarch's heartstrings and purse-strings endangers all of her subjects, first emerged as a stereotype in English writing near the end of Queen Elizabeth's reign.[13] By the time the word *favorite* took hold in seventeenth-century England, favoritism was thriving both as a practice and as a controversial—and vastly appealing—topic of discourse. According to absolutist doctrine, the right of the elite to select favorites followed naturally from the presumption encoded in the idea of prerogative and most forcefully in the divine right of kings: that it was good and right for everyone if those with the best blood—and therefore born to rule—pursued their innately superior inclinations, with respect to secrets and companionship no less than other kinds of decisions. Yet, insofar as it also entailed empowering others, potentially without regard to the quality of their blood, the practice also seemed at odds with this ideology. Addressing favoritism as a pan-European phenomenon, Elliott explains:

> Discourses on the favourite, attacks on the favourite and apologias for the favourite arose out of a perceived disjunction between the notion of ideal kingship and the troubling realities of a world in which all too often monarchs seemed for one reason or another incapable of exercising to the full their monarchical authority, and devolved substantial parts of it on to a single individual who might or might not be qualified for the task. Either way … this meant the interposition of a third party between the sovereign and the subject. This, inevitably, was a situation that gave rise to violent polemic, and generated vigorous attempts both to legitimize and to delegitimize the [favourite].[14]

In this view, then, even the most dedicated and orthodox monarchists felt at least a modicum of ambivalence about favoritism in the abstract, however much they approved of the specific individuals their monarch singled out, because these intimate alliances highlighted the gaps between the theory and practice of absolute rule, raising questions about how political power was best diffused and distributed among royal subjects.

Curtis Perry nuances this view of the early modern discourse of favoritism for the English context. "It helps to think of the ongoing debate over favoritism [in England] not (or not only) as a precursor to more modern forms of political thought but as the manifestation of a fissure built into the edifice of English constitutional monarchy," Perry writes. "The English king, ruling 'politically'—with parliament and by means of native common law—triumphs as a ruler by suppressing his own will, thereby minimizing its potential to lead him into tyranny."[15] Though royalist ideologues and a dazzling court culture suggested otherwise, English monarchs did not reign unchecked. The imperial will had to keep in step with established laws and Parliament. Ambivalence over favoritism in early modern England thus also entailed grappling with the structural limitations to English monarchy. Perry observes how widely compelling the topic of favoritism became across English society. Stories about favorites "clearly appealed to a broader cross-section of the population than the direct rivals of the favorites themselves."[16] Though the relationships began and evolved largely out of view, the twists and turns of royal favor had implications for the stability and direction of the state as a whole. Evaluating or speculating about the monarch's voluntary relationships was justified since they impinged more or less directly on all English lives and security.

The embodied dimensions of courtly closet intimacies were especially fascinating. Generally speaking, the boundaries around same-sex physical contact were loose throughout the early modern period. Alan Bray points out that it was common then for friends to signal their connection with physical gestures, like kissing and embracing, or sharing a bed. Because of "the greater extent to which in that culture, in comparison to our own, the life of the body—in the daily cycle of working, eating and drinking, the bodily functions and sleeping—was carried on outside the marital home," Bray writes, "bodily intimacy became an instrument by which social relationships could be established and given meaning."[17] As Thomas King proposes, this general pattern of embodied connection was heightened and made distinctly hierarchical at court: courtiers showed off their submissive proximity to royal power as "the mark of their favor."[18] In their search for precursors to contemporary gay relationships, historians of male sexuality sometimes elide court favoritism with pederasty—sexual relations between older and younger men or boys. However, they also stress that relationships of the courtly closet could be suffused with erotic feeling whether or not sexual contact was involved. As studies by Alan Stewart and Richard Rambuss help to underscore, the discourses of favoritism and secret love intersected in the early modern period and, in their shared associations with the closet, they seem in retrospect to predict contemporary metaphorical resonances of the closet as a space of homoerotic secrecy.

Alan Stewart focuses on the connection between elite men and their male secretary-favorites, finding that, though the intensity of these relationships stemmed in no small part from the high stakes of the information they managed together, a hidden or forbidden love affair often seemed the most effective way to figure the men's interdependence. For example, in *The State and Dignities of a Secretorie of Estates Place*, Robert Cecil writes: "As long as any matter of what weight soever is handled onely between the Prince and the Secretary: Those Councells are compared to the mutuall affections of two lovers, undiscovered to their friends."[19] In Angel Day's manual, *The English Secretorie*, the closet's physical structure of secrecy serves as a metonym for the intensity of the secretary's loyalty and obligation to his master: "To a Closet, there belongeth properly, a doore, a locke, and a key: to a Secretorie, there appertaineth incidently, Honestie, Troth, and Fidelitie."[20] Adapting the traditional idea of the monarch's representative double-ness, Stewart proposes that the secretary "might be said to have two bodies: the body personal and the body archival," adding that, "While the death of the secretary destroys the personal relations, the body archival—the contents of the closet and the technologies of the closet—remains intact, a textual legacy that clearly gives rise to anxiety."[21] Who should replace a long-standing secretary? And by what means could his knowledge of the closet's contents be passed along? The uncertain afterlife of the relationship only intensified the master or mistress's sense of vulnerable dependence on this particular favorite.[22]

The associative links between closets, favorites, and eroticism also made their way into the religious writing of the period. Richard Rambuss argues that the English prayer closet became the main receptacle for the religious passion that had been more generally expressed in early modern England: "Erotic devotion—religion speaking of and as sex— does not suddenly disappear sometime in the seventeenth or the eighteenth century. But it does appear to be increasingly rezoned, with its all-exciting, unsettling flexions of amplified affect, to the closet."[23] Significantly, though it's not Rambuss's concern, the courtly closet seems to have provided an important reference point for this rezoning of religious passion. In *The Privie Key of Heaven, or, Twenty Arguments for Closet-Prayer*, for example, which Rambuss cites extensively, Thomas Brooks figures the Christian man's private relationship to God as both a royal petition and a clandestine encounter in a courtly closet. Closet prayer produces outcomes as efficiently as courtly closet conversation: "you know that many times a Favourite at Court gets more by one secret motion, by one private request to his Prince, than a Trades-man, or a Merchant gets in twenty years labour and paines, &c. So a Christian many times gets more by one secret motion, by one private request to the King of Kings, than many others doe by Trading long in the more publick Duties of Religion."[24] And closet prayer has the erotic intensity of courtly closet conversation. Brooks draws on a traditional image of the feminine soul to evoke its fundamentally intimate nature: "Lovers love much to be alone, to be in a corner together. What place can be so proper for the Soul to meet her Beloved in, as the Closet where there shall be nothing to disturb or interrupt their Heavenly Conversation? ... Here she may enjoy him, as fully as possibly she can in this Life.... Oh the secret kisses, the secret embraces, the secret whispers, the secret cheerings, the secret sealings, the secret discoveries ... that God gives to his people when alone."[25]

Whereas Cecil, Day, and Brooks celebrate passionate attachment as a positive, even virtuous, consequence (or cause) of closet conversations between a prince or the King of Kings and his favorites, for many other commentators, sexual contact was the most dangerous medium and expression of loyalty between patron and favorite. Sodomy was a broadly defined crime in the early modern period. Reproduction between married couples, the basis of dynastic succession, was the only form of sexuality not potentially construed as an illegal act and political threat.[26] In Christopher Marlowe's late sixteenth-century history play *Edward II*, which focuses on the medieval king's attachment to Piers Gaveston, Gaveston's enemies call him a "night-grown mushrump." Not only, like fungus springing up from dirt, has this favorite risen to public prominence as if from nowhere and improbably fast, but his "rump," it is suggested, has been a crucial factor in his ascent.[27] As Perry points out, accusations of eroticism between monarchs and favorites were always political in their valences because of what they suggested about the sovereign's unfitness to rule: "Imagining favoritism as political intimacy based on sexual contact has a built-in utility as an unofficial language of corruption, for it taps into the commonplace analogy between failed self-government and the inability to govern others, thereby rendering concerns about political corruption in terms of the personal intemperance of the monarch."[28] A sovereign who had sex with favorites or adored them extravagantly was more likely to be excessively partial, whether weak and easily manipulated or tyrannical and overeager to exercise his power, possibly at the expense of the state—or both.

Memoirs of Count Grammont

If the commentary on relations of the courtly closet had been politically charged since the sixteenth century, it was intensely so in the early years of the eighteenth century, when Anthony Hamilton was writing his secret history of the Restoration court.[29] In 1688 Parliament had deposed James, Charles's openly Catholic brother, after a reign of just three years. The Act of Settlement had recently been passed, insuring that if no Protestant Stuart was eligible to hold the throne, it would go instead to one of the Stuarts' relatives from the House of Hanover. James's Protestant daughter, named for her mother, Anne Hyde, was queen. But, unable to produce a living heir, it seemed increasingly likely that Anne would be the last Stuart to reign. Focusing concern over the demise of absolutism and the rise of party politics, the competition between Queen Anne's first favorite, the Whig Sarah Churchill, and Churchill's cousin, the Tory Abigail Masham, was a popular topic of gossip and debate.[30]

R. O. Bucholz describes the widespread feeling of tides turning at this time: "Just as the constitutional sovereignty of the monarch had been challenged and—in some areas—usurped, so had the sovereignty of her court in the worlds of art, fashion, business, and politics."[31] Even Whitehall Palace was gone, having burned down in 1698. The building where Charles II had established his enormous household thus became, retrospectively, a poetic symbol of absolutism's last blast in England: "Its memory was kept alive by an endless stream of popular anecdotes, anti-court propaganda, and Grub Street memoirs, culminating in those of Count Grammont," Bucholz notes.[32] Philibert de Comte de Grammont, for whom Hamilton composed his secret history, was from a noble Gascon family, and an illegitimate grandson of Henry IV. Now in his eighties and long since back in France, Grammont still loved recounting his memories of Charles II's court, where during his brief stay he met and eventually married Hamilton's older sister Elizabeth. The Hamiltons were Anglo-Irish nobility of Scottish extraction, whose Catholic family had waited out the Interregnum in Paris, followed Charles II back to London in 1660, then returned to France after James's exile. Though he had been a child during the Restoration, Hamilton found in his brother-in-law's stories fertile ground for historical reflection and political projection. Alert to the shifting priorities of the new century, he tempers his delight in Grammont's tales of the excesses of Charles's court with skeptical bemusement.

Early on in the *Memoirs*, Hamilton targets Charles's way of distributing royal favor, making it clear that, for him, as for Grammont, the King of France, Louis XIV, has set the standard for the embodiment of sovereignty. The Sun King exemplifies the tenet that a discriminating will is both a cause and an effect of a strong, stable state. Under Louis XIII, Cardinal de Richelieu had really held the reins in France and, as a result, the "fortune of great men depended solely on ministerial favour."[33] But Louis's son has reinvigorated the French monarchy by concentrating power in his own hands, and the nobility has fallen back in line: "the great lost their consequence before an absolute master; and the courtiers approached with reverential awe the sole object of their respects, and the sole master of their fortunes.... [F]avours, according to the king's pleasure, were sometimes conferred on merit, and sometimes for services done to the state; but to importune, or to menace the court, was no longer the method to obtain them."[34] Now the distribution of power and privilege is—as God intended—the purview of the king and the king alone, and Louis rewards excellence and performance above all.

Count Grammont develops his own code of conduct in relation to these standards, refusing to become a sycophant, bully, or liar, and choosing "to attach himself solely to the king in all his views of preferment; to have no regard for favour unless when it was supported by merit; to make himself beloved by the courtiers ... ; to dare to undertake any thing in order to do good, and to engage in nothing at the expense of innocence."[35] For a good while Grammont's integrity, wit, and frank competitiveness are a winning combination at the French court. The absolute monarch draws a clear line around his sexual property in women, however, and is intolerant of infractions. Thus when Grammont oversteps his bounds with one of the king's mistresses, Louis immediately banishes him. Grammont leaves the country without a fuss, "not finding any place in France which could console him for what he most regretted, the presence and sight of his prince."[36]

In Hamilton's portrait, the affable English king doesn't exercise his prerogative half so well. Softhearted and often lazy, Charles loves Grammont for his sparkling conversation but is not usually so astute in choosing where to bestow his favor.[37] Hamilton comments, for instance, that Charles Berkeley, the Earl of Falmouth, whom the king promoted for his service to the exiled Stuart court, "had nothing very remarkable either in his wit, or his person; but his sentiments were worthy of the fortune which awaited him, when, on the very point of his elevation, he was killed at sea."[38] Nor is Hamilton particularly impressed by the king's attention to his own elder brother, describing him as "the man who of all the court dressed best: he was well made in his person.... [N]o person danced better, nor was anyone a more general lover: a merit of some account in a court entirely devoted to love and gallantry."[39] Hamilton implies that the potential for a more rigorous Stuart reign lies in wait in the person of the Duke of York—an "entirely different" character to Charles, to whom the court attributes "undaunted courage, an inviolable attachment for his word, great economy in his affairs, hauteur, application, arrogance, each in their turn." As a "scrupulous observer of the rules of duty and the laws of justice," the future king is "accounted a faithful friend, and an implacable enemy."[40] In the meantime, Whitehall is taking a comic—almost farcical—turn. Whereas Louis XIV banishes Grammont for crossing the line with his mistress, Charles indulges, even encourages, erotic rivalries. As evidenced by the traits that make both Grammont and Hamilton's brother appealing to the king, at the Restoration court a facility for playing the game of love, or talking about it, or both, is taking the place of the established virtues of favorites. Qualities that directly support noblemen's friendships and alliances, such as devotion, courage, and discretion, are losing sway to those that drive sexual competition between them.

THE HOBART AFFAIR

Hamilton brings absolutist structures of intimacy vividly to life in an episode involving the Duchess of York, her favorite, Miss Hobart, her favorite's favorite, Miss Temple, and the Earl of Rochester, the most notorious libertine of the period and another of the king's favorites. The longest of the intrigues recounted in the *Memoirs*, it does not convey historical facts so much as the mood and spirit of the Restoration, as Grammont and Hamilton relive it four decades later.[41] Rumors about Miss Hobart begin to fly after Miss Bagot, another maid of honor to the Duchess of York, refuses to return Hobart's affections and successfully redirects them to Sarah, the young niece of their governess: "the report, whether true or false, of [Miss Hobart's] singularity, spread through the whole court," writes Hamilton, "where people being yet so uncivilized as never to have heard of that kind of refinement in love of ancient Greece, some imagined, that the illustrious Hobart, who seemed so particularly attached to the fair sex, was in reality something more than she appeared to be." Though the Duchess of York has "too much generosity not to treat as visionary" the insinuation that Hobart is a man in disguise or a hermaphrodite, she does "remove her from the society of the maids of honour, to be an attendant upon her own person," a post that includes superintendence of the duchess's baths. Worried about Sarah, the governess solicits Rochester's opinion of Hobart. He "advise[s] her to take her niece ... out of the hands of Miss Hobart, and contrive[s] matters so well, that she [falls] into his own."[42] Hobart now turns her attention to the newest of the Duchess of York's maids of honor, Miss Temple, whom Rochester is courting too. Because Temple is as pretty and dull as Hobart is witty and sharp, the duchess assigns her bathing-closet mistress the task of ensuring that Temple's relationship with Rochester has no "dangerous consequences." Spurred on by Rochester, Sarah reconciles with Hobart so that she can spy for him.

When Temple visits Miss Hobart one afternoon, hot and tired after a day of riding, asking for sweetmeats and permission to "change her linen," Hobart undertakes her duty.[43] She dismisses the chambermaid, undresses Temple, and invites her to retire to a couch in the antechamber of the bathing closet, "where we may enjoy a little conversation, secure from any impertinent visit" (figure 14).[44] Here she lectures Temple on the many trials that noblewomen face in courtship and marriage then sings her a lampoon, which she tells Temple that Rochester has written about her, but which in fact Hobart herself has adapted from a ballad he has written for a less attractive maid of honor, "whose person he took to pieces in the most frightful and hideous manner imaginable."[45] Unbeknownst to them, however, Sarah has overheard their whole conversation from behind the curtained partition separating the bath from the couch. She informs Rochester that the women have planned to masquerade as one another one evening so that Temple can discover his true intentions. Thus when he meets them on the Mall, Rochester is prepared with a counterplot. Temple, masked and dressed as Hobart, is approached by Rochester's friend, the playwright Thomas Killigrew, who, pretending to have been fooled, warns her that she will fail to seduce the innocent Miss Temple and that a former servant is telling anyone who will listen "that she is with child, [and] that you are the occasion of her being in that condition."[46] Afraid that she could be "contaminated by them," Temple runs back to her palace chambers to tear off Hobart's clothes.[47] Hobart follows her into her room, but Temple screams and the governess and her niece come running (figure 15). Temple soon gets married and leaves Whitehall. Briefly the butt of new jokes at court, Hobart remains in the duchess's service.

Although the *Memoirs* as a whole have not received much attention in recent decades, a handful of literary historians of sexuality have singled out the Hobart-Temple affair.[48] Harriette Andreadis proposes that the

CHAPTER IX

C. Delort.inv.   Printed by Lemercier.Paris   L. Boisson sc

FIG. 14. Miss Hobart helps Miss Temple to change. (Engraving by Charles Édouard Delort, *Miss Hobart and Miss Temple*. Reprinted from Anthony Hamilton, *Memoirs of Count Grammont*, ed. Sir Walter Scott [London: J.C. Nimmo, 1889].)

FIG. 15. Merging the moment when Temple calls for help with the earlier scene of intimacy in the bathing closet, Boisson also recasts the governess and her niece, who run to Temple's aid, as voyeurs. (Léon Boisson [after Delort], *Miss Hobart and Miss Temple*. Reprinted from Anthony Hamilton, *Memoirs of the Count de Grammont*, ed. Henry Vizetelly [London: Vizetelly & Co., 1889]. Courtesy of Mount Allison University Library.)

episode signals the transition from an earlier model of female intimacy, in which erotic contact is understood to be continuous with other forms of affection, to a modern paradigm in which virtuous female friendship must be chaste. Hamilton seems to mock those who believe that the older lady in waiting is "something more than she appeared to be," Andreadis argues, yet his references to the court gossip actually invite readers to take a "salacious" and "voyeuristic" view of Hobart's desire for her favorites.[49] Elizabeth Wahl focuses on the growing coherence of female homosexual identity over the course of the eighteenth century. For Wahl, the episode exemplifies one of the key satirical plot patterns that emerged to "mitigate the more threatening implications of female homosexuality": the lesbian dupe outsmarted by a man. "Hobart proves no match for Rochester," Wahl observes: "From the beginning of his account, as Hamilton introduces the reader to Miss Hobart and begins his tale of her machinations with Miss Temple and Lord Rochester, he suggests that the outcome is a foregone conclusion."[50] Emma Donoghue argues that the offhand way that Hamilton weaves the rumors about Hobart through his narration demonstrates the changing value of a biomorphological view of eroticism between women in this period. Thanks in part to vernacular translations of classical texts, the belief that women who desired other women had "abnormal or double-sexed genitals" continued into the eighteenth century not as empirical fact but rather as a sensationalist, disciplinary fiction: "It is a measure of the persistence of the lesbian-as-hermaphrodite motif that [Hamilton], considering himself too sophisticated to believe the myth himself, still chooses to allude to it to colour his satire," Donoghue remarks.[51] David Robinson proposes that Hamilton's pose of indifference follows an enduring pattern of homophobic rhetoric: "In contrast to the men and women of Charles II's court, the narrator affects to be thoroughly blasé about sex between women. At the same time, the gossipy rhetorical strategy flatters the reader, gives her the illusion of being in the know, able to recognize and decode authorial hints and suggestions, and thus superior to simpletons who need things spelled out."[52] According to Robinson, Hamilton draws on a kind of deferred or secondary homophobia: rather than debunking Miss Hobart's alleged "singularity," he uses it to ground his own and his readers' sense of relative sophistication.

Significantly, through this set of detailed interpretations, Hobart has gained critical currency as an object of scandal who has been doubly exploited—first by the Restoration courtiers who cling to obsolete explanations of her desire, and then again in the early eighteenth century by

Hamilton, who capitalizes on the entertainment value of these explanations, though he doesn't really believe them. In her field-shaping *Epistemology of the Closet*, Eve Sedgwick argues that, contrary to the apparently self-evident and much-lauded power of knowledge, it is in fact ignorance, whether actively cultivated or unconscious, that has very often shored up homophobia and heterosexism in Western societies, past and present. Focused on the authorial power that Hamilton gains by keeping false knowledge about Hobart's desire in circulation, Donoghue, Wahl, Andreadis, and Robinson share the view that the epistemology of the closet—and in particular "the epistemological privilege of unknowing"—is at the core of Hamilton's interest in the Hobart-Temple affair.[53] The coda of this book will undertake a more thorough reconsideration of the relationship between the eighteenth-century architecture of intimacy and the twentieth- and twenty-first-century idiom of the queer closet. Here, however, attending to the political valences of the eighteenth-century architecture of intimacy will revise the dominant critical perspective on the Hobart episode by emphasizing Hobart's successful navigation of Whitehall's closet culture, on the one hand, and, on the other, by designating as the primary object of Hamilton's irony not Hobart herself but the political turmoil that her pursuit of same-sex intimacy represents in the early eighteenth century—not coincidentally, at a time when Anne Hyde's daughter occupied the British throne.

THE BATHING-CLOSET LECTURE

In *Memoirs of Count Grammont*, the closet is the place where courtiers most often talk and connect with people of their own sex. However, because, in Hamilton's version of Whitehall, men and women alike focus so much of their attention on the other sex, many homosocial bonds now seem to depend on the jolt of heterosexual scandal. The *Memoirs'* longest male closet exchange is a version of the same story that Sandwich recounted to Pepys about the Duke of York's marriage to Anne Hyde. At the start of Hamilton's account, Falmouth voices fears about Clarendon's influence over Charles: "an insignificant lawyer, whom the favor of the sovereign had lately made a peer of the realm without any noble blood, and chancellor, without any capacity."[54] Since James's marriage to Anne would permanently seal the king's new bond with Clarendon, Falmouth gathers a group of courtiers eager to support his efforts to convince James to annul the match. Meeting with him in secret in the king's closet,

Falmouth and his crew vie with one another in the extravagance of details in their accounts of their supposed affairs with Anne Hyde. One courtier claims that he met with Miss Hyde once at Clarendon's closet when he was away and "not paying so much attention to what was upon the table as to what they were engaged in, they had spilled a bottle full of ink upon a despatch of four pages, and that the King's monkey, which was blamed for the accident, had been a long time in disgrace."[55] Another affirms that "he had found the critical minute" with Miss Hyde in a privy—"in a certain closet built over the water"—avowing that "three or four swans had been witnesses to the happiness of many others, as the lady frequently repaired to that place."[56] On the face of it, Falmouth's plot fails—the next day the Duke of York will publicly announce his marriage and the newly recognized Duchess of York, a shrewd politician in her own right, will go on to "praise [the] zeal" of Falmouth and his cabinet counsel, telling them that "nothing was a greater proof of the attachment of a man of honour, than his being more solicitous for the interest of his friend, or master, than for his own reputation."[57] Yet the men's collective act of imagination serves a greater purpose, transforming this conjugal impediment into an opportunity to recharge their relationships to James and to one another.

The sexual double standard makes the court an especially fraught place for women, as a bad move can bring not only ridicule, but also, potentially, redundancy. Miss Jennings, the future Duchess of Marlborough's older sister, collects "salutary maxims" on the subject of female self-preservation at Whitehall: "A lady ought to be young to enter the court with advantage, and not old to leave it with good grace," she "[can] not maintain herself there but by a glorious resistance, or by illustrious foibles," and "in so dangerous a situation, she ought to use her utmost endeavours not to dispose of her heart until she [gives] her hand."[58] Moreover, it is not only men who pose a threat to female courtiers. Female sexual shame is the primary medium of power and pleasure in closet exchanges between women as well. Hamilton's cousin, Lady Muskerry, has a big belly and mismatched legs. Hamilton's sister Elizabeth retires to her closet with her siblings to hatch a plot to humiliate her at the queen's masquerade ball, then returns with her cousin, feigning surprise when Muskerry divulges that she plans to attend the ball in disguise, though her husband has strictly forbidden it.[59] When a box of love letters addressed to one of her maids of honor comes into the Duchess of York's hands, she opens it in front of several ladies "who happened then to be in her closet." [60] The duchess knows that once the incriminating contents of the box have been exposed, the young woman will no longer be viable as a maid of honor. But entrusting the other ladies with evidence of the secret affair further obliges their loyalty. While elite men show off as adulterers and cuckolds, elite women trade in female sexual shame in order to strengthen the emotional current between them and establish or maintain their place in the court's pecking order.

At a glance, the scene in the Duchess of York's bathing closet seems to fit the basic pattern of triangulated closet relations quite well: Hobart's play for intimacy with Temple is streaked with defamation and manipulation, and oriented toward the barbed, exclusive public of the court. Upon closer inspection, however, it is a reversal of the prevailing model. Rather than using female sexual shame to fire up their alliance, as other women at Charles's court tend to do, Hobart hopes to connect with Temple by breaking down the heterosexual impositions on their relationship. Hobart's special role in the duchess's bathing closet indexes her preferred status. Because Hobart has been given the position immediately following rumors that she is "something more than she appeared to be," the duchess may appear to be trying to hide her maid of honor away. Yet this assumption underestimates both the well-established honor of service in the courtly closet in general, and the duchess in particular, whom Hamilton characterizes as having "so just a discernment of merit, that, whoever of either sex were possessed of it, were sure to be distinguished by her."[61] As the incident involving the love letters makes clear, the duchess has no qualms about dismissing anyone in her service who discredits her. A courtier's degree of favor in the early modern court was "directly proportional to access to the closets," and a lady of the bedchamber, to which bathing-closet steward was roughly equivalent, ranked above a maid of honor.[62] Skeptical of Charles's rakish reinterpretation of courtly virtues, Anne understands that, along with her intelligence, Hobart's lack of appeal to and lack of interest in men in fact makes her especially well qualified for the role of confidante and agent. In bringing Hobart into her private apartments, the duchess promotes her, and Hobart, in turn, uses this privileged access to cultivate a favorite of her own.

In the pivotal scene, Temple lounges in her shift, more than halfway ready to be led to the bath. But the older woman wants to talk first. Her ensuing polemic—which Northrop Frye characterized as a "long improving moral lecture"—draws on eighteenth-century feminist theory to expose the limits of courtship and marriage for women and to advocate for female favoritism of the old-fashioned variety. "In the first place, then, you ought to set it down as an undoubted fact that all [male] courtiers are deficient either in honesty, good sense, judgment, wit, or sincerity," Hobart begins. Men may appear or claim to be compelled by love alone, but "interest or pleasure are the motives of all their actions": either they seek profitable marriages or (more likely and worse) the passing gratification of a conquest.[63] If a maid of honor does succeed in finding a husband at court, she must exchange the royal household for a far less glamorous form of domesticity. Two recent Whitehall matches are heartbreaking cases in point. The new Lady Yarborough now lives in the netherland of Cornwall with a "great country bumpkin," and the new Lady Falmouth left London "in a coach with four such lean horses that I cannot believe she is yet half way to her miserable little castle." The only way to withstand the vortex of male sexual desire is to refuse it altogether, Hobart advises: "However brilliant the phantom may appear, suffer not yourself to be caught by its splendour, and never be so weak as to transform your slave into your tyrant."[64] A young woman may feel invincible during courtship, but she is lost forever if she loses her honor, becomes dependent on one man, or, as a wife, is exiled from the court.

Mary Astell had recently proposed in her *Reflections on Marriage* that the only way for a woman to escape male tyranny in this world is to remain single. A devout Anglican and monarchist, Astell challenges the hypocrisy of John Locke's argument against absolutism in his *Two Treatises of Government*, calling out the way Locke glosses over the oppression that wives and daughters continue to face in their households: "If Absolute Sovereignty be not necessary in a State, how comes it to be so in a Family?" Echoing Astell, Hobart points out that noblewomen who do not allow men to court or marry them acquire a unique form of authority of their own: "As long as you preserve your own liberty [from men], you will be mistress of that of others."[65] And she illustrates this argument with a cautionary tale about an actress and one of the highest-ranking men in England. Enchanted from afar, the Earl of Oxford had gone to great lengths to woo the "graceful" Roxolana, an actress known by that name after performing the part "to perfection" in William Davenant's heroic drama, *The Siege of Rhodes*.[66] When the actress "proudly rejected the addresses and presents of the Earl," his passion was enflamed to such a degree that he found himself unable to enjoy the amusements of the court—even gambling and smoking lost their allure. "In this extremity, love had recourse to Hymen," Hobart remarks. First steadfastly refusing her pursuer's signed promise of marriage, the actress agreed to and then consummated the union after "the earl himself came to her lodgings attended by a clergyman." But the earl had outperformed and coerced her: the pretended priest had been one of his trumpeters and a witness, his kettle-drummer. When the young woman discovers that the earl has no intention of owning her as his wife, she looks to the king for amends, but her petitions fail: "In vain did she throw herself at the king's feet ... she had only to rise up again without redress; and happy might she think herself to receive an annuity of one thousand crowns, and to re-sume the name of [Roxolana], instead of Countess of Oxford."[67] This arrangement brings some financial security but, in place of rank, a for-malized identification with her character. She is now a mistress in the subjected sense, without any of the social status afforded to a married woman.[68]

A popular figure in late seventeenth- and early eighteenth-century writing, Roxolana's historical prototype was the woman who rose from slavery to share the sultan's throne in the mid-sixteenth century, the Ot-toman Empire's most powerful period.[69] Brought to Constantinople from what is now Russia ("Russelana"), she became the preferred harem slave of Emperor Solyman the Magnificent. Fiercely ambitious, according to Richard Knolles's sixteenth-century account, she taunted the sultan by feigning piety until he agreed to free her from bondage, then denied him sex until he agreed to marry her.[70] Living arrangements at the Grand Seraglio were altered: "Women moved with [Roxolana] from the Old Palace, built by Mehmed the Conqueror, to the Seraglio harem, and ap-proached the seat of power."[71] The union was thought to be the first of its kind.[72] Though sultans could officially take up to four wives, before Solyman none of the Ottoman emperors had wanted any. As a rule, the sultan kept an unlimited number of female slaves in his seraglio, af-forded some privileges to any who gave birth to boys, and passed on the right to rule to the first-born or favorite son. For Western political theo-rists, his was the purest embodiment of prerogative imaginable. With neither a hereditary nobility nor a parliament under him, authority was concentrated solely in his hands and those of the janissaries he had se-lected to represent him. As a wife, a free woman, Roxolana influenced, absorbed, and benefited from his imperial power in ways that no other woman—and perhaps no other person—could. As seventeenth-century English historian and diplomat Paul Rycault understands it, sultans gen-erally "take no feminine companion of their Empire in whom they may be more concerned than in Slaves" because, they believe, were the cus-tom of marriage in use, "the chief Revenue of the Empire would be ex-pended in the Chambers of Women, and diverted from the true Channels in which the Treasure ought to run for nourishment of the Politick body of the Common-wealth."[73]

Hobart's version of the Roxolana scandal does not explicitly refer to the famous sixteenth-century marriage. Instead it's presented as a kind of allegory-in-reverse that appeals to readers to compare the fate of the historical Eastern Roxolana to that of her local counterpart. When the English actress withdraws and withholds sex, she takes more or less the same gamble as the Ottoman concubine, leveraging her desirability to a powerful man. But whereas the real Roxolana wins the gamble, the latter has misjudged her context. A fellow duke's company player mocks, "The Sultana [Roxolana] might have supposed, in some part or other of a play, that she was really married."[74] The bitter irony of Hobart's allegory-in-reverse is that Eastern despotism turns out to afford better opportunities for an ambitious woman than the pragmatic and marriage-minded English court. Sex with a man can be a vehicle for upward mobility in the Ottoman seraglio, where, the English imagine, desire runs to sublime heights. But for a young woman of humble birth venturing into the petty English court, it cannot. Moreover, Restoration court culture triangulates her relationship with the earl through the king, who readily sides with his male courtier and cruelly renames the actress for her incongruous effort at modesty.

The applied moral of the tale is that in allowing Rochester to entice and flatter her, Temple, like the now defamed English actress, is in danger of inflating the power she gains as an object of male desire at Whitehall. Hobart finally spells it out for her: "No woman gives ear to [Rochester] three times, but she irretrievably loses her reputation. No woman can escape him, for he has her in his writings, though his other attacks be ineffectual; and in the age we live in, the one is as bad as the other in the eye of the public."[75] She punctuates her point by reciting her adaptation of Rochester's lampoon. Under Charles's libertine rule, relationships with men are an ineffective means for women to secure protection and privilege. Temple should learn from Hobart's own example that more lasting strength may be gained through the intimate economy of the closet. She should give her ear, and her affection, to Hobart alone.

THE DESPOTIC EROTICS OF THE BATH

More than previous critics of the episode have allowed, Hamilton's Jacobite sensibility inclines him toward Hobart and the traditional form of favoritism that she endorses. But she is not exempt from his satire altogether. Previously, literary critics have taken Hobart's alleged hermaphrodism and her protolesbianism to be the main targets of Hamilton's mockery. The unusual setting of Hobart's lecture provides a different, explicitly political, frame of analysis. The duchess's bathroom resolves a practical problem in the narration of this ostensibly historical episode. Its lockable, curtained partition makes it possible for Sarah, bathing unseen, to overhear Hobart's lecture, lampoon, and her plot against Rochester. In this way, the setting accounts both for how Rochester learns about Hobart's plan in time to subvert it, and how Hamilton, via Grammont, can recount her long speech in such confident detail.

Alongside probability, however, ideological and aesthetic associations are engaged here. With its divided chamber, curtains, and couch, the Duchess of York's bathing closet is in the height of fashion for its time. Couches—"new forms, hybrids between the bed and the chair"—had come to England from France, where in the mid-seventeenth century, they were built in response to "the new emphasis on comfort and sociability," as Madeleine Dobie explains: "Benches and church pews aside, they were the first [European] seats designed for several occupants."[76] Moreover, experiments in pumping and gravity in the second half of the seventeenth century had led to improvements in palace plumbing.[77] Shortly after the Restoration, and in keeping with his general interest in intimate spaces and rituals, Charles transformed the largest of his three bathrooms into a place for relaxing in luxurious seclusion, a kind of spa lounge. Whitehall works' accounts show that, in 1663, "The room was panelled and embellished with carvings, curtains and a screen were provided for the bath and a painting was set up over the chimney. A palisade was erected in the privy garden before the windows of the rooms to maintain the King's privacy."[78] The same year, "soft furnishings" were brought in, including hangings and a feather bed. An account from September 1668 lists expenses for laying a forty-nine-square-foot floor in its sunken-pool bath. Five years later, the water system was improved, and the room's walls and ceiling were covered in mirrors. While there is no certain record of the first Duchess of York's early lodgings, Simon Thurley records that the king's mistress Barbara Castlemaine had new panels installed in her bathing closet at around the same time.[79]

So rare were such rooms even at Whitehall that bath steward was not one of its conventional offices. However, travel writers had made it well known that opulent baths were essential features of the imperial court at Constantinople. The Koran's injunction to wash in preparation for prayer and after sex or excretion had given the bath a cultural value in the Muslim East that it didn't have in England, where cleanliness was a minor element in elite civility, a way to prevent not disease or vice but ridicule. Going to a bath one day, after "long being within doors in the dirt," Elizabeth Pepys "pretends to a resolution of being hereafter very clean," but Samuel is doubtful, "—how long it will hold, I can guess."[80] The disgracefully minimal notion of cleanliness that Hobart attributes to one of Miss Temple's rivals, who "attend[s] to those parts which must necessarily be seen, such as the neck and hands," was in fact standard throughout European courts in this period.[81] As historians of European privacy have explained, cleanliness had "little to do with water" and was "largely unconcerned with the body, except for the hands and the face, the only parts that showed."[82] The more thorough cleanliness that Hobart attributes to Temple affirms the values of a seventeenth-century court obsessed not with hygiene but with producing and displaying intimate knowledge. Paul Rycault explains that the *Hamaungee Bashee*, "chief over the Baths," was one of the twelve offices to which an educated male slave might be promoted, one of the few attending "immediately on the Person of the Grand Signior." Hobart's stock of sweetmeats—often exchanged between elite English women in the period—also points to the East, the oldest English source for sugar, and to the seraglio in particular, where a male slave might earn the post of the *Kiler Kiahaiasi*, "overseer of the provisions of *Sherbets*, Sugar, sweet-meats, &c."[83] Even the couch had an exoticized Eastern aura: "The oriental, feminine names commonly conferred on them, such as *lits de repos, canapés, sofas, ottomanes, turquoises,* and *duchesses* evoked a distanced impression of the Turkish divan, the row of cushions arranged against a wall the European travelers encountered in Constantinople."[84]

The Grand Seraglio in Constantinople, much bigger than any English palace, was a common metonymy for the sultan's potent will in seventeenth- and early eighteenth-century European writing. Italian ambassador Ottaviano Bon uses a verbal tour of this building to introduce the methodical despotism of the whole of the Ottoman Empire. First describing thick walls, watch-towers, and tiers of armed guards, then moving through terraces and halls, Bon finally arrives at the living areas and the people enclosed within them: "All they which are in the *Seraglio*, both men and women, are the Grand Signiors slaves (for so they stile themselves) and so are all they which are subject to his Empire. For, besides that he is their Soveraign, they do all acknowledge that whatsoever they do possess, or enjoy, proceedeth meerly from his good will, and favour:

and not onely their estates but their lives also are at his dispose."[85] Political and architectural structures of subjection were especially intricately
interconnected in representations of the seraglio's harem or women's
quarters, where the sultan reputedly had stocks of virgin slaves trained
and at the ready to indulge his every whim. Ruth Yeazel views the conceptual conflations in the English meanings of *harem* and *seraglio* as evidence
of a Western obsession with women's sexual imprisonment in the period.
Though these women's quarters were not locked as a rule, European
writers imposed that idea: "In Turkish, *haremlik* literally means the place
of the sanctuary," Yeazel explains. The term *seraglio*, more completely a
Western construction, also evokes sexual slavery: "Europeans mistakenly
associated the Turco-Persian word for palace, *saray*, with the Italian *ser-
rare*, to lock up or enclose—by which false etymology the English 'seraglio' and the French *sérail* came to signify not only an entire building (as
in 'the Grand Seraglio' at Constantinople), but the apartments in which
the women were confined and even the women themselves."[86] Rycault
assumes that his description of the *haremlik* will be the highlight of the
tour of the Ottoman court offered in his book, teasing that the reader
"may chance to take it unkindly, should I leave him at the door, and not
introduce him into those apartments, where the Grand Signiors Mistresses
are lodged."[87]

The segregation of slaves, necessary to securing the sultan's control
over alliances and reproduction, enforced a homosocial substructure in
the Grand Seraglio, which compelled Western images of men and especially women lacking access to "natural" outlets for their lust.[88] Travel
writers of the period understand eroticism among young slaves of the
same sex in the Seraglio as a way of making do with what's available:
"wanting the society of" (Bon) or "deprived of Conversation with" (Le
Stourgeon) the other sex, the "amorous disposition of youth" is, Rycault
writes, "transported to a most passionate admiration of beauty where-
soever it finds it."[89] The Turkish practice of bathing communally made
the association of shared subjection and gratuitous homoeroticism especially slippery when it came to women. As Billie Melman puts it, "The
women's baths were identified as the *loci sensuales* in the erotically charged
landscape of the Orient."[90] A sixteenth-century diplomat's memoir, *Embassy into Turkey,* reports, for instance, "amongst the women of Levan[t],
ther is very great amity proceding ... through the frequentation & resort
to the bathes: yea & somtimes become so feruently in loue the one of the
other as if it were men, in such sort that perceiuing some maiden or
woman of excellent beauty they wil not ceaste [*sic*] vntil they haue found

means to bath with them, & to handle & grope them euerywhere at their pleasures, so ful they are of luxuriousnes & feminine wantonnes."[91] A half century later, another Western writer reports that "filthie lust" is "committed daily in the remote closets of ... darkesome [Turkish] Bannias: yea women with women" "a thing uncredible, if former times had not given thereunto both detection and punishment."[92] As their language of lust, chance, and impulse suggests, Europeans presume that in the bath female slaves enact a mode of arbitrariness that, in contrast to that of the sultan, emerges from their valuelessness and exchangeability in the absence of his favor. The association between the bath or *hammam* and this effortless mutual yielding was exacerbated by the Western belief that immersion in hot water inflamed the passions and diminished the capacity to reason in equal measure.[93] These were purely sensual bonds, utterly devoid of political traction.

Shortly after having been redesigned for the Restoration court in the spirit of Eastern decadence, the bath made its way into English historical fictions where, consistent with previous associations, it underscored the sexual subservience presumed to be expected of women under despotic rule. In Aphra Behn's *Oroonoko*, a tyrannical African king tries to force a young woman to marry him in the royal bath, using it as locked harem chamber, court, and *bagnio* in one. In Delarivier Manley's *The New Atalantis*, in an effort to secure the loyalty and protection of the aging Cicero, Thais fills her mansion with "She-Slaves ... amorous Devotees, whom she caus'd to be fetched from *Greece*, when they were too Young to have a true Sense of Decency or Vertue" and stages elaborate, vicarious seductions in a bathing closet.[94] Notably the "wanton" girls of Thais's hammam-harem, as "delicious," "panting," and "ready" for love as their prototypes in orientalist travelogues, have neither identities nor desires except for the sensual ones that they immediately satisfy. In Hamilton's own early experiment with the oriental tale, *Les Quatre Facardins*, a white princess poses with African slaves in her bath to captivate a male onlooker (figure 16).[95]

Thus in the early modern period and throughout the eighteenth century, the bath evokes images of nameless female captives, who, rendered pliant by steam and heat, fall into one another's arms thoughtlessly, performing their inconsequentiality in fleeting, meaningless pleasures. Without disrupting the basic historical realism of the *Memoirs*, Hamilton's intimate bathing closet setting brings these fantasies and fears home, as it were, as interpretive lures. In Hobart's Orientalist allegory-in-reverse, Turkey features as England's utopian foil, a faraway land where the imperial

Pag. 33o.

LES QUATRE FACARDINS.

J. M. Moreau le j. inv.   E. De Ghendt sculp.

FIG. 16. The princess frames her whiteness against the apparently interchangeable black bodies of her attendants to entice the man looking in. (J. M. Moreau, from *Les Quatre Facardins*. Reprinted from Anthony Hamilton, *Les Quatre Facardins, Oeuvres, Tome Second* [Paris: A. A. Renouard, 1812]. Courtesy of Université de Sherbrooke.)

will is so expansive that relations with men may, on rare occasions, be worth the gamble. But the particular Whitehall room where Hamilton has her tell the tale contradicts this imaginary feminist geography. The bathing closet evokes the rule that, in the British imagination, defines the original Roxolana's exceptional achievement: women's state of complete subjection in the Ottoman Empire. Comparing the Duchess of York's bathing closet to the despotic hammam raises questions about the structure and status of women's relationships at the English court too. Viewed in contrast with the purely sensual homoeroticism attributed to the Ottoman bath, the bathing closet points up the ambitious nature of Hobart's desire. Clearly, loyalty to the duchess has propelled her toward Temple. But isn't Hobart's own desire to top Rochester a factor too? To what extent do the connections between female favorites and their mistresses mimic the power-soaked courtships and marriages that Hobart claims they can replace? If Hobart did manage to seduce Temple, would this physical intimacy help to solidify their alliance and Hobart's dominance? At the same time, as a mirror reflection of the West, the Eastern bath suggests the precariousness of Hobart's bonds with both Temple and the duchess. Can a woman really guarantee another woman's liberty for life? Given the legal and political inferiority of all women but the queen—as firmly established in the West as in the East— how could female favoritism ever substitute for marriage? Hobart may be as misguided about the prospects of ambitious women as the English Roxolana of her morality tale.

Knowing what he knows about Charles's belated bid for control over his court and Parliament, and about all of the limitations on royal authority to come after 1688, Hamilton portrays the backroom escapades at Restoration court with both delight and regret. It was fun while it lasted, but couldn't the Stuarts have lasted a little longer if only Charles could have been, with respect to clientage, a bit more like Louis—or the Duchess of York, for that matter? The striking setting of the Hobart-Temple episode puts a gendered spin on the ambivalent recollections of the *Memoirs* as a whole. Early in the eighteenth century, some of the most outspoken and imaginative defenders of royal prerogative were feminists, who, notwithstanding their patriarchal extremes, found in absolutism, and sometimes also in the unlimited privileges associated with Eastern despotism, compelling examples and models of female agency, autonomy, and desire. The Hobart-Temple affair both celebrates and mocks this apparently contradictory discourse. Avoiding stinging critique and definitive positions, Hamilton instead sends readers' minds spiraling from the Whitehall room to its exotic counterparts and back, again and again, to contend with the instability and ongoing influence of favoritism, especially between women, during this period of political transition.

VIRTUAL FAVOR: READING THE SECRET
HISTORY IN MANUSCRIPT AND PRINT

The decline of the court and absolutist values came hand-in-hand with the growth of the print market and the public sphere in the early eighteenth century, as Habermas and many others have shown. In general, literary historians see the popularity of the genre of the secret history as both an effect and a gauge of the crucial new interrelationships between print publics and politics in this period. Procopius's account of the debauchery and excess at Justinian's Eastern Roman court was first published in English translation in the late seventeenth century. The *Anecdota* or *Secret History*, which describes such incidents as the Empress Theodora inviting courtiers to watch geese peck barley grains from between her legs, was not just of antiquarian interest but also provided a striking model for contemporary writers hoping to pique curiosity about what the English monarchy and nobility had been getting up to behind closed doors. Originally written in Greek in the sixth century and rediscovered in the Vatican a thousand years later, it garnered far more attention throughout Europe than the previous translations of Procopius's eight official military histories had done. *Anecdota* literally means unpublished things. But even in its original moment, long before the invention of the printing press, this title was somewhat contradictory and ironic, since from the start the book's express purpose had been to share royal secrets.

Curtis Perry has characterized all early modern treatments of favorites—including those that are apparently affirming—as vehicles for raising "questions concerning the nature of the relationship between monarch and subject" and therefore as means of defining and consolidating the critical orientation of the emerging modern public sphere.[96] To expose kings and queens' practical and emotional dependence on their inferiors was necessarily to begin to close the gap between sovereign and subject, and thus to license the criticism of the former by the latter. Several literary historians have argued that the secret history, as the literary genre most committed to representing closet intimacies and other court secrets, provided an especially apt channel for the critique from below of traditional elite codes of privacy and secrecy.[97] As Erin Keating observes in her study of the two earliest secret histories of the English court, "The interactions among secret histories and the communities of readers that coalesced around them helped to shape new notions of who had the right to speak and judge in political society."[98] When such texts circulated in print, they underscored readers' distance from official state actors. Rebecca Bullard thus defines the eighteenth-century British secret history as the exemplary genre of the new medium: "Against the clandestine world of the backstairs and closet, secret history pits the populist medium of print. While secrets are created in private, passed on through whispers or manuscripts that can be destroyed at a moment's notice, secret historians expose secrets in a printed and therefore highly public form. The medium in which their texts appear is thus central to their iconoclastic political aims."[99]

Yet *Memoirs of Count Grammont* directly supports populist values neither explicitly in its narrative nor implicitly in its mode of transmission. Hamilton composed the text, like the rest of his writings, to be circulated only in manuscript, and defines his own authority in relation to this traditional medium. In the opening chapter, he announces that his closet intimacy with his nobler, older, and more charming brother-in-law is the essential precondition of the book, thereby casting himself not as a professional, self-interested author or creator, but rather as Grammont's secretary: "I only hold the pen, while he directs it to the most remarkable and secret passages of his life."[100] While Grammont lived in England, Charles II had received him with warmth and provided him with a regular pension.[101] His brother-in-law owes the "most remarkable and secret passages of his life," stories he has often shared in conversation but never written down, to the fact that he had been in position to get a close-up view of Whitehall in its prime. Thus Hamilton implicitly establishes his own (lesser) authority by way of their intimate association. As dutiful servant to Grammont, Hamilton has been honored with imaginative, narrative access to the hidden corners of the Restoration court, and his act of transcription passes along a still more limited version of this privilege to others who know and love his brother-in-law as well as a few acquaintances at some slight remove from Grammont's inner circle. The hand-written text, which Hamilton called "Fragmens de la Vie du Comte de Gramont," extended the King's favor to a very select circle of readers with strong ties to the French or English courts. Hamilton's biographer, Ruth Clark, reports that Hamilton's sister Elizabeth read the manuscript "with great delight" in 1712, then immediately "had a copy made for the Duchess of Hanover, who professed to be no less 'diverted.'"[102]

However, Hamilton's investment in this traditionally circumscribed social imaginary is complicated not only by the transgressive energies of the secret history as such but also by his text's appearance in the emergent mass medium of print. Given the wide appeal of secret histories of the Restoration court and the limitations of authorial copyright in the period, Hamilton cannot have been terribly surprised when a French publisher began selling *Mémoires de la vie du Comte de Grammont contenant particulièrement I'Histoire Amoureuse de la Cour d'Angleterre sous le Regne du Roi Charles II*, with no named author, in 1713. Nor the following year, when London journalist Abel Boyer packaged his English translation as a *roman à clef*. Nor in 1715, when a new English edition with a key appended appeared.[103] Clark is certain that the appearance of the *Memoirs* in print was unplanned and unwelcome to Hamilton: "It was all very well to circulate the manuscript among a few friends; it was a different thing to divulge it to the public at large ... it could hardly please Hamilton to contribute to the amusement of the bourgeoisie by a work that was not intended for it and to have his family affairs discussed by a class for whom he had always entertained a profound contempt."[104] The original edition's obfuscation of both his authorship of the text and the identities of many of the courtiers in question would not necessarily have felt like protection, as these modes of secrecy could easily be interpreted as coy signals of the scandalous nature of its contents, given that secret histories tended explicitly to "constitute themselves as (potentially) libelous histories that need to sustain their own secrecy by obscuring the identity either of their authors or of the figures they aim to expose."[105] Though Hamilton did not seek this particular mode of political and legal edginess, in print his text nevertheless acquired it.

Thus the episodes come to signify somewhat differently in a commercial publication than they do in the manuscript. For invited aristocratic readers, the minutiae of court life documented on every page—that Frances Stewart is susceptible to fits of laughter, that Miss Blague swirls yellow ribbon through her hair when she dresses for the queen's masquerade, or that Lord Arlington uses a little plaster to cover the scar across his nose—are inside jokes that underscore both their proximity and their obligations to the court, reminding them that the text has effectively made them favorites of Grammont and, via Grammont, retrospectively, of the Stuarts as well.[106] Members of the larger and more heterogeneous audience of the printed secret history, by contrast, feel neither personally entitled to nor socially responsible for this sort of information. For them, all of the quirky details serve as abstract, if entertaining, evidence of the foolishness and vanity of the political body that they generally view from afar. Since, in his narration of the Hobart-Temple affair, Hamilton mocks Hobart's strident confidence in female favoritism, such readers may have felt this episode particularly empowered them to question the virtue and value of absolutist intimacies, even as they were trying on a new textual extension of this sort of connection.

When narrating the secret history's influence on the foundation of a modern reading public, literary historians have been interested in how this genre of British political writing shaped the development of the domestic novel. This literary history has particularly hinged on representations of heterosexual intimacies for obvious reasons. In his extensive account of the secret history's role as a crucial generic link in the evolution of the modern novel, McKeon proposes that this form "domesticates state politics through the 'sexual politics' of amatory intrigue and erotic romance: in a nation-state like England, where royal sovereignty depends on familial-dynastic inheritance," there is a "metonymic contiguity" between the political and the heterosexual.[107] Exploring the courtly closet as a key site for favoritism shifts attention to the vital role played by same-sex alliances within both the secret history and the social imagination it was helping to shape. It is interesting to consider, for example, how Samuel Richardson's *Pamela*, which for many literary and media historians represents the linchpin in the rise of commercial print and liberal ideology, may be reread with an eye to the homoerotic orientations of the elite closet.[108] Critics focused on the marriage plot have variously considered how Mr. B models the development required of the novel's own readers. As the libertine learns to read Pamela's letters to her parents as valid and touching expressions of personal experience rather than, as before, an unauthorized, even treasonous, secret history, he learns to value the affective autonomy which, Richardson aims to show, is the ideal basis for wifely submission.[109] Yet Pamela's dangerous visibility in the Bedfordshire estate, indeed her very literacy, has depended on the many hours she had spent with Lady B in her mistress's dressing room, being taught to read widely, write, and embroider all of the accomplishments of a fine lady. After Lady B's death, Mr. B's sister, Lady Davers, is unwilling to inherit this relationship, and Mrs. Jervis, the housekeeper, is herself too dependent to match the level of protection provided by Pamela's first mistress. In a sense, Pamela has no choice but to marry her master. Insofar as Richardson finally asks readers to celebrate Mr. B's reform and his sincere love for Pamela, the novel undoubtedly shores up the subversive political power of the secret history. But if we imagine *Pamela* as a sequel to the Hobart episode in *Memoirs of Count Grammont*, a melancholy shadow narrative about the decline of female favoritism glimmers into view.[110]

Houses of office

Pepys refers to a small room reserved exclusively for excretion as a *house of office*. He had one such room on an upper level—probably outside on the leads—of his Seething Lane home, likely an area of about fifty square feet, with a wooden opening over a vault that emptied into the cellar.[1] He expresses satisfaction when the vault is cleared out from time to time, but it's only tangential to the various home improvement projects he dreams up and carries out throughout the diary. Especially relative to his fascination with the potential social and symbolic value of other kinds of private space, the house of office holds little interest.

The vagueness regarding the house of office is probably more a reflection of the fact that he rarely has to go there than of any prudishishness about bodily functions in general or excretion in particular. Ongoing problems with constipation and gas keep him attuned to his own cycles of suffering and release, which he often records in his journal, such as in this October 1663 entry: "And so rose in the morning in perfect good ease. But only strain I put myself to to shit, more then I needed. But continued all the morning well, and in the afternoon had a natural easily and dry stoole, the first I have had these five days or six, for which God be praised."[2] Following the general practice of wealthier Londoners, he uses a ceramic chamber pot inside, sometimes tucked into a decorated wooden box, then passes along the task of emptying and cleaning it to others. After great success with a laxative pill one morning, he records that his wife and their maid Ashwell actually have a bonding moment en route to the house of office: they "between them spilt the pot of piss and turd upon the floor and stool and God knows what, and were mighty merry washing of it clean."[3]

Morover, he's capable of waxing philosophical about waste. With his neighbors, William Batten and John Mennes, he contemplates the cultural relativism of excretory practices on discovering that in Portugal "they scorn to make a seat for a house of office. But they do shit all in pots and so empty them in the river."[4] When one of King Charles's dogs spontaneously relieves himself on the deck of the boat taking the Stuarts back to England, Pepys registers, with pleasure, how the occurrence signals the limits of hierarchical categorizations of human and animal bodies: the dog "made us [all] laugh and me think that a King and all that belong to him are but just as others are."[5] However, this openness is not really evident in his approach to his own privy or those belonging to the other residents of the housing complex. Unlike the king's dog, a pet eagle that Pepys and his wife apparently kept in their privy is condemned for its waste and soon given away. "We were glad to be rid of her, she fouling our house of office mightily," Pepys writes.[6]

Structural features at Seething Lane make it difficult decisively to attribute authority over the spaces at the bottom and at the top of the building, where the houses of office have the greatest impact on other residents. Pepys confronts the practical and social difficulties of these shared peripheries shortly after moving in. As he wanders in the cellar considering where to put in a new window—a replacement for the one that William Batten has had bricked up—Pepys steps "into a great heap" of another neighbor's shit, "by which I found that Mr. Turners house of office is full and comes into my cellar."[7] Because it's not always clear which will be the fastest and fairest route for clearing out an individual sewage vault, the negotiations around waste removal sometimes get heated, especially as the residents become more proprietary over their borrowed space over the years. On an evening when he himself happens to be "full of wind," Pepys purposely "sit[s] up a little longer than ordinary" to keep an eye on the men clearing Thomas Turner's sewage "out of my cellar." When they figure out how to take "the turds up through Mr. Turners own house," he goes to bed.[8] A few weeks later, Pepys exchanges "some high words" with Lady Batten about the planned cleaning of his house of office, before he "at last agree[s] that it should be done through my office, and so all well."[9] Ultimately, Pepys is again pleasantly surprised that the laborers do the work "with much more cleanness than I expected."[10]

There are also occasional negotiations over bad smells on the rooftop area. When Pepys is having the upper terrace renovated, William Penn informs him that John Mennes, who lives right next door, is worried that the Pepys's project is going to get in the way of his own family's house of office.[11] Pepys immediately goes to reassure him. A few years later, Pepys is enjoying the completed terrace with some guests when they are "driven down again with a stink by Sir W. Pen's shying of a shitten pot in their house of office close by."[12] The forms of intimacy, ownership, status, and obligation that Pepys intuitively associates with other closets are premised on the possibility of clear boundaries to be temporarily dropped only at the will of their owners. Such boundaries are obviously complicated by the processes for which houses of office are designed. However welcome the visitors themselves might be, they leave burdensome gifts that can disrupt the usual flow of good will and favor.

Yet the antisocial quality of the house of office gives it a kind of edgy glamor too, as in the case of "a pretty story" that Mennes tells him about a mutual acquaintance who has twice escaped from prison, once dressed in women's clothing and another time "through a house of office."[13] And these spaces also sometimes serve as makeshift sites of privacy or secrecy. He and Elizabeth are heartbroken to discover that their youngest servant, Will, has stolen six shillings out of another servant's closet, "and hid it in the house of office."[14] Feeling vulnerable at the height of the Second Anglo-Dutch War, Pepys contemplates "flinging" some of his own money there.[15]

3

Lady Acheson's Privy for Two

It is not simply that the writer makes a "gift" of his work by laying it out at the patron's feet. In some sense the work always was his—the poet simply restores it to its rightful parent or owner.

—Dustin Griffin[1]

On the whole, the history of plumbing, and of technology generally in English country houses, has been one of installing gadgets which fail to work. It is a two-steps-forward one-step-back story.

—Mark Girouard[2]

Where there is dirt there is system.

—Mary Douglas[3]

Revisiting Market Hill

The English word *privy* has as full and fertile a history as *closet*, which it predates by at least a hundred years. Beginning in the thirteenth century, *privy* could denote a private room or small building for urinating or defecating in; a favorite or close companion, including a sexual intimate; or any person, thing, or action kept secret or hidden. All of these senses of the word inform Jonathan Swift's earliest scatological poem. Written in 1730, "Panegyric on the Dean in the Person of a Lady of the North" is a tribute to Market Hill, the country estate in County Armagh, Northern Ireland, where Swift stayed for three summers in a row between 1728 and 1730, to his hosts Lord Arthur Acheson, Irish politician and baronet, and his wife Lady Anne Acheson, daughter of the Lord Chancellor of Ireland, and especially to the pair of outhouses, or earth closets as they were then sometimes known, that he built there.[4] The "Panegyric" was not intended for print publication: it was a gift for his patroness, Lady Acheson, who is also the poem's putative speaker. In the poem, Lady Anne finally concedes that the earth closets Swift has made are better than indoor privies, but not before imagining at length a golden age of excremental freedom under the sun and stars, a time before time, when nymphs and swains didn't feel the need to hide themselves in structures like this or of any sort.

Soon after the "Panegyric," Swift wrote "A Lady's Dressing-Room," "A Beautiful Young Nymph Going to Bed," "Strephon and Chloe," and "Cassinus and Peter," a group of poems that sealed his reputation as a writer obsessed with bodily waste, especially its role in the intimate imagination.[5] Since the mid-twentieth century, criticism of Swift's first scatological poem, as of his later excremental writings, has tended to emphasize the abstract symbolism and antisocial or antiromantic feelings, whether despair, disgust, or, at best, playful narcissism, of the poem's vivid references to outhouses and shit, sometimes leaning on psychoanalytic concepts of sublimation and infantile anal eroticism that take excrement as a marker of culture's raw, unstable borders, or as the primal material of human creativity.[6] For instance, Carole Fabricant sees the "Panegyric" as "part of Swift's idiosyncratic and extremely complicated version of *Civilization and Its Discontents*.... Viewed in ideological terms, the verse dramatizes the ironic tensions between the 'Tory' and the 'anarchist' elements that are ever present in Swift; that is, between his theoretical belief in the societal need for sublimation and his temperamental antipathy to all forms of restraint."[7] Everett Zimmerman argues that locating an authorial center, always difficult with Swift, is especially tricky in this poem because its apparent idealization of nature "collapses in the ubiquity of excrement."[8] Kelly Anspaugh notes the visceral force of Swift's excremental theme: "We are all uneasy in the presence of the turd, which is what makes it so effective as a satirical trope. It is effective precisely because it is so *affective*—gets us in the guts, so to speak."[9] Frederich Bogel proposes that the fundamental project of all satire is to interrogate categorical distinctions and suggests that Swift's scatological writings, including the "Panegyric," serve this broader agenda: "Dramatic and insistent as the question of excrement sometimes is," Bogel writes, "in Swift, it is nevertheless part of a larger fascination with the problematics of boundaries and transgression, separation and contamination, inside and outside, and with the complexity and ambiguity that so often surround them."[10] Sophie Gee argues that the poem's treatment of waste serves to underscore Swift's "earthly poetics."[11] Most recently, Peter Smith has suggested that the nihilism and elitism of Swift's scatological satires put them "temperamentally" in line with those of his predecessor Rochester.[12] But when and where to go were not only abstract questions in Swift's day. As it elucidates the "Panegyric"'s prescient exploration of the material culture of excretory privacy and of the architecture of intimacy more broadly, this chapter highlights some of Swift's more concrete and affective concerns. Over the course of the poem, the pair of earth closets become a setting and symbol of changing social, bodily, and textual relations as potent and layered as the bathing closet in the *Memoirs*. A satirical monument to the erosion of traditional country house values, the double privies at once encapsulate Swift's awkwardness around literary patronage and serve to reinvigorate his relationship to Lady Acheson.

THE RISE OF THE WATER CLOSET

The early eighteenth-century material culture of excretion is best illuminated by setting it against the longer history whose outcome is familiar today: the emergence of a technology capable of instantly flushing away waste. When it was coined in England in the mid-eighteenth century, the term *water closet* reflected both a long-standing interest in designing out-of-the-way interiors especially for excretion, and the modern plumbing systems that could minimize their smell—in theory, without any additional human labor. By the twentieth century, indoor toilets with plumbing had of course become predictable features of domestic architecture throughout much of the Western world. In England and Ireland, both the rooms and the apparatuses they contain are still called water closets.

The eighteenth-century water closet had distant predecessors in monastic privies and feudal garde-robes. The religious versions had smelled better. As Lawrence Wright puts it, in the middle ages, "the monasteries were the guardians of culture—and of sanitation."[13] In fact, in Britain, as with bathing, the concept of sanitation is anachronistic with regard to excretion until well into the nineteenth century, when sewage was first approached not simply as an olfactory inconvenience but a major public health concern.[14] Exceptionally, medieval monasteries were situated near rivers and streams to ensure that they would have a running water supply. Not only did monks wash before and after meals, but they urinated and defecated in structures built solely for this purpose. Privies were distanced from other buildings, sometimes linked to the monks' sleeping quarters by way of long ventilating bridges, and subdivided inside—with partitions between back-to-back or rows of seats—to accommodate a collective and punctual regime of bodily discipline. A seventeenth-century account of an ancient monastery at Durham describes

> a large and decent place, adjoining to the West-side of the ... Dorter [dormitory], towards the water, for the Monks and Novices to resort to, called the Privies ... Every Seat and Partition was of Wainscott, close on either side, so that they could not see one another when they were in that place. There were as many Seats on either side as there were little Windows in the Wall to give light to the said Seats.... At the West-end of it there were three fair glass Windows; which great Windows gave light to the whole House.[15]

In *The Life of St. Gregory*, the privy "is the retreat recommended for uninterrupted reading."[16] Vertical shafts below each seat funneled waste into a walled-in sewer pipe through which water flowed, either directly or indirectly, from a natural source.

In palaces, castles, and manor-houses of the medieval period, the privy or privy house might be designed along the same lines as those in monastic privies: multiple stalls were grouped together and each seat opened over a shaft. Estates without access to rivers and streams turned to moats or large earth pits as sewage receptacles, which were more rank because more stagnant. After the Protestant Reformation and the dissolution of Catholic institutions in England, the new aristocratic inhabitants of the former convents and monasteries tended to use the privies exactly as had been done before. But in the sixteenth century, around the same time that closets were becoming more prominent in elite households and courts in England, the privy, also known as the garde-robe, withdraught, jakes, latrine, necessary, convenience, gong, closet of ease, or house of office, was often placed near an important chamber of the household, with several seats side by side and, like the privy above Pepys's home, stacked over a sewage pit. When they were tucked away in the building's walls, Girouard points out, from the outside, "the series of projections built to contain the privies and their shafts could be an impressive feature."[17]

As enclosed, shared spaces, privies made occupants intensely aware of differences of station and quality, and more so, or differently, than in other closets because of the acutely embodied focus of their use. In general, the meaning of privy intimacy varied even more extensively than that associated with other kinds of private space leading up to and throughout the long eighteenth century. In the medieval period, an abbot at the

Redburn Priory had a private latrine constructed because the brother-hood disliked communal excretion when it included their superior: "for-merly one building had served [the abbot] and the brethren there, where-fore they were ashamed when they had to go to the Necessary in his presence."[18] Witnessing a superior in this position was not necessarily an honor at court either. In the late fifteenth and early sixteenth centuries, the groom of the stool or stole, who was assigned the care of the royal privy, was not a role for a great favorite. Yet after the Tudor monarchs moved the royal bed from the great chamber into the privy chamber (the room next to the privy), the status of this office improved somewhat. It improved further still, Girouard explains, when,

> in the later sixteenth and seventeenth centuries, as part of the con-stant series of retreats that make up the history of palace planning ... [what had been the privy chamber] became a private dining and re-ception room, with a suite of private chambers beyond it, all collec-tively known as the privy lodgings. The groom of the stole remained in charge of the whole sequence; an official whose original job had been to clean out the royal latrines had become one of the most pow-erful and confidential of royal servants.[19]

Though the social position of grooms of the stole improved to the extent that their duties extended beyond the basic management of human waste, it is also significant that such duties came to be seen as continuous with and as honorable as other forms of care for the royal body.

It was at this point that an innovative new kind of privy became imag-inable. Sir John Harington, a godson of Elizabeth I, is credited with being the first to reconceive it.[20] Punning on a jakes or jack, two other common names for the privy (and ancestor to our john), Harington's *Metamorphosis of Ajax* is an extensive treatise on excretory cultures past and present that also offers practical advice on how to "[free] this noysome place from all annoyance" by means of a flush and a valve (figure 17).[21] To construct the flushing device, an illustrated guide instructs: "In the Privie that annoyes you, first cause a Cesterne ... to be placed either be-hind the seat, in any place, either in the roome, or above it, from whence the water may, by a small pype of leade of an inch be convayed under the seate in the hinder part therof (but quite out of sight); to which pype you must have a Cocke or washer, to yeeld water with some pretie strength when you would let it in."[22] The guide provides further detailed advice as to the construction of the privy vessel. It is to be a slanted oval bowl,

This is Don AJAX house of the new fashion, all in sunder;
that a workman may see what he hath to do.

Here is the same, all put together; that the work-
man may see if it be well.

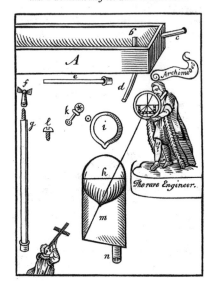
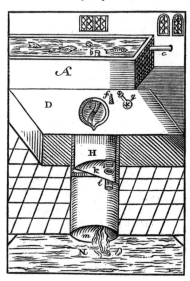

FIG. 17. A how-to guide appears in the second of Harington's book's three parts. (Illustrations reprinted from Sir John Harington, *An Anatomy of the Metamorpho-sed Ajax* [Chiswick: C. Whittingham, 1814], 10, 13. Courtesy of Osler Library, McGill University.)

dressed with some impermeable substance, to the bottom of which is fastened a lockable brass washer, which shuts out the smell of the privy shaft below. "If water be plentie, the oftener it is used and opened, the sweeter; but if it be scant, once a day is inough, for a need, though twenty persons should use it.... And this being well done, and orderly kept, your worst privy may be as sweet as your best chamber."[23] The garderobes in palaces and great houses were sometimes manually cleaned with rainwater—but to little effect. Harington's simple and elegant design, which he had constructed on his own estate, was far more effective in preventing unpleasant odors from permeating the room.

In addition to providing practical instructions for privy improvements, the *Metamorphosis* seeks to elevate excretion as a topic of discourse.[24] Harington had been banished from court after circulating a risqué episode of *Orlando Furioso* among the queen's maids of honor and won back Elizabeth's favor only after dedicating his complete English translation of this romance to her. By the time he was disseminating his new work on privies under the pseudonym Miscamos, he had also already had his invention installed for the queen at Richmond Palace.[25] Harington predicts that detractors will be offended by his project not because of excrement's intrinsically disruptive qualities or associations but because of its indecorous triviality, and he weaves a rebuttal to these objections into his prefatory materials. In a opening letter, Miscamos's cousin and patron, Philostilpnos, urges him to write and publish the book: "all my feare is that your pen having bene inured to so high discourse, / *Of Dames, of Knights, of armes, of loves delight* / will now disdaine to take so base a subject, / *Of vaults, of sinkes, privies & draughts to write* / But," Philostilpnos pleads, "herein let a publik benefit expell a private bashfulness."[26] The *Metamorphosis* characterizes this traditional approach to excretion in a later passage: "some will object, that [the privy] was never of that importaunce, but that it was left to each mans owne care to provide, for that which concerned his own peculiar necessitie."[27] In his roughly contemporaneous *Four Books of Architecture*, the Italian architect Andrea Palladio compares the elements of built space to the parts of the body in an analogy that aligns and privileges the qualities of beauty, visibility, and grandeur: "As our Blessed Creator has ordered these our members in such a manner, that the most beautiful are in places most exposed to view, and the less comely more hidden; so in building also, we ought to put the principal and considerable parts, in places most seen, and the less beautiful in places as much hidden from the eye as possible; that in them may be lodged all the foulness of the house."[28] When Harington worries that certain readers will think that he has inflated the "importaunce" of the privy, he acknowledges the new influence on the English elite of Palladio's neoclassical spatial cosmology.

It took nearly a hundred years for the technical innovations that Harington described to catch on. By the mid-seventeenth century, the classical splendor of large open spaces competed with more various and specialized methods of apportioning space. Water, flowing more efficiently than ever before, came into fashion, in the form of fountains, marble basins, buffets, and baths, and some privies benefited from the installation of pipes and sophisticated drainage systems. After a tour through Windsor Castle in the late seventeenth century, travel writer Celia Fiennes records that, in the apartments of Prince George of Denmark, she had observed "a little place wth a seate of Easement of Marble wth sluces of water to wash all down," and in Queen Anne's apartment directly above it, "Just such marble seates of Easem^t wth the sluces of water as that below." Fiennes's detailed description may have been the sort of thing Swift had in mind when, in his *Mechanical Operations of the Spirit*, he mocked those who assumed the authority to depict significant places on the basis of having seen one or two inconsequential parts: "As if a Traveller should go about to describe a *Palace*, when he had seen nothing but the *Privy*."[29]

But it took nearly a hundred more years before water closets were regular features of English architecture. In 1775, Alexander Cummings took out the first patent for a valve closet, much like the one Harington had invented in the late sixteenth century. In 1777, Samuel Prosser patented a privy that used a ball float to control the flow of clean water into the basin. An advertisement for Prosser's privies boasted that they "[f]ar excel any ever made, or invented for SWEETNESS, and Ease to be kept in repair," adding that "the different Noblemen ... in the three kingdoms having used them with satisfaction, will be a means of promoting them."[30] The smell is the immediate problem water closet designers want to rectify, voicing a growing concern for the degree of "satisfaction" users can take in the experience and in domestic comfort more generally. A year later, watchmaker and jeweller Josiah Bramah found a new solution to the problem of backwash by using two valves, one to bring water into the basin and the other to remove it.

Though in retrospect the water closet can be made to play a leading role in a coming-of-age story about the triumph of domestic hygiene, its future was uncertain in Swift's day.[31] In fact, Girouard characterizes the middle of the eighteenth century as a plumbing slump: "By 1730 ... any country house could in theory have running water on all floors, and as many baths and water-closets as its owners wanted or could afford. But comparatively little use was made of this technology in the next fifty years.... Water-closets became, if anything, less common."[32] Similarly, Wright observes that "even in the great houses" water closets were "rather rare and rude."[33] In his mid-eighteenth-century plans for the massive Kedleston Hall, Palladian architect James Paine included only one indoor privy. In 1734, William Kent designed "only a windowless 'two-holer' in an odd corner of the hall" at the Earl of Leicester's country house in Norfolk. If the elite who cared enough did have their privies designed with special care, these facilities elicited the same combination of wonder and suspicion as other novelties in this period. When in 1718 Royal Society member John Aubrey saw "a pretty machine to cleanse an House of Office" at an estate in Surrey, he described its operation with scientific precision. He noticed that the "pretty machine" jetted "a small stream of water no bigger than one's finger, which ran into an engine made like a bit of a fire-shovel, which hung upon its centre of gravity, so that when it was full a considerable quantity of water fell down with some force."[34] Horace Walpole was struck by the number and sophistication of the built-in stools he glimpsed on a tour of Aelia Laelie Chudley's house, reporting in a letter to a friend: "But of all curiosities, are the conveniences in every bedchamber: great mahogany projections ... with the holes, with brass handles, and cocks, &c.—I could not help saying, it was the *loosest* family I ever saw!"[35]

A much more basic means of dealing with waste in the household still suited the minority of people wealthy enough to contemplate the addition of water closets. Well into the eighteenth century, the most common path to the sewer was not via the privy shaft but via the chamber pot, also known as the *commode* or *close stool*. Chamber pots and commodes were more mobile and versatile than their built-in counterparts, and their construction, use, and labor varied dramatically across different social groups. As Pepys's *Diary* attests, the maintenance of built-in indoor privies could entail some degree of labor management as well as occasional social and spatial negotiations by owners. However, the main effort involved in transporting waste matter to the cesspit was absorbed by users, who walked to the privy then let gravity—or water and gravity—take care of the rest. By contrast, the elite use of chamber pots reinforced the traditional social hierarchy much more often and much more intimately. Whereas the poor emptied their simple clay pots themselves, sometimes straight out the window of their lodgings, the elite used more elaborately decorated commodes and close stools and constantly offloaded the labor of disposal onto their servants, drafting them into an endless, stinking exchange. As Fabricant puts it, "In eighteenth-century England and Ireland ... the relationship between the upper and lower classes, between master and servant, was defined, at least in part, excrementally."[36]

The seventeenth century had seen the advent in courts and noble households of private staircases leading directly to and from the most remote rooms in elite apartments. The backstairs were understood to be the ideal site for the entrance and exit of anyone, or anything, that the owner preferred to keep from general view—including chamber pots. For Alan Bray, the structures and practices of excretory concealment mark the beginning of a general descent in status and significance of this sort of daily physical contact with a royal or noble patron: "Such service began to be regarded not as indicative of [an honorable mode of] intimacy but as menial or degrading."[37] Swift's own unfinished mock-instruction guide, *Directions to Servants*, derides the new social economy of service that chamber pots and backstairs reinforce. Speaking as a butler-instructor,

Swift encourages the housemaid to exploit the contrast between her mistress's furtive use of her commode and the potential hypervisibility of its contents during their disposal:

> I am very much offended with those Ladies, who are so proud and lazy, that they will not be at the Pains of stepping into the Garden to pluck a Rose, but keep an odious Implement sometimes in the Bedchamber itself, or at least in a dark Closet adjoining, which they make Use of to ease their worst Necessities; and, you are the usual Carriers away of the Pan, which maketh not only the Chamber, but even their Cloaths offensive, to all who come near. Now, to cure them of this odious Practice, let me advise you on whom this Office lies, to convey away this Utensil, that you will do it openly, down the great Stairs, and in the Presence of the Footmen; and, if any Body knocks, to open the Street-door, while you have the Vessel filled in your Hands. This, if any Thing can, will make your Lady take the Pains of evacuating in the proper Place.[38]

While Swift implicitly disciplines the passive-aggressive housemaid, the satirical instruction is clear and direct in its condemnation of the "proud and lazy" noblewoman she must serve. The servant is encouraged to make use of her negligible power to expose the pot and its contents to the footmen who pass her on the "great Stairs" as well as to the people of quality who call at the front door. Though the servant is cunning—shaming her mistress without resorting to a face-to-face confrontation that would likely cost her her position—the lady is much worse: a hypocrite, who fills her "odious Implement" in her private apartments rather than going to the garden, the "proper Place" to "ease the worst Necessities," according to the speaker. Underlying the lady's efforts at excretory secrecy are the several desires—for physical comfort, seamless domesticity, and (the appearance of) a closed and fully autonomous body—that would soon come together to fuel the modern rise of the water closet.

Privy Prayers

When Swift built the outdoor privies at Market Hill, he was participating in a new trend. As the construction of water closets briefly lapsed, "a fashion started for outdoor earth closets" among country-house owners, Girouard explains.[39] Generally without plumbing, these outdoor spaces, sometimes called earth houses or boghouses, were designed with an eye to some of the same concerns that more sophisticated facilities were supposed to provide: that is, ensuring a pleasant, "sweet and clean" experience for the user and freeing the house from the lingering odors of the privy shaft. A Norfolk gentleman's specifications for the "little house" he was having built in the garden of his estate show that above all he wanted the place to feel fresh: "I would have it as light as possible. There must be a good broad place to set a candle on, and a place to keep paper ... though the better the plainer, it should be neat."[40] Swift obviously also reflected on his little houses as he was making them. To what extent is privacy during excretion a natural and reasonable desire, Swift wonders in his "Panegyric," and to what extent is it a desire indicated by and indicative of a new kind of selfish orientation? Throughout the poem, he praises himself in the voice of his friend, Lady Acheson, "the Lady of the North," as she rambles from her house through its adjoining farm into the countryside, then back home again for dinner.[41] Along the way he has her contemplating the architecture of excretion, ultimately picturing privy privacy as the essence of humanity's modern fall into the iron age—into culture, sin, and shame.

According to the poem's semifictional premise, Swift's generosity and gallantry as a house guest have occasioned its composition: "Resolved my gratitude to show ... / ... now in all our sex's name, / My artless muse shall sing your fame," Lady Anne begins.[42] "In each capacity I mean / To sing your praise" (43–44). Swift has contributed in many ways to life at Market Hill. Addressing him directly, Lady Anne first lists his actions and qualities that have improved relations with the surrounding community: his respectful treatment of the neighborhood ladies—"By your example and assistance, / The fellows learn to know their distance" (55–56); his erudition as a preacher—"How your superior learning shines / Above our neighbouring dull divines" (63–64); his sharp conversation—"Your style is clear, and so concise, / We never ask to hear you twice" (73–74); and his manners—"such address, and grateful port, / As clearly shows you bred at court" (82–84). Next she considers the services he performs so well in and around the household: he plays butler's mate (selecting wines), guide and seamstress (leading hikes then darning the socks ruined en route), tutor (improving Lady Anne's reading and speech), and jester (making jokes to please everyone, whether "A duchess or a kitchen girl").

There is a slightly bitter or brittle tinge to these initial compliments. Is Swift perhaps a bit too pleased with himself? Too solicitous or officious? A bit too paternalistic with all the women? The suspicion that Lady Anne's flattery is backhanded is confirmed when she looks to the farm

and lands at Market Hill where Swift works as "thatcher, ditcher, gar-
dener, bailie" (157) and "dairy handmaid" (167), noting that "to a genuis
so extensive, / No work is grievous or offensive" (157–58). Though not
yet in view, the outhouses are already in the air. One set of projects that
the dean "ponder[s] long" "with anxious thought" (161) includes building pig sties, rat-proofing a vault, and cleaning the chicken coop (159–
66). He also invents a method for separating butter from whey in a time-
consuming process involving a bottle (167–86):

> Three morning hours you toss and shake
> The bottle, till your fingers ache:
> Hard is the toil, nor small the art,
> The butter from the whey to part:
> Behold; a frothy substance rise;
> Be cautious, or your bottle flies.
> The butter comes; our fears are ceased;
> And, out you squeeze an ounce at least. (179–86)

The pains Swift takes to squeeze out a tiny pat of butter reminds Lady
Anne of the hours he passes, nearly fruitlessly, "bent upon some smart
lampoon" (189):

> You toss and turn your brain till noon;
> Which, in its jumblings round the skull,
> Dilates, and makes the vessel full:
> While nothing comes but froth at first,
> You think your giddy head will burst:
> But squeezing out four lines in rhyme,
> Are largely paid for all your time. (187–96)

Swift's brain is like the butterbottle; the indiscriminate mass of ideas he
quickly generates is the froth; and the two couplets worth keeping after
a hard morning at the writing desk are the meager bit of butter.

Onerous and anticlimactic, Swift's creative efforts suggest not only
impotence but also constipation, setting the tone for the skeptical treatment of the earth closets to come. "Palladio was not half so skilled in /
The grandeur or the art of building," Lady Anne announces, examining them:

> Two temples of magnific size,
> Attract the curious traveller's eyes,

That might be envied by the Greeks;
Raised up by you in twenty weeks. (199–203)

Just as before she has mocked the pitiful ratio of stuff produced to effort made, here her hyperbole and concerns with labor and time undercut the apparent praise of the outhouses. While the privies' exteriors at least have the potential to dignify the public face of Market Hill, their façade is belied by the interior space, which turns occupants' attention away from the social world of the estate:

Here, gentle goddess Cloacine
Receives all offerings at her shrine.
In separate cells the he's and she's
Here pay their vows with bended knees;
(For, 'tis prophane when sexes mingle;
And every nymph must enter single;
And when she feels an *inward motion*,
Comes filled with *reverence* and *devotion*.) (205–12)

Swift may have been ahead of the curve in designating each of the two privies for only one sex. "Perhaps the first mention in history of 'Ladies' and 'Gentlemen' in this connection is in the report of a great Ball in Paris in 1739," Wright remarks, "which tells, as of a remarkable innovation, that [the hosts] had even taken the precaution of allotting cabinets with inscriptions over the doors, *Garderobes pour les femmes* and *Garderobes pour les hommes*, with chambermaids in the former and valets in the latter."[43] Pious disciples bequeath "offerings" in Swift's separate houses of worship. They have been called to the outhouse because they are, like the gassy enthusiasts in his *Mechanical Operations*, "filled" with piety.[44] While the imagined devotees in the "Panegyric" pay "vows" to Cloacine, the Roman goddess of the sewers and conjugal love, the "separate cells" of the privies also facilitate the solitude and inwardness usually reserved for the Protestant prayer closet in this period.

In his *Metamorphosis of Ajax*, Harington had already presented the privy as a site of spiritual privacy in a poem about a conflict between a clergyman and the devil:

A goodly Father sitting on a draught,
To doe as neede, and nature hath us taught;
Mumbled (as was his maner) certen prayr's,
And unto him, the Divell straight repayr's,

And boldly to revile him he begins,
Alledging that such prayr's are deadly sins;
And that it shewd, he was devoyd of grace,
To speake to God, from so unmeete a place.
The reverend man, though at the first dismaid;
Yet strong in faith, to Satan thus he said.
Thou damned spirit, wicked, false and lying,
Dispairing thine own good, & ours envying:
Each take his due, and me thou canst not hurt,
To God my pray'r I meant, to thee the durt.[45]

Harking back to the English privy's ecclesiastic origins, Harington's little verse-parable maps the Christian split of good and evil, spirit and matter, heaven and hell, purity and profanity onto the vertically oriented closet and shaft, insisting, finally, that, "Pure prayr ascends to him that high doth sit, / Down fals the filth, for fiends of hel more fit" (figure 18).[46] Harington was writing not long before the King James Bible's new version of Matthew 6.6 had enjoined Protestants to pray specifically in closets. In "mumbl[ing] … certaine prayers," the reverend perhaps exhibits the kind of unthinking piety that Protestant authors of closet-prayer guides sought to prevent. For instance, in *Duties of the Closet*, William Dawes had surmised, "If we keep our Minds within our Closets, we shall find it an easy matter to fix them upon such Objects as are proper for those Places; and if we let them go out of them, and ramble about the World, it is not for want of Power and Opportunity, but want of Will and Endeavour, to Restrain them." Understanding consciousness to be entirely within the thinker's control, Dawes counsels his readers to

Sprinto non spinto.   More feard than hurt.

A godly father, sitting on a draught,
To do as need and nature hath us taught,

D

FIG. 18. The reverend father insists that a privy is a decent place to pray. (Illustration reprinted from Sir John Harington, *The Metamorphosis of Ajax* [Chiswick: C. Whittingham, 1814], 33. Courtesy of Osler Library, McGill University.)

direct their minds with special care in their closets: "Resolve ... with thy Self to set a watch upon thy Thoughts, and to make Advantage of thy Retirement, by sending up thy Mind, which may now easily disengage it self from Earth, to Heaven."[47] When the devil distracts the "goodly Father" as he prays alone, Harington's poem enacts one of the paradoxical rationales of this practice. As Thomas Brooks would later put it: "If Closet Prayer be not an indispensible duty that Christ hath laid upon all his people, why doth Satan so much oppose it, why doth he so industriously and so unweariedly labour to discourage Christians in it, & to take off Christians from it?"[48] Harington justifies his improvements to the privy with a pun on its more abstract signification: "If we wold amend our privie faults first, we should afterward much the better reforme the open offences."[49] And Harington plays up the correspondence between spiritual interiority and the private depths of the house in a mnemonic couplet: *"To keepe your houses sweete, cleanse privie vaults, / To keepe your soules as sweete, mend privie faults."*[50] These axioms echo in Brooks's basic rationale for praying in private: "Secret-Prayer sweetly enclines, & strongly disposes a Christian to all other religious duties and services" (figure 19).[51]

Like Harington, Swift elevates his invention as a conduit to two kinds of sweetness at once. Michael Edson has recently argued that eighteenth-century poets commonly fused ancient pagan or secular ideas of retreat with newer Christian ones. Edson especially notes the influence of the "native tradition" of closet prayer on British retirement poetry: "For the increasingly middle-class audiences of such poetry, without a classical education but schooled in Protestant piety, 'retirement' evoked not the Sabine farm but the prayer closet. The growing stress on meditation, along with changes in the setting of poems after 1690, reflects the impact of a Protestant ideal of retirement as a withdrawal from worldly preoccupations for the purposes of spiritual reflection."[52] Though Swift prayed in private every day, he wasn't above looking critically at this (or any)

FIG. 19. In the corner of Harington's instructional diagrams, a priest blesses the water closet. (Detail from *An Anatomy of the Metamorpho-sed Ajax*, 10. Courtesy of Osler Library, McGill University.)

religious practice.[53] One of Swift's original closet prayers emphasizes that the very recognition of a capacity for and the benefits of intimacy with God depends on God's grace: "Lord, since we cannot know thee but by often drawing near unto thee, and coming into thy presence, which in this life we can do only by prayer, O make us, therefore, ever sensible of these great benefits of prayer, that we may rejoice at all opportunities of coming into thy presence, and may ever find ourselves the better for it and more heavenly minded by it."[54] Showing the resemblances between classical and contemporary, excretory and spiritual modes of retirement in the "Panegyric," Swift reiterates the point that simply separating oneself from the rest of the household does not automatically lead to moral or spiritual elevation.

The Privy Pastoral

After Lady Anne wanders past the privies to the meadows surrounding her estate, a longing sets in. She "sigh[s] to think of ancient days" (226): "Thee bounteous goddess Cloacine, / To temples why do we confine?," she muses, "Forbid in open air to breathe; / Why are thine altars fixed beneath?" (229–32). And she begins to conjure a mythic golden age of excremental libertinism, before the invention of human law, before the enclosure of the commons, when, no sooner than the impulse struck them, nymphs and swains "placed / Their sacrifice [to Cloacina] with zeal and haste" (239–40), whether at the "margin of a purling stream" (241), in the "shelter of a shady grove" (246), or "in some flowery vale." Cloacina then reigned over not a human-made network of sewers but the whole "earthly globe," and her pagan "votaries" were repaid for their spontaneous offerings with lovely blossoms, including "many a flower abstersive"; flowers, that is, whose purgative properties help to sustain humans' humble role within an ecological cycle of ingestion, excretion, fertilization, and growth.

Lady Anne's portrait of the dawning of a dystopian iron age superimposes images of ancient political imperialism and contemporary cultural imperialism. Whereas in libertine pastorals such as Thomas Carew's "A Rapture" and Aphra Behn's "Golden Age," the fall into culture, Christianity, and shame is specifically a fall into sexual repression, in the "Panegyric," excremental repression precipitates human decline. When Jove, Roman god of law, state, and society, triumphs over Saturn, god of agriculture, it is Gluttony, the usurper's "bloated harpy sprung from hell"

(269), who "confine[s]" free-spirited Cloacina "to a cell" (270); and the hell from which Gluttony emanates is evidently France. Wedging herself into "a spacious elbow-chair," a large soft recliner designed for Louis XV's court, and gorging on a "treble share" of food, Gluttony plots to convert "harmless" natives to her ways—to supersize them.[55] She "sends her priests ... / From haughty Gaul ... ,"

> ... to make ragouts
> Instead of wholesome bread and cheese,
> To dress their soups and fricassees;
> And, for [their] home-bred British cheer,
> Botargo, catsup, and caveer.[56] (263–68)

Harington had taken a lighthearted view of the effects of intemperance: "He that makes his belly his God, I wold have him make a Jakes his chappell."[57] The more his new machine was used, the better. Lady Anne's vision is darker. "Infecting [their] hearts by stealth" (280), Gluttony's chefs—with their heavy sauces, stews, and relishes—upset the "home-bred" digestive balance. "Ah! who in our degenerate days / As nature prompts, his offering pays?" (287–88), Lady Anne sighs.[58] Gluttony's most zealous converts trample over our innate excretory equality by creating an exclusive mode of excremental indulgence indoors, keeping commodes and chamber pots in their secluded closets to use as they please and exploiting an underclass of servants who must empty them, even though "nature never difference made / Between the sceptre and the spade" (289–90). The new excretory customs, which willfully prioritize comfort and vanity over health and modesty, suddenly seem self-indulgent:

> Why will you place in lazy Pride
> Your Altars near your Couches Side?
> When from the homeliest Earthen Ware
> Are sent up Off'rings more sincere
> Than where the haughty Dutchess Locks,
> Her Silver Vase in Cedar-Box. (293–98)

In Swift's most famous scatological poem, "The Lady's Dressing Room," Strephon, having been misled by the appearance of her chamber pot, learns the hard way that "Celia, Celia, Celia shits."[59] "[H]aughty Celia"'s commode—covered "With rings and fringes counterfeit / To make it seem in this disguise, / A cabinet to vulgar eyes"—is like the one Lady Anne imagines that a "haughty Dutchess" (297) would use.[60] A simple ceramic chamber pot is to her "more sincere," that is, better suited to its lowly purpose, than a fussy "Silver Vase in Cedar-Box."[61] Like Strephon, Lady Anne has had her own close encounter when, some miles from Market Hill, she stumbles upon waste left by some northern "swains." But she isn't disgusted like Strephon. Rather the "offerings" that "in golden ranks / Adorn our crystal river's banks" and "grace the flowery downs" with their "spiral tops" and "copple-crowns" (299–304) are welcome hieroglyphs of a happier, freer time. At first glance Lady Anne had admired the buildings where every *"inward motion"* (212, 209; italics in original) can be solemnly, silently revered, where the "bashful maid" can "hide her blush"—where "unobserved, she boldly goes" (213–15). But the ramble expands her horizons and now the privies actually seem profane:

> None seek thee now in open Air;
> To thee no verdant Altars rear,
> But, in their Cells and Vaults obscene
> Present a sacrifice unclean. (281–84)

Viewed through her newly sharpened pastoral lens, all variety of excretory interiors become subsumed under the rubric of "Cells and Vaults obscene," not only Swift's privies, but also water closets, unplumbed indoor closets of ease, and any other private place where a lady or lord might use a chamber pot.

When Lady Anne returns to the manor house at the end of the "Panegyric," however, she comes home to the present moment and a more pragmatic mindset. In the second to last stanza she quotes advice she has been given in a dream by Phoebus—presumably a stand-in for Swift:

> At nicely carving show thy wit;
> But ne'er presume to eat a bit ...
> Let never at your board be known
> An empty plate except your own. (335–37; 338–40)

Resisting Gluttony's insidious influence, Lady Anne is counseled to distribute the meats on her table "nicely," filling rather than heaping her guests' plates, while, for her own part, "ne'er presum[ing] to eat a bit." If excremental privacy of some sort is pretty much inevitable for moderns, one can at least strive to minimize the need for it.[62]

Literary critics such as Everett Zimmerman have stressed how difficult it is to pin down Swift's intentions in the "Panegyric." Yet the vision of excretion "in the open air" as the essential, now lost, communal pleasure that is attributed to Lady Acheson in the poem is evidently not without a certain appeal to the poet as well.[63] To appreciate the prescience of Swift's curiosity about privy privacy, it's instructive to compare the "Panegyric" to an earnest antiquarian treatise by Archdeacon Samuel Rolleston that was published two decades later. Appearing in a single edition in London in 1751, *A Philosophical Dialogue Concerning Decency* combines a classical debate with a catalog of excretory objects and spaces from biblical and other ancient writings.[64] The catalog, which Rolleston claims is the first of its kind, features what may be the earliest printed use of the term *water closet*. In stark contrast to Harington, Rolleston presumes that "places of Retirement for necessary Occasions" is an important topic, and cannot fathom its age-old neglect. "I have not in the whole course of my studies met with any dissertation written upon this subject, which is as worthy of our consideration as any point of antiquity whatsoever," he remarks; moreover, he "very much wonder[s] at" the fact that his own learned society has never yet tackled the topic.[65] Rolleston has discovered what he believes to be the Bible's first reference to a room set aside specifically for excretion in Judges 3.24. Ehud discovers his enemy, the king of the Moabites, sitting alone, and murders him. Guards eventually begin to wonder why the king has been gone so long and try to go to him, "upon which some imagin'd, as the door was lock'd, that he might be easing himself." Traditional translations call the room where the guards seek the king a "summer chamber," but Rolleston disagrees: the room "was in all probability what we call a water closet."[66] (For Rolleston, evidently, "what we call" a water closet does not need to have plumbing.) Though the expression must have already been quite common in spoken English, the *Oxford English Dictionary*'s first citation for water closet comes from *Connoisseur* magazine four years later: "It was always my office to attend him in the water-closet when he took a cathartic." Significantly, both of these early written usages highlight the close association between the water closet and the courtly closet as potential sites of intimacy.

In Rolleston's *Philosophical Dialogue*, two gentlemen, Philoprepon and Eutrapelus, visit their friend in the country, a doctor of divinity, presumably Rolleston himself. The men are in an open field with a public road alongside it, returning from a long hike, when the doctor is "violently seiz'd upon" by indigestion, "attended with a necessity of going to stool."

He has recently built a new outdoor privy on his estate, and he thinks of it now. "I wish I was now at home; that I might ease myself in the neat apartment I have lately made in my garden, for I hate to do such things in publick," he complains. Despite the exigency of his situation, he starts a conversation with his friends about his inhibitions. "I have heard you say that you cannot even make water if you think any one looks upon you—" he says to Philoprepon. "Very modest indeed!" Eutrapelus interrupts, "surely, Gentlemen, the necessities of nature must be attended to; and nature requires us to empty, as well as it does to fill."[67] Thus begins a debate about the origins of excretory shame, which the doctor's guests continue as he runs on ahead.

Philoprepon and Eutrapelus hold divergent views on the issue. Eutrapelus is a relativist. Alluding indirectly to Diogenes's notorious acts of defecation in the theater and masturbation in the marketplace, Eutrapelus is inspired by the classical Greek philosopher's famous contention that anything that is in itself lawful can be done lawfully in public, understanding the embarrassment his friends feel at the mere thought of being caught in that act as nothing other than the fear of flouting custom. To support his argument against the naturalness of excretory shame, he points to the diversity of excretory manners, attitudes, and practices in Britain and around the world. The desire for privacy varies by nation: "I believe the Mossinians ... both men and women made no scruple of easing nature both ways in the publick streets."[68] It varies by status: in Venice "they esteem it a part of noble liberty to discharge where and before whom they please."[69] And it varies by sex: "Our Ladies in England are asham'd of being seen even in going to, or returning from the most necessary parts of our houses.... Now if this shame or modesty be founded in nature, why should not a man be asham'd of such a thing as well as a woman."[70] The notion that there exists some sort of universal excretory code defies significant evidence to the contrary.

Inclined to propriety, Philoprepon objects that the fact that certain groups or types favor more open practices does not confirm their naturalness. Philoprepon subscribes to a classical, elitist ideal of nature. That which is natural to do is right and good to do, but it doesn't follow that everyone's inclinations will therefore necessarily point them in that direction: rather, naturalness is a quality that our actions all too often fail to achieve. After working to dismantle Eutrapelus's assumptions, Philoprepon takes his own argumentative flight. He contends that at the heart of our natural excremental modesty is a universal taboo on public sex, known in positive terms as a love of decency:

Men by seeing women, and women by seeing men in those circumstances and in such a situation would have their passions rais'd and
might sometimes be suddenly hurry'd by the violence of their lust,
thus set on fire, to break the laws of nature, and to do what in cooler
thoughts they would judge iniquitous and wicked. In short, without
the decency I am speaking of there would be an end of all continence
and chastity; rapes, fornication, adultery, and all uncleanness would
appear at noon day, and be common in our publick streets.[71]

Philoprepon thus reasons that the roots of excretory privacy lie in our
potent unconscious wish for and fear of libidinal excess. On the one
hand, we possess a primal urge that exceeds our rational control. In
merely "seeing" a person of the other sex excreting in public, men and
women "would have their passions raised" to a dangerous degree and
might be "suddenly hurry'd by the violence of their lust." On the other
hand, Philoprepon classifies the desire to keep sex off "our publick
streets" as one of "the laws of nature." The draw of excremental privacy
stems from the same foundation as our repulsion at the thought of living
in a society where "rapes, fornication, adultery, and all uncleanness ...
appear at noon day." The doctor, having finished his business and re-
joined his friends again, sides with Philoprepon in principle but refrains
from reasoning out his position as they approach his house. He prefers
to make his case concretely, following the *Dialogue*, in a lecture, written
for his antiquarian society, on the history of objects and spaces of excretion, which reveals consistent long-standing efforts to hide these bodily
functions across several Western cultures.

   Reading the *Dialogue Concerning Decency* alongside the "Panegyric"
underscores the moral complexity attributed to various settings and practices of excretion in the period. Both Rolleston and Swift sense that the
limits of human compassion and sociability, the nature of privacy and
publicness, and indeed of nature itself, are all urgently implicated in this
everyday experience. Where Rolleston situates contrasting views of privy
privacy in different characters, Swift's "Panegyric" draws on classical
epochal divisions to set out its myth of privy origins. Lady Anne's golden
age (roughly) correlates to Eutrapelus's view that excremental shame is
cultural and that, under the right conditions, the whole world could be
liberated from it. By contrast, her iron age, the dawning of a pervasive
desire for privy privacy, correlates more closely with Philoprepon and
the doctor's insistence on the universality of excretory shame: modernity
has left a permanent mark on not just our (changeable) habits but on

our very nature. As she describes this postlapsarian moment, Lady Anne is wary of the excremental retirement that Rolleston's *Dialogue* ultimately celebrates. The interiors that hide the effects of our indulgence are no panacea: rather they can make us even more susceptible to laziness, over-weening pride, introversion, even more alienated from our own bodies.

At the Edge of the Country House

Along with the pastoral, "Panegyric on the Dean" plays with interrelated conventions of georgic and country house poetry. Surveying the socio-economic and architectural concerns raised by these poetic modes, and contextualizing them with an eye to Swift's whole career, reveals how the double privies embody his ill-defined bond with Lady Acheson. Produc-tive labor in the out of doors is a major and variable trope both of clas-sical georgic poetry and, as Alastair Fowler points out, of early modern English country house poetry, a subset of the georgic that also remained influential throughout the eighteenth century. The classical georgic is a point of origin for the motif of spontaneous abundance, where "crops and fruits offer themselves *sponte ... sua* to the happy husbandman," as well as the contrasting motif of entropy, which stresses the constant vig-ilance needed to keep pace with environmental cycles and make things grow, as when Virgil compares the farmer's fight against rot to the man who rows upstream: "if he chance / His arms to slacken, lo! with head-long force / The current sweeps him down the hurrying tide."[72] Swift tends to favor this latter view when it comes to describing his labor at Market Hill. Significantly, when Swift represents his own writing as a kind of constipated intellectual work, he layers in a capitalist calculus of productivity: "You toss and turn your brain till noon / ... / ... squeezing out four lines in rhyme, / Are largely paid for all your time" (187; 195–96). Here what seems to impair his creative process is the prospect that his poem for his patrons might be construed as a measurable, marketable product.

How the value attributed to literature was affected by the growing print market had been a challenging issue for Swift throughout his ca-reer, one that he explored extensively in such texts as *Tale of a Tub* and "On Poetry: A Rapsody." It was a practical problem as well. As Stephen Karian has recently shown, though Swift did seek the commercial distri-bution of many of his writings, his participation in commercial publi-cation was generally at arm's length. He assigned to friends the task of negotiating with and receiving payment from publishers, and since provocative, potentially libelous texts were a greater legal liability for all concerned if their author was known, his publications were generally anonymous. Later in his career, beginning around the time of his visits to Market Hill, Swift began actively withholding some poems from publication. Writing for manuscript circulation meant that he didn't have to appease publishers or internalize their concerns.[73] Yet, however cynical Swift was about the emerging commercial system of authorship and the forms of circulation associated with booksellers and printers, nor was he particularly enamored with the older but still thriving hierarchical system of authorial dependence associated with patronage and the manuscript tradition.

Linking writers from across the social spectrum to the most elite members of society, literary patronage was a traditional form of social connection akin to and often intersecting with court favoritism. As Dustin Griffin argues, in late seventeenth- and eighteenth-century England and Ireland, the vast majority of authors, whether or not they were publishing commercially, had royal and noble patrons from whom they received a wide range of benefits, including: places at court or appointments in the church or at a university that gave them security for literary pursuits; money and other gifts; hospitality, in either the short or long term; protection from lawsuits or other sorts of attack; introductions; encouragement; and, significantly, an enabling form of deferred or second-hand authority.[74] "The patron is not only the guarantor of wit, reassuring the hesitating bookseller or bookbuyer," Griffin explains, "but is himself the source of it. It is only by acknowledging that authority, and in effect drawing on its power, that the client-writer may speak."[75] Authors also benefited vicariously from "familiarity" with their patrons, Griffin's term for the provisional intimacy across social divides of the sort that was frequently and acutely realized in elite closets: "Persons of talent are permitted to cross a line, under controlled conditions, that normally separates the ranks of a hierarchical society. To be admitted to a lord's 'conversation' does not simply bring the opportunity to hear well-bred remarks.... It implies a rise in status."[76] Patrons stood to gain a lot in turn. They served as masters not only of the texts whose creation they had nurtured, but also of the authors themselves, who were often effectively considered, like wives and servants throughout this period, part of their property. Author-servants were expected to entertain, amuse, and enlighten patrons, and, above all, to promote their family names, titles, estates, and interests, including any party-political interests, in and around

the court. More broadly, in supporting authors, elite patrons in the eighteenth century aimed to reaffirm their role as the primary audience for and
authority over literary culture in the face of the growing, and increasingly socially diverse, group of readers of print.[77]

The course of Swift's career had been shaped by patronage, well before
he met the Achesons. His earliest education was sponsored by his father's
brother Godwin Swift. As a young man he held the post of secretary to
Sir William Temple at Moor Park; his first clerical posts were thanks to
his promotion by Lord Berkeley; Queen Anne later placed him as Dean
of St Patrick's Cathedral in Dublin; and his writings were in various ways
supported by the Earl of Oxford, among others. Yet, as Griffin points
out, Swift was loathe to acknowledge this dependence, and, especially
after his hopes of securing a preferment at court were dashed in 1714, he
tended to represent relations of patronage as at least as debasing to writers as marketplace transactions, if not considerably more so.[78] Probably
Swift's most scathing image of the quest for patronage is in Part One of
Gulliver's Travels. Lilliputians wanting consideration as "Candidates for
great Employments, and high Favour, at Court" must learn acrobatic
arts from an early age: "When a great Office is vacant, either by Death or
Disgrace (which often happens,) five or six of those Candidates petition
the Emperor to entertain his Majesty and the Court with a Dance on the
Rope; and whoever jumps the highest, without falling, succeeds in the
Office." However playful these diversions may seem, they "are often attended with fatal Accidents, whereof great Numbers are on Record."[79]
Sensing the personal bitterness leaching through this image, Griffin reads
the episode as a kind of revenge fantasy directed at ministers of state such
as Oxford and Bolingbroke and colored by Swift's own disappointment:
"Since they treated me as little more than an entertainer, and then threw
me away, let them suffer, let them pay."[80] In a poem contemporaneous
with "Panegyric," Swift pictures the poet-client as a sexual procurer:

> For, as the Appetites to quench,
> Lords keep a Pimp to bring a Wench;
> So, Men of Wit are but a kind
> Of Pandars to a vicious Mind;
> Who proper Objects must provide
> To gratify their Lust of pride.[81]

A secret historian like Anthony Hamilton highlights his personal connections to Whitehall in order to lend authority to the intimate stories he

tells about it. Nevertheless, those stories remain, by definition, unofficial ones, not the ones that the king, in his sovereign capacity, would have asked him to disseminate. Country house poetry, on the other hand, is a fundamentally self-referential and deferential genre, which both emerges from and solicits the hospitality and generosity of the patron. Yet the usual status of the country house poem as a gift from below is complexly reworked in Swift's "Panegyric." Almost all of Swift's Market Hill poems, including "Panegyric," followed the traditional pattern insofar as they were composed with a very limited audience in mind. As Peter Schakel explains, what Swift wrote during the day would be read aloud in the evening, often by whomever Swift had cast as speaker, for the amusement of the Achesons and the rest of their household: the "social context required his poems to be conversational rather than literary and allude to immediate family events—like Lady Acheson having stepped in dung while on a country walk."[82] Nevertheless, Lady Acheson often couldn't resist showing her copies of the poems to friends, and, following the same roundabout trajectory of *Memoirs of Count Grammont* and many other texts of this period, quite of few of the Market Hill verses did soon make their way into the hands of publishers. Early on in the "Panegyric," Swift mocks his patroness's practice of sharing his poems, when he pictures her directly seeking this poem's commercial publication, in her own name:

> My gratitude the world shall know:
> And, see, the printer's boy below:
> Ye hawkers all, your voices lift;
> "A panegyric on Dean Swift."
> And then, to mend the matter still;
> "By Lady Anne of Market Hill." (31–36)

In fact, Lady Acheson was probably not instrumental in the publication of the "Panegyric," which first appeared in print in 1735 in George Faulkner's authorized edition of Swift's *Works,* "where it was one of the 'inoffensive' new items inserted in the corrected state of the volume to replace controversial poems."[83] But this image of Lady Anne as at once the poem's subject, author, and promoter—in cahoots with the printers and hawkers who sell the poem for money—underscores the larger issues: Who owns a poem you wrote explicitly for someone else, and while living under her roof and eating her food? What's the difference between a gift and a product, and under which category does poetry fall now that the commercial impetus of the print market is gaining such momentum?

Might the specific images and occasions of a piece of writing and the medium by which it circulates affect the answers? A playful personal dig at her, the image of Lady Anne's appropriation of the poem's authorship also reflects Swift's uneasy awareness that their relationship is caught between the collapsing distinctions between manuscript and print as well as their respective paradigms of favor and profit.[84]

Formal precedents also further illuminate the subversive architectural symbolism of the privies. Country house poets, like secret historians, recognize that where and how elite favor is granted can be telling. However, unlike secret historians, country house poets, keyed to communal concerns, usually focus on sites and situations in which groups of people from across the social strata meet. Girouard sums up the principle of hospitality enacted in country house rituals from the time of their feudal origins: "To have crowds of people continuously coming to the house, to have drink flowing in abundance, to serve up far more food than could possibly be eaten, and to feed the poor waiting at the gate with the leftovers was all evidence of power, wealth and glory."[85] With the kitchen and parlors extending from it in two opposing wings, the great hall was the most common place for members of the patrons' extended family, their household guests and servants, and often tenants as well to gather and eat (figure 20). In fact, as G. R. Hibbard points out (and in contrast to Habermas's narration of its disappearance as an eighteenth-century phenomenon), due to the influence of more symmetrical and elaborate European neoclassical architecture, the native medieval great hall was already out of fashion by the time country-house poetry was emerging in the early seventeenth century.[86] Nevertheless, these ceremonial halls were still prominent in older estates that had not been extensively renovated, and the room and its rituals still held a strong symbolic appeal for poets.[87] For example, the lavish, limitless banquets in two definitive early modern country house poems implicitly celebrate the great hall as the center of feudal community and generosity. Your "liberal board doth flow / With all that hospitality doth know;" Ben Jonson tells his patron in "To Penshurt":

> Where comes no guest but is allowed to eat,
> Without his fear, and of thy lord's own meat;
> Where the same beer and bread, and selfsame wine,
> This is his lordship's shall be also mine,
> And I not fain to sit (as some this day
> At great men's tables), and yet dine away.

Here no man tells my cups; nor, standing by,
A waiter doth my gluttony envy,
But gives me what I call, and lets me eat.[88]

In "Panegyrick to Sir Lewis Pemberton," Robert Herrick likewise exalts,

   all, who at thy table seated are,
  Find equall freedome, equall fare;
And Thou, like to that *Hospitable God*,
  Jove, joy'st when guests make their abode
To eate thy Bullocks thighs, thy Veales, thy fat
  Weathers, and never grudged at.
The *Phesant, Partridge, Gotwit, Reeve, Ruffe, Raile*,
  The *Cock*, the *Curlew*, and the *quaile*;
These, and thy choicest viands do extend
  Their taste unto the lower end
Of thy glad table: not a dish more known
  To thee, then unto anyone.[89]

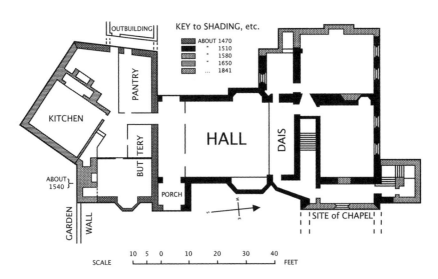

FIG. 20. At Horham, the great hall, the huge central room that provided both the spatial and the social axis of the early modern manor house, survived three centuries of renovations. (Architectural plan of Horham Hall. Reprinted from WikiCommons. Courtesy of user: The Man in Question. Reproduced in accordance with CC BY-SA 3.0. https://creativecommons.org/licenses/by-sa/3.0/deed.en.)

At the heart of Swift's "Panegyric," by contrast, are the earth closets, and the shared evening meal is an afterthought, for which, moreover, restraint is prescribed. Carole Fabricant remarks that, throughout the Market Hill series, the whole of the Achesons' estate stands for "the passing away both of a private Augustan community ... and of the public world necessary to sustain such a community."[90] Moreover, Fabricant notes that Swift's longing for this kind of community may have been particularly acute while composing the "Panegyric." In the summer of 1729, he had announced he would build himself a house, to be named "Drapier's Hill" after the persona of his successful political pamphlets, on land near Market Hill that he had bought from Lady Acheson's husband. But by October of the same year, he had given up, writing to Pope: "I will fly as soon as build; I have neither years, nor spirits, nor money, nor patience for such amusements."[91] In his poem "Vanbrug's House, *Built from the Ruins of White-Hall that was Burnt,*" Swift contrasts John Vanbrugh's grandiose vision to the tiny house he eventually produces: "A Thing resembling a Goose Py." Fabricant proposes that, "in broader terms," this early poem mocking the renowned architect of Castle Howard and Blenheim Palace "depicts a world in which neither traditional country houses nor the poems that traditionally commemorate them can any longer be created except in burlesque form."[92] The diminished scale is part of the point with the privies too. Enclosing self-indulgent, self-involved subjects, body and soul, the two stand-alone cells are parodic inversions of the expansive, welcoming interiors celebrated by seventeenth-century country-house poets.

LADY ANNE AND PRIVY INTIMACY

Though the outhouses at Market Hill give shape to Swift's sense of loss and despair regarding the changing material conditions of literary patronage and rural sociability, they also, like Hamilton's bathing closet, partly compensate for it. Like other sorts of closets, privies also had a history as places where royalty or nobility could quickly and sometimes surreptitiously forge bonds with favorites. Moreover, having less lofty associations than other closets, the privy could accommodate especially marginal connections, the dirtiest of secrets. In the cabinet council against James's marriage to Anne Hyde in *Memoirs of Count Grammont*, one of the courtiers smirks that not only did he experience "the critical minute" with Miss Hyde in "a certain closet built over the

water" but also that "three or four swans had been witnesses to the happiness of many others, as the lady frequently repaired to that place."[93]
Harington points out that while latrines were casually sociable places in
ancient Rome ("in Martials time, [people] shunned not one the others
companie, at Monsieur A JAX"), at the Elizabethan court they assist
in erotic assignations.[94] This is the subject of a scandalous verse called
"Against *Cayus* that scorn'd his Metamorphosis," included in Harington's
treatise:

> Last day thy Mistris, Cayus, being present,
> One hapt to name, to purpose not unpleasant,
> The Title of my mis-conceived Booke:
> At which you spit, as though you could not brooke
> So grosse a Word: but shall I tell the matter
> Why? If one names a Jax, your lips doe water.
> There was the place of your first love and meeting,
> There first you gave your Mistris such a greeting,
> As bred her scorne, your shame, and others lafter,
> And made her feele it twenty fortnights after;
> Then thanke their wit, that makes the place so sweet,
> That for your Hymen you thought place so meet.[95]

The courtier's public display of censure actually masks an illicit experience of pleasure from which he wants to distance himself. At the sound of
the word "jakes," goes the poem, Cayus's mouth waters in a lustful, not,
as he claims, disgusted, intuitive response. Though he and his mistress
will be dishonored "twenty fortnights after" by the birth of an illegitimate child, the name of the place of their "first love and meeting" summons erotic memories. Harington unmasks Cayus's pretense because he
wants to defend and promote his improvements to the privy, which have
"[made] the place so sweet" that it appeals to adulterers.[96] Predicting
Philoprepon's logic in Rolleston's *Dialogue Concerning Decency*, Harington imagines that the heightened embodiment of the privy further fuels
physical intimacies. He also remarks that, in European courts, privies are
especially valued as settings of courtly preferment: "I have heard it seriously told, that a great Magnifico of Venice being Ambassador in France,
and hearing a Noble person was come to speake with him, made him
stay til he had untyed his points; and when he was new set on his stoole,
sent for the Noble man to come to him at that time; as a verie speciall
favor."[97] Rolleston's Eutrapelus has heard the same anecdote.[98]

"Panegyric on the Dean" is hardly a love poem. Throughout his oeuvre, Swift tends to represent the delusion and clumsiness entailed in romantic love as both universal truths and, in poems like "Cadenas and Vanessa," a personal specialty. Like many of his other poems for or about specific women, the "Panegyric" takes up the pastoral theme of love and desire between nymphs and swains, but substitutes pedagogy for sex as the main medium of interpersonal connection. As Nora Crow Jaffe and others have argued, Swift repeated with Lady Acheson, who was probably twenty-five years younger than him, the pattern of gruff flirtation established in his previous relationships with Esther Johnson (Stella) and Esther Vanhomrigh (Vanessa). "Lady Anne was the last in Swift's 'triumfeminate,' as [he] would call it," Jaffe writes, "When he met her, in 1728, Vanessa was dead and Stella had just died . . . , we might still say he created Lady Anne in their image."[99] This included casting her, as he had them, as an unlikely muse—a rough diamond in need of his polish. In the "Panegyric," Swift has Lady Acheson recording his advice about how to perform at the dinner table and improve her verbal skills, activities she is instructed to prioritize over gambling with the neighborhood ladies in the evening (141–44). The whole poem pays homage to the long walks that he insisted she take with him to improve her health. Swift claimed in a letter to his friend Alexander Pope that "she teased him to write about her and kept all the copies of the poems."[100] But the verses for Lady Acheson focus on her flaws, loading apparently flattering poetic forms with decidedly unflattering content. In "Death and Daphne," Lady Acheson is skeletally skinny and so cold that even Death won't marry her. "Epistle to a Lady," probably the best known of this series, thematizes Lady Acheson's desire for Swift to write about her, and the poet's inability to satisfy the beloved's request for a heroic verse is figured as a sexual failure that, significantly, only improves his capacity to mentor her. Initially, Swift had been equally close to Sir Arthur, a baronet and Anglican churchman who had recently taken a seat in the Irish House of Commons. But over the course of his several long visits to their estate, the emotional balance between three had shifted. Usually somewhat bored by country life, Lady Acheson was happy for the distractions Swift provided, and her introverted husband was happy for them too. In the "Panegyric," Swift has Lady Anne describing his attentions to her as salutary to their marriage:

Sir Arthur, since you set the pattern,
No longer calls me Snipe and Slattern;
Nor dare he, though he were a duke,
Offend me with the least rebuke. (57–60)

Whose pattern has Swift set? The ambiguities in the first couplet allow that, while Lady Anne's conduct has been improved such that her husband's insults no longer apply, Swift may have also provided a model of "spousal" respect for Sir Arthur. In any case, under Swift's watch, Arthur no longer "dare[s]" to insult her. The theme of triangulation recurs in the later Market Hill verses, notably "The Grand Question Debated," in which the couple's opposing views about what should be done with an unused part of their estate hinge on their predictions about how the change will affect their relationship with Swift. It's worth noting that, after the Achesons began living apart in the 1730s, Swift never returned to Armagh and only saw Lady Acheson infrequently in Dublin, instead "divid[ing] his need for female company among a number of [other] women," as Swift's biographer Irvin Ehrenpreis puts it.[101] The poems for her stopped as well.

Yet Swift does acknowledge the erotic potential of excretory favoritism in the intimate form of the "Panegyric." In attributing to his lady-speaker a passionate interest in apparently obscene matters, Swift experiments with the strange reciprocity between shame and affection that the double voice enhanced. The edgier his account of Lady Acheson's thoughts and feelings, the more palpable the charge of their attachment in the poem, and, potentially, the less likely she would be to want to share it. The privies thus both serve and symbolize this effort to circumscribe the circulation of the poem-gift made exclusively for her and keep it out of the marketplace, whose bottom-line and individualist values were undermining the quality of life in the country no less than in the city. What connected him to Lady Acheson bore only a dim resemblance to the idealized version of ancient hospitality commemorated in country house poetry. Nor was the Achesons' generosity in opening their house to him anything like the more substantial forms of career patronage that he had spent much of his life both yearning for and decrying. But while it lasted, the relationship was meaningful and Swift was grateful for it. Concretizing the poem's redoubled voice, the his-and-hers earth closets at Market Hill pay tribute to and reinforce Swift's passing bond with Lady Acheson, making a new/old place for them, alone together, between the house and the fields, and at the uneasy boundaries between domestic propriety and pastoral bliss, labor and service, aggression and kindness.

Peter Schakel proposes that "until the Market Hill poems, Swift's poetry was largely monophonic," and that writing for the Achesons led to his most original formal innovations. In particular, from the time of its first print publication in 1735, the "Panegyric" has confronted readers with an intricate psychological exercise. Knowing that Lady Acheson is the poem's intended audience—not us—we are challenged to keep track of the likely differences between Swift's representation of Lady Anne's feelings, Lady Acheson's actual feelings during the events represented in the poem (insofar as they really occurred), as well as her subsequent re-action(s) to hearing her intimate thoughts represented or misrepresented in this way. Whereas the uninvited readers of Hamilton's published secret history try on a vicarious form of favoritism, the anonymous readers of Swift's published mock–country house poem are plunged into the mire of a patron-artist dynamic that, in theory, excludes them. The irony—of which Swift was surely aware—is that encountering the poem in print does nothing to diminish the "Panegyric"'s intimate poetics of obliga-tion and humiliation.[102]

Breaking and entering

Many closets and cabinets had an appeal that extended well beyond the group of people who might expect an invitation. In any case, both the high stakes and shifting social foundations of closet intimacies meant that guest lists would often change. Running through Pepys's account of the Restoration culture of the closet are many instances of uncontained desire, trespass, and betrayal.

Things are taken from and hidden in other people's closets. Pepys is intrigued to hear about the stealthy theft of documents from the Duke of York's closet in 1668 and from that of a Dutch statesman the following year.[1] After William Batten recovers some of his wife's missing jewels under a china cup in her closet—"where he hath servants will swear they did look in searching the house"—Pepys enjoys speculating with his neighbor Elizabeth Turner about what has happened. Perhaps the childless Lady Batten, who has recently been very ill, had passed the jewelry along to some friends, then asked for it back once she'd realized she wasn't going to die after all? One of her servants, meanwhile, has been imprisoned for the crime.[2] In another long gossip session a month later, Mrs. Turner tells Pepys that she has heard from Mrs. Griffith, the housekeeper's wife, who has heard from Lord Brouncker's maid, that her "lewd and nasty" master has, at the king's expense, acquired "of Foly, the ironmonger, 50*l*-worth in locks and keys for his house, and [the price] is from the fineness of them, having some of 4 and 5*l* a lock, such as is in the Duke's closet"—and that these fine locks have aided Brouncker in extorting money from his own staff. He "do keep many of [the maid's] things from her of her own goods, and would have her bring a bill into the office for them," Mrs. Turner reports to Pepys, who duly notes the misconduct in his journal.[3]

The thresholds of closets and cabinets sometimes become especially loaded sites of conflict over lost authority or broken promises. When pregnant in the summer of 1667, Lady Castlemaine is rumored to have "nearly hectored [the king] out of his wits," threatening "to bring all his bastards to his closet-door" or to bring the new baby, after it is born, "into the White Hall gallery, and dash the brains of it out before the King's face."[4] The year before, Pepys had experienced a closet shaming of his own when a crowd of women staged a protest in front of the navy's offices, demanding compensation and assistance for their husbands— naval officers who were held as prisoners of war in Holland.[5] As the crowd disperses, Pepys calls just one of the bereaved women back to his office closet to give her some money in private. In this case, there is no record of what it cost her.

If unexpectedly showing up at someone's closet signaled aggression, a readiness to share secrets more widely than the owner would wish, then being granted unexpected access could, conversely, signal that the pro- prietor's defenses had been lowered, or that former secrets might now be shared. When William Coventry hopes to counter his reputation for profiting from the sale of naval posts, he privately presents Pepys with "a list ... wherein he reckons up ... 236 offices of ships which have been disposed of without his taking one farthing." Pepys intuitively under- stands his colleague's gesture: "He opened his Cabinett on purpose to shew me [this list], meaning, I suppose, that I should discourse abroad of it, and vindicate him therein; which I shall with all my power do."[6]

Frequently given as gifts, freestanding cabinets of wood or iron re- inforced the same bonds of favor and obligation as visits to closets, and were, because of their smaller size and greater mobility, even more vul- nerable to misdirection and misconstruction. Elaborately carved and dec- orated cabinets and chests of drawers were aesthetic objects in their own right. Inside them, valuable artifacts, letters, gems, documents, books, and letters could be arranged for storage and display, and later locked and tucked away for safekeeping, ideally inside a lockable closet. In the diary, Pepys records at least eight cabinet exchanges, in half of which he is involved directly either as giver or receiver.[7] Some of these cabinet exchanges have a romantic or sexual drift. He gets Betty Michell a dress- ing box, lingering with her at the shop to watch the cabinet-makers put on the finishing touches—"some exceeding good work, and very pleasant to see them do it"—and allowing the "mistress of the shop" to "[take] her for my wife, which I owned and her big belly."[8] In an effort to appease the guilt over his sexual compulsions, he buys Elizabeth an expensive walnut cabinet as a New Year's gift two years later.[9] When Pepys accepts "a pretty Cabinet" from one of his suppliers about halfway through the diary—"which I gave my wife—the first of that sort of goods I ever had yet—and very conveniently it comes for her closet"—it's another strong signal of his good reputation and career success.[10]

The outrage that ensues when these gifts are mishandled makes their customary value especially clear. After William Batten fires William Hughes from his position as rope-maker for the navy, Hughes "[cries] out upon Sir Wm for his Cabinet."[11] Hughes had given Batten the chest of drawers in gratitude for the employment, but, as the subsequent regret and the ambiguous possessive third-person pronoun suggest, the gift had in a sense belonged to both men, a symbol of reciprocal commitments. Later, Mr. Hempson, another man whom Batten has turned away, accuses Batten of regularly requiring advance gifts "of a piece of Sattin and cabinetts and other things from people that deal with him," reporting that in fact "hardly any body goes to see or hath anything done by Sir W. Batten but it comes with a bribe."[12] The difference between the customary exchange of favors or perquisites and this bribery is that the latter is an entirely self-serving ritual: here the receiver values only himself and ignores the promise of ongoing reciprocity with which such gifts are supposed to be imbued.

4

Miss C——y's Cabinet of Curiosities

An infinity of devices could be had from an ingenious lock-smith. A London ironmonger supplied brass locks, iron rimmed locks, spring locks, spring plate locks, stock locks, drawback locks, closet locks, hatch locks, pew locks, cupboard locks and box locks in 1686. The lock and key, however, was no foolproof system.

—AMANDA VICKERY[1]

The other Cabinet Miss C——y had, and which coming in to my Hands I broke open, was very curious ...—I turned the various Papers in it over and over, and determined to publish such as were the most to my Liking.

—"TRISTRAM SHANDY"[2]

It is important to point out that the taste for peeking into other people's lives, and using mediated experience to satisfy this drive, may have existed since long before the rise of reality TV programs.

—LEMI BARUH[3]

CLOSETS WITHOUT WALLS

As closets and cabinets multiplied in eighteenth-century architecture, so too did they proliferate in English writing, not only as evocative settings and symbols but also as textual structures in their own right. Though conservative authors like Anthony Hamilton and Jonathan Swift tried to restrict the circulation of closet stories to limited elite circles, in fact, as they well knew, nothing could stop the flow of desire from without, not even in the short term. An important outlet for this desire was the plethora of textual collections explicitly designated as *closets* or *cabinets* that were published in seventeenth- and eighteenth-century England.[4] There were recipe and remedy books, such as *The Queen-Like Closet, or Rich cabinet stored with all manner of rare receipts*; political polemics, such as *The Devils Cabinet-Councell Discovered, Or the Mistery and Iniquity of the Good old Cause*; spiritual tracts, such as *The Golden Cabinet of true Treasure: Containing the summe of Morall Philosophie*; literary anthologies, such as *The Cabinet of Genius*; do-it-yourself guides, such as *Every Woman Her Own Midwife, or, A Compleat cabinet opened for child-bearing women*, and many others besides. Only a few literary critics have discussed examples of this now-obsolete textual category, and fewer still have explored its unity and breadth.[5] Yet, in the seventeenth century, *closet* and *cabinet* were far more prevalent than *miscellany* or *anthology* as names for published collections and, even as *miscellany* took over as the principal designation for a textual compilation in the eighteenth century, *closet* and *cabinet* remained much more common than the now dominant *anthology*. The cohesiveness of the media discourse generated through these textual closets underscores the many conceptual continuities between the various architectural spaces to which they referred. First surveying the frontispieces, dedications, and prefaces of this large and diverse set of texts, then focusing on the recurring figure of the voyeur in the subset of erotic cabinets of love, most extensively one called *Miss C——y's Cabinet of Curiosities*, this chapter discovers a flexible rhetoric of intimacy at a distance that facilitated the early, tentative self-authorization of print.[6]

Commercial print undoubtedly displaced manuscript as the dominant mode of knowledge circulation in eighteenth-century Britain, emerging as the first mass medium. Yet the growth of print commerce "led ... to a mordant concern about the dissemination of literary goods," as Jonathan Kramnick puts it.[7] Book and media historians emphasize that the shift to print, like most historical transformations, was gradual and uneven, full of hitches, glitches, and false starts. In Clifford Siskin and William Warner's words, the story of the rise of print is "also a story of apparent delay in which the fifteenth-century technology of inscription— printing through the use of moveable type—took hundreds of years to implicate and modify an already existing media ecology of voice, sound, image, and manuscript writing."[8] Moreover, media historians remark that because print has ultimately been so successful—because it has so thoroughly saturated post-Enlightenment ideas of knowledge, accessibility,

and authority—it can be hard now to see it as a historical innovation that
developed out of and in relation to the much older (though also evolving) practices and values of manuscript exchange. David McKitterick observes, "Infatuation with the printed book and with the history of printing
led not just to [the notion of] a divorce between manuscript and print,
but also, and more seriously, to misunderstandings concerning the relationships between the two that have so far been only partially recovered."[9]
Adrian Johns tackles head-on the apparently self-evident superiority of
print by showing that seventeenth- and eighteenth-century stakeholders
understood that the medium of their livelihood would triumph only if
they succeeded in creating the impression that it was a seamless font of
truth: "Print was dedicated to effacing its own traces, and necessarily so:
only if such efforts disappeared could printing gain the air of intrinsic
reliability on which its cultural and commercial success could be built."[10]
But, Johns explains, the backdrop to these efforts was widespread skep-
ticism and fear. Perceiving the printed text as inherently "destabilizing
and threatening to civility," many contemporaries looked to established
social codes in order "to determine the appropriate kind and degree
of faith to vest in this unfamiliar object": "Their worries about literary
credit were often resolved, as a matter of everyday practice, into assessments of the people involved in the making, distribution, and reception
of books. Readers worried about who decided what got into print, and
about who controlled it once it was there."[11] Most people who bought
books at a shop, borrowed them from a lending library, or skimmed
them at the coffee house had little to no direct contact with the people
involved in their production. How to reckon the value of prepackaged
ideas and information?

Closet and cabinet were among the most common textual categories
used to provide a conceptual link from the established hierarchical cultures of learning and patronage to the emerging culture of print commerce. In this respect, they bear comparing with the group of publications
that Roger Chartier has called *bibliothèques sans murs*, libraries without
walls.[12] In early modern France, *bibliothèque* referred most commonly to
a room or building in a palace or on a noble estate where books were
gathered. Increasingly, it also denoted a book or series of books in which
numerous works in a given genre, such as fiction or travel narratives, were
published together, or a book or series of books in which all of the books
contained in other physical or textual *bibliothèques* were cataloged.[13] Taking a special interest in this last sort of virtual library, Chartier argues
that the producers of such master-catalogs were adapting an age-old de-

sire for a fully inclusive collection to a new context of shifting media. The tension produced by the "proliferation of titles and editions" in print in the seventeenth century manifests in the mediated fantasy space of the textual *bibliothèque*. Because of this proliferation, the universal library

> cannot be other than immaterial, reduced to the dimensions of a cat-alog, a nomenclature, or a survey. Conversely, any library that is actually installed in a specific place and that is made up of real works available for consultation and reading, no matter how rich it might be, gives only a truncated image of all accumulable knowledge. The irreducible gap between ideally exhaustive inventories and necessarily incomplete collections was experienced with intense frustration. It led to extravagant ventures assembling—in spirit, if not in reality—all possible books, all discoverable titles, all works ever written.[14]

In Chartier's view, though the compilers of textual *bibliothèques* may appear, from our vantage, to have been optimistic, they were spurred on by a maddening compulsion to manage what was, even to them, clearly an unmanageable volume of books.[15]

Eleanor Shevlin suggests that "particular titling practices, especially the recurrence of selected keywords, can be instrumental both in shaping reader responses to individual texts and entire genres and in constructing new markets and expanding existing ones."[16] Given that many actual closets and cabinets were dedicated wholly or in part to the storage and display of books, as architectural referents they overlapped with *bibliothèques*. These terms also overlapped significantly as orienting metaphors of early modern and eighteenth-century print culture insofar as closet and cabinet, like *bibliothèque*, underscored the idea that printed texts are also sites for the storage and display of knowledge. Thus, like the *bibliothèques sans murs*, the analogical relation of closet and cabinet to published text helped authors and booksellers to finesse thinking about what books could or should contain, how contents should be organized, and how readers might enter, exit, and navigate the physical space of the book. However, unlike the libraries without walls, which manifested and at the same time exacerbated frustrations over the uncontrollable quantity of books in circulation, textual closets and cabinets were especially keyed to anxieties over quality, over the social credentials of printed knowledge. Libraries without walls, while appearing to provide a new level of control over information overload, in fact contributed to the problem by generating more books, and the need for catalogs of catalogs. So too were the provisional solutions to concerns over social quality put forth in textual closets without walls ultimately incomplete and, in certain respects, contradictory. By making explicit their personal connections to elite closets, book editors and producers were hoping to underscore the social capital of their publications. Yet in so doing they also raised troubling new questions about the entitlement of ordinary readers to access and engage with printed knowledge.

LEARNING *IN SITU*

To understand how the intersecting tropes of the closet and cabinet contributed to the conceptualization of textual relations in the eighteenth-century British print market, it helps first to register their centrality and fluidity as embodied and emotionally charged sites of learning. The kinds of ideas, information, narratives, and things examined, accumulated, and shared in actual closets and cabinets were as wildly various as the category of knowledge itself in a period when coherent distinctions between arts and sciences, religious and secular life, fact and fiction, private and public were just beginning to be systematized and theorized. Closets were key sites of both formal and everyday literacy: witty letters and weighty tomes alike were read and composed there; manuscripts and books of all sorts were organized and stored there; and journals, accounts, recipes, and commonplace books were perused and updated. Furthermore, where the royalty or aristocracy were concerned, any and all texts associated with closets and cabinets, from signed peace treaties to laundry lists, stood as political information potentially worth sharing with a favorite or leaking in a secret history. Beautiful in themselves, and inviting the exhibition of paintings, drawings, sculptures, miniatures, maps, plates, vases, coins, medals—anything the owner deemed pleasing to look at—closets could also be spaces of aesthetic appreciation and evaluation. For alchemists, apothecaries, cooks, physicians, and midwives, who kept their equipment, manuals, and sundry substances in closets, these rooms were associated with ancient practical knowledge and perhaps the training of apprentices. As prayer closets, they served in the daily production of theological knowledge through the habits of spiritual self-reflection they encouraged, which included reading the Bible and other religious texts, and engaging with them deeply, whether only in the mind or in writing as well. Cosmetics, accessories, wigs, and perhaps a love letter or two might be kept in dressing rooms or on dressing tables in closets that served multiple functions, along with texts of instruction in fashion and manners. As cabinets of curiosity, closets invited the organization, examination, and display of what we would now call scientific, historical, or archeological objects: natural specimens, rocks, minerals, and gems; ancient clothing, weapons, tools, artifacts from around the world.[17] And anyone who didn't have a room of their own might nevertheless have a freestanding and lockable cabinet to accommodate a more limited number of such things.

The ongoing use of the generic terms *closet* and *cabinet* throughout the period, even as more specific designations were coming into use, might remind us that, generally speaking, most people still didn't determine in advance exactly what they would keep or do in their private spaces. Initially, the underlying condition of this material and conceptual breadth had been owners' elevated status within the household and within society at large. Later, as cabinets became increasingly available to people living under others' roofs, these receptacles dispersed the opportunity for secret knowledge formerly available only to the elite. The control over access that closets and cabinets permitted was another part of their appeal. Feelings of closeness between owner and guest arising from or intensified by physical proximity were further amplified by the processes of exchanging, refining, and defining all kinds of ideas and information together—whether this entailed preparing a letter, identifying a specimen, admiring the likeness of a portrait, or selecting a pair of earrings to wear to dinner. Some modes of interpersonal closet and cabinet exchange were relatively formalized. Apprentices, secretaries, grooms of the stole, and other ongoing private attendants interacted with their masters and mistresses according to specific protocols that had evolved over many centuries. As Alan Stewart argues, the intensity of connection between master and secretary in particular was generated not only by the high stakes of the information that the secretary managed on his master's behalf, but also by the built-in obsolescence of the secretary's skills in storing and retrieving that information—localized, internalized skills that were at once more valuable and, in many cases, less durable than the closet's actual contents.[18] The Protestant clergy represented communion with the supreme patriarch in the prayer closet as akin to such courtly closet encounters, insisting that God heard and rewarded only those supplicants whose punctual, private communications struck just the right chord. Other kinds of knowledge sharing—such as those associated with cabinets of curiosity—were so frequent yet so novel that collective parameters had to be explicitly set, leading to the advent of virtuosic clubs, such as the Society of Dilettanti and—most notably—the Royal Society of London for Improving Natural Knowledge.[19] Whether entirely improvised or partly scripted, closet exchanges equated the privilege of access to knowledge not with power exactly, but with the decision, generally under the purview of the most powerful person in the room, temporarily to suspend formal power dynamics.

A teasing letter from the young essayist Elizabeth Montagu to her patroness, the Duchess of Portland, encapsulates the closet's importance as a place where intellectual exchanges interfered with and transformed the usual patterns of obligation and deference. Montagu alludes to John Locke's metaphor for the empirical mind as a storage-place of ideas as she imagines her patroness's closet as both the setting and the vehicle of their intimate connection. "Pray do not compliment my head; such as it is it is at your Service," she begins:

> It is not a head of great capacity, but a great part of the space is unfurnished. I only beg if you furnish it, it may be with a little more order than your Closet; for with heads as with drawers, too full one can never find any thing when one looks for it. A head made up with the variety of your Closet must be excellent for making dictionaries, writing grammars, for all the languages spoken at Babel, or a natural History of the Creatures in Noah's Ark, or for drawing plans for the Labyrinths of Dedalus. What a cunning confusion, and vast variety and surprising Universality must the head possess that is but worthy to make an inventory of the things in that Closet. So many things there made by Art and Nature, so many stranger still, and very curious, hit off by chance and casualty. Shells so big and so little, some things so antique, and some so new fashioned, some excellent for being of much use, others so exquisite for being of no use at all; accidental shapes that seem formed on purpose; contrivances of art that appear as if done by Accident. But how should I describe it? [20]

Adopting a reverse psychology not unlike that of Swift's "Panegyrick on the Dean," Montagu alternately targets herself and her patroness, at once forecasting and performing their mutual state of dependence. Her initial abstract image of the private space of her mind—a mental closet that is empty due to her youthful inexperience—soon merges with a concrete image of the architectural center of her relationship to her patroness. Because spending time with the duchess in her closet is the experience that will most contribute to her own cognitive development, the chaos of things crammed into the room at first gives her pause: "I only beg if you furnish [my mind], it may be with a little more order than your Closet." But when Montagu proceeds to elaborate just how unprepared she is to cope with this "cunning confusion," her clever sketch of the duchess's collection proves just the opposite. In the jumble of books and objects pictured in her mind's eye, Montagu evidently perceives all kinds of meaningful differences. The duchess's books, she notes, could provide the substance for a variety of linguistic, natural-historical, and mythological catalogs. Whether human-made or not, the duchess's curiosities can also be distinguished by such properties as size, age, and functionality. Montagu especially showcases her own talent for observation and analysis when she considers, finally, how the most awe-inspiring things in the collection defy familiar distinctions between art and chance: "Accidental shapes ... seem formed on purpose" while "contrivances of art ... appear as if done by Accident." Though Montagu's inadequacy for the task of helping the duchess to classify and arrange the things in her closet is obviously a pose, when she asks, finally, "But how shall I describe it?," the question is not entirely disingenuous nor merely rhetorical: she has only just begun the formidable task. However, Montagu's backhanded compliment and self-praise are meant to reassure her patroness that the job will eventually get done—and exceptionally well, too, because their talents are so complementary. Just as the favorite's mental emptiness belies a vast curiosity and potential to learn, the clutter of the patroness' closet belies her virtuosity. They will produce ordered splendor together.

Printed Closets and Cabinets: Authorizing Media Shift

Catering to and soliciting widespread curiosity about elite private spaces, the publication of numerous collections called closets and cabinets in seventeenth- and eighteenth-century England contributed to the development of a range of modern anthology forms, including encyclopedias, epistolary narratives, cookbooks, and erotica. Undoubtedly, the titular tropes promised that these texts held quantities of information, instructions, ideas, or stories. But the fascination with status in the framing discussions of so many of these closet and cabinet collections suggests that authors, publishers, and editors were at least as compelled to establish the fundamental social quality of the knowledge that they were making widely available. Echoing Marshall McLuhan, Lisa Gittelman remarks, "Each new medium represents its predecessors."[21] Looking back to look forward, purveyors of print were trying to bridge the gaps between their own increasingly accessible, anonymous mode of communication and recognized elitist modes of learning. By picturing printed texts as sites of knowledge exchange over which the original owners had, generally unwittingly, lost control, booksellers provided new openings for the desire and curiosity of those usually excluded from elite closets. In so doing, they also inadvertently brought into sharp focus the peculiar indirectness and indiscretion of print readership.

There are significant parallels between closet and cabinet justifications and other forms of self-authorization commonly used to bolster the reputation of print in the seventeenth and eighteenth centuries. Closet and cabinet claims are especially comparable to other kinds of truth claims, on the one hand, and dedications to patrons, on the other. Though the process of commercial print publication necessarily wrenched content away from its social and embodied points of origin, prefatory claims to historicity tried to compensate for this separation by reassuring readers that mass-produced books referred directly to the real world. Thus, when a supposed editor calls *Robinson Crusoe* "a just history of fact" or asserts *Pamela*'s "Foundation in Truth and Nature," Daniel Defoe and Samuel Richardson, respectively, were hinging the worth of their narratives in part on the premise that they represent actual people and occurrences.[22] Though such heroism had not often been seen in literary characters of low birth, the remarkable resilience of Robinson Crusoe and Pamela Andrews was not the stuff of romance.[23] The related trope of the discovered manuscript or book drew authority from the authenticity of sources rather than events. For instance, in the preface to the first edition of *The Castle of Otranto*, Horace Walpole's translator-persona asserts that the tale that he has now put into English was likely first written down in Italian during the Crusades, then published as a book in Naples in the early sixteenth century, before having been recently rediscovered in the library of an ancient Catholic family in northern England. In this case, the current print publication has been sanctioned by the auspicious durability of the story it transmits, which, though it dates back to the dark ages, has repeatedly been revived and repackaged. Since closet and cabinet justifications ground the value of texts in elite private spaces, both general and specific, or in one or more of the interpersonal processes of amassing and sharing knowledge associated with them, they could attribute both event- and text-based credibility as well. Yet, because authors and booksellers used closet and cabinet claims to acknowledge debts to and derive status from real or fictional superiors, they were comparable to formal dedications to patrons as well, which also remained common, since literary patronage remained common, throughout the period.

However, the trope of the textual closet or cabinet differs from these better-known forms of referential authorization insofar as the structural metaphor of elite private space both sustains an originary social hierarchy of learning and considers how this hierarchy is dismantled as elite knowledge is transferred to a standard, bound-paper format for wide distribution. In particular, closet and cabinet justifications often place less emphasis on the original elite owner than on the role played by some intermediary—such as a former favorite, servant, or apprentice, or even a closet thief—who may or may not also be the published book's author, editor, or bookseller. Significantly, discussions of these tropes say little to nothing about the trade and craft of bookmaking, focusing instead on the winding social paths, and sometimes the novel or uncomfortable actions, such as retrospectively betraying one's master or mistress, that bring private knowledge to anonymous readers. At the same time, even when they also denote specific private spaces external to the text, many of the titles of published closets and cabinets, like those of the *bibliothèques sans murs*, also refer to the book itself as a tangible object, deflecting attention from the specialized and mechanized labor of remediation to the action of entering a private space in the absence of its owner, an experience that most people across the social spectrum would have found much easier to imagine.

If all published closet and cabinet compilations were secret histories of a sort insofar as they claimed to pass along confidential knowledge to those who might not otherwise have had access to it, this generic link was especially apparent when editors or booksellers referred to a specific, well-known royal or noble closet or cabinet as the point of origin for the contents of a published book. Indeed, sometimes the link between a published collection and the genre of political disclosure was made explicit, such as in *The Cabinet Open'd, Or the Secret History of the Amours of Madam de Maintenon, With the French King* (1690). In its account of the affair and secret marriage of Louis XIV and Françoise d'Aubigné, Marquise de Maintenon, *The Cabinet Open'd* juxtaposes both first-person/epistolary and third-person narration. In the preface to the reader, the author-editor rationalizes the decision to share personal writings taken illicitly from Madam de Maintenon's cabinet:

> Altho' several persons, having wrote upon the like subjects, have deliver'd nothing but pure Romance, nevertheless what I have Wrote is

an unquestionable truth; for the better part of the Memoires from whence this Little History is drawn, came out of the Cabinet of Madam de Maintenon, and were partly written with her own Hand. These we recovered of a certain Gentlewoman, who lived a considerable time with her, and who had not served her this trick, but only to avoid a greater mischief which was designed her.[24]

The editor has received Madam de Maintenon's personal writings from an unnamed "Gentlewoman, who lived a considerable time with her," presumably one of Madam de Maintenon's most intimate servants. In contrast to the common literary critical view of the anti-elitist orientation of the published secret history, this framing discourse assumes a royalist reader who is right to be suspicious of print.[25] It's only because fanciful and scandalous accounts of the affair are already in circulation that this new version, and the insubordinate act of theft or "trick" on which it is founded, are at all justified. The authority of *The Cabinet Open'd* crucially inheres in the private archive on which the book is based and in the close relationship between the mistress and servant that first developed in and around it.

The Queens Closet Opened (1655) is framed by a similar claim to closet origins and the same defensive rationale of print publication. In the letter to the reader that introduces this popular seventeenth-century cookbook, Henrietta Maria's former secretary stresses that its recipes were all first collected in the former Queen's closet at Whitehall: "Since my Soveraign Mistress her banishment, ... I found no less then two other Copies [of her recipes] abroad ... my friends ... advised me to dispatch my original copy to the Press to prevent these false ones; for otherwise I should not have thought it less then Sacriledge, had not the lock been first pickt, to have opened the Closet of my distressed Soveraign Mistress without her Royal Assent."[26] That the contents of this royal room are worthy of saving goes without saying. However, the secretary-turned-editor maintains that he regrets that print publication is the only way to ensure the continued integrity of that now historical space. Identifying himself by initials, W.M. acknowledges the possibility that this exposure will be misread as treasonous in spirit and remarks that he wishes he could write a memoir, as a kind of prelude or paratext to the manual, in which he could reassure readers of his absolute loyalty to the Queen: "My particular relation for many yeares to her Majesties service might easily, should I write my own history, rid thee of all scruples touching the truth of this collection, there being few or none of these receipts presented to her Majesty, which were not transcribed into her book by my self, the Original papers being most of them preserved in my own hands, which I kept as so many Reliques, and should sooner have parted with my dearest bloud, then to have suffered them to be publick." This intimate work of first copying the recipes and then "preserv[ing] them in [his] own hands" after Henrietta Maria's exile has infused them materially with the aura of patron and client alike: the recipes are "Reliques" of the Queen and, if pirated copies had not already been in circulation, W.M. "should sooner have parted with [his] dearest bloud, then to have suffered them to be publick." Though elsewhere he briefly mentions "the general good" that the recipes might do among English readers, the thrust of W.M.'s closet discourse, like that of Madam de Maintenon's editor, is to suggest that print is a medium of last resort. The authenticity of this complete yet penetrable version of the Queen's treasured private collection depends, paradoxically, on his reluctance to produce it.[27]

Other printed cabinets and closets focus less on original elite collections than on the specialized processes and social networks that these sites of intimate exchange encouraged and accommodated. For example, in the title page of a book of medicinal recipes, *Modern Curiosities of Art & Nature Extracted out of the Cabinets of the most Eminent Personages of the French Court* (1685), publishers Matthew Gilliflower and James Partridge invoke the text's origins in largely unspecified elite private spaces but then turn to its author. The book's cures have been "Composed and Experimented by the Sieur Lemery, Apothecary to the French King," and the book's authority rests on Lemery's expertise: "Look not on this as a Rapsody of Impertinent Recipe's catch't up by some Drudge of the Press, who never try'd other Experiment than that of Imposing upon the easie, as well Bookseller as Buyer, but rather (as indeed it is) a Collection of Approved Experiments, made by the Sieur Lemery, famous for his Excellent Course of Chymistry, who, as Apothecary to the French King, had great opportunities of communicating to, and receiving from divers Personages of the French-Court and others, many curious Secrets and Experiments."[28] At once naming and aiming to assuage readers' fears that the book is a hack job by "some Drudge of the Press" with nothing on his mind but the bottom line, the publishers underscore the author's "famous" expertise in "Chymistry" as well as his close relationships with Louis XIV and "divers Personages of the French-Court," many of whom are also apparently closet experimenters.

A somewhat more confident vision of print relations can be glimpsed in Hannah Woolley's housekeeping manual, *The Queen-Like Closet; or,*

Rich Cabinet (1670), and Nicholas Haym's catalog, *British Treasury: Cabinet the first of our Greek and Roman antiquities of all sorts* (1719). The title pages and dedications of both books gesture to a set of generic architectural spaces where their author-editors have spent many years developing their skills in elite company. But they also look forward to the new relationships that will be cultivated through publication. In his extensive autobiographical preface, Nicholas Haym explains that in the first place it was thanks to the patronage of Lord Halifax that he has had the opportunity to visit and make drawings of some of the finest cabinet collections in Britain. However, Haym is also aware that any individual collection must be limited. While improving his own knowledge of antiquities in a variety of actual closets, he produces a textual cabinet in the exhaustive spirit of the *bibliothèque sans murs*, with an eye to projected readers' desires to see those coins and medals that "have never yet been printed" and have been "observed but by few."[29] Similarly, in her dedication, Hannah Woolley highlights not only the quality of the people whom her recipes have already pleased but also the considerations that she has shown to her new audience: "I do assure you all, that they are very Choice Receipts, and such as I have not taken up on the Credit of others, but do Commend them to you from my own Practice, who have had the Honour to perform such things for the Entertainments of His late MAJESTY, as well as for the Nobility. I could have enlarged the Volum very much, had I not picked out only such as I thought to be the very best; and such as hath cost me much time, and great pains to gather together."[30] Insofar as Woolley does distinguish between social and culinary factors, she privileges the latter, selecting for her unknown readers "only such as I thought to be the very best." Yet Woolley's personal assessment of the quality of the recipes still largely depends on the rank of the people whom the recipes have already pleased.

Sometimes booksellers' closet or cabinet justifications serve to disavow emerging capitalist standards of measure and to realign texts for sale with traditional qualitative economies of value. Authors and editors of printed collections of spiritual knowledge seem to be particularly taken with images of sparkling jewels and precious metals for this reason. The worth of these gorgeous, impervious, inorganic materials, which were often collected in locked closets and cabinets, is widely understood to be in excess of their market value and rather to lie in their capacity to seal and symbolize enduring bonds across generations. In the dedicatory epistle of an early example of this subgenre, *The Golden Cabinet of true Treasure: Containing the summe of Morall Philosophie* (1612), the translator, appropriately named William Jewell, admonishes: "All things, for the which men labour and trade in this world, may bee reduced unto one of these three points, Honour, Riches, or Pleasure and yet notwithstanding, the greatest part of men are often beguiled of their purposes, because their election erreth in the meanes, whereby they might attaine unto the same.... For this reason," he continues, "have I spent my best endeavours, to set befor your eyes that end and scope, whereunto all the actions and aberations of mankind should be directed: and not that alone, but the meanes also which conduce unto it.... And these are the pretious and rich Iewels which are contained in the *Golden Cabinet of true Treasure*."[31] Jewell's volume should help his readers to discriminate between selfish aims and the intangible "pretious and rich Iewels" of salvation. Indeed, the struggle to distinguish between "true" (Christian) and self-interested notions of "honour," "riches," and "pleasure" parallels the difficulty in choosing the right path with which the book as a whole purports to help. *The audi filia, or a rich cabinet full of spirituall iewells* (1620), composed by "the Reuerend Father, Doctour Auila," Thomas Brooks's *Cabinet of Choice Jewels Or, A Box of precious Ointment* (1669), "Being a plain Discovery of . . . what men are worth for Eternity, and how 'tis like to go with them in another World," and Charles Bradbury's *Cabinet of Jewels Opened to the Curious, by a Key of Real Knowledge* (1785), all use the same metaphor to signal the incalculable worth of a spiritual life.[32]

The apparently timeless value of gemstones and precious metals also made them attractive to publishers of other kinds of specialized knowledge. One vast miscellany of practical information called *The Golden Cabinet* (1773) begins with advice on how to gild things. Another *Golden Cabinet* (1790) lays bare the art of clairvoyance. In the front matter to *Rich Cabinet with Variety of Inventions in several Arts and Siences* (1658), John White underscores how "rich"—both diverse and invaluable—book learning can be. The frontispiece engraving celebrates the possibility of encountering vast stores of knowledge (figure 21). Globes and nautical instruments, people dueling, monsters, and mermaids are all accounted for here. In an accompanying poem, "The Authour to his Book," White likens readers growing intellectually in relation to his text—the way they "content [their] mind[s]," as he puts it—to elite women at their dressing tables:

As in a glasse herein you may behold
A goodly Cascate set with pearls and gold;
Not petty Gugau's to adorn the Brest,

The Neck, the Arm, but jewels of the best,
And choicest Learning such herein you'd find
Will please your fancy & content your mind;
Some for delight and recreation,
And some for serious contemplation;
Some in Arithmetick that lofty Art,
Some likewise in Geometry are taught,
Some in Astronomy that Art most hie,
Others teach how to decorate the Skie,
With splendent Stars, silver & golden Showers
Which are th'effects of Philosophick powers.[33]

White's volume is "a glasse" insofar as it provides a clear, if two-dimensional, view of myriad fields of learning. And readers, looking into it, satisfy their own tastes as they take up the "jewels of the best, / And choicest Learning" that most suit them. In his dedication, White retools the metaphor. "I have here unlock'd and open'd to your view a rich Cabinet of varieties," he announces: "If there be any thing therein contained that may yield you profit, solace of the mind, recreation of the spirits, or content, I shall think my labour well bestowed, and be glad; If it be otherwise, I shall be sorry that I have nothing therein to please your mind, intreating you to shut down the lid again." Playing up the physical resemblance between textual and elite material structures for gathering knowledge, White imagines his book as a receptacle that might just as easily be closed as opened.

Even when not concretized in this way, the idea that printed closets and cabinets had been unlocked or broken open, or their contents discovered, abounded throughout the genre and gave form to a range of perspectives on the accessibility of print. In the *Queen's Closet Opened* and *The Cabinet Open'd* cited above, the tropes support a conservative rhetoric of publication in which dutiful favorites reluctantly expose secret documents in print as a defense against scandalous, inaccurate versions that are already making the rounds. More commonly, the tropes of the closet and cabinet participate in the period's increasingly positive discourse of print publication, and help to rationalize the exposure of private knowledge on political or scientific grounds. In these iterations, the exhibition of elite intimate spaces provides a tangible point of focus around which new kinds of intellectual collectives can begin to gather, organize, and define themselves.

In the preface to *The Kings Cabinet opened: Or, Certain Packets of Secret Letters & Papers; Written with the Kings own Hand, and taken in his Cabinet at Nasby-Field* (1645), probably the most consequential English printed

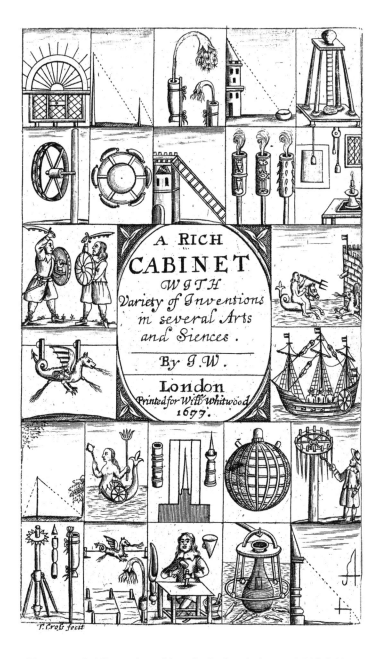

FIG. 21. The squares holding various objects in the frontispiece to *A Rich Cabinet* suggest reams of cut paper or uniform drawers in a built cabinet and evoke the desire for an endlessly expanding catalog of knowledge. (Frontispiece reprinted from John White, *A Rich Cabinet* [London: William Whitwood, 1668]. Courtesy of Beinecke Rare Book and Manuscript Library, Yale University.)

cabinet, the book's Parliamentarian publisher suggests that Charles I's personal letters have been printed by divine ordinance. The act of exposing the letters is a sacred reversal of the monarch's dangerous secrecy: "By Gods good providence the traverse Curtain is drawn, and the King writing to Ormond, and the Queen ... is presented upon the stage. God grant that the drawing of this Curtain may bee as fatall to Popery, and all Antichristian heresie here now, as the rending of the vaile was to the Jewish Ceremonies in Iudea, at the expiration of our Saviour."[34] In the logic of this image, it is no human agent but God's invisible hand remaking the king's cabinet as a public theater, that authorizes the exposure of Charles's disloyal religious and political proclivities and demands that good Protestants rise up together to call his bluff.

Publishers of printed closets and cabinets found a secular rationale for the publication of formerly private knowledge in the new scientific discourse of the period. In the preface to *Novum Organum*, Francis Bacon had emphasized the importance of first-hand experience over ancient wisdom, the crucial principle of English empirical philosophy, by calling on "true sons of learning" to accompany him past the "outer halls of Nature, which any number of men have already trodden, to where at length the way into her inner chambers shall be revealed."[35] Later in the century, in his description of England's first scientific institution, *The History of the Royal Society*, Thomas Sprat put a more concrete and practical spin on Bacon's images of architectural penetration and exposure. Though independent experimenters should willingly allow "all, or the greatest part of ... domestick Receipts and Curiosities" to "flow into" the "publick Treasurie," if necessary, the new scientists can take more active measures: "the Royal Society will be able by Degrees to purchase such extraordinary Inventions, which are now close lock'd up in Cabinets; and then to bring them into one common Stock."[36] In this formulation, the Royal Society itself serves as a cabinet of cabinets, a universal macro-cabinet, whose "Stock" has been purchased and then, crucially, made fully accessible, being, as Sprat imagines, "upon all Occasions expos'd to all Men's Use."

The emergent scientific concern with sharing knowledge in order to advance it also helped to promote more inclusive and extensive private cabinet viewings throughout the period and ultimately gave rise to the public museum. In general, printed closets and cabinets provided textual complements to museum curators' efforts to authorize the display of once-private material collections to large audiences. In some instances, they were also supplementary texts and virtual museums in their own right, providing records and guides to collections already on display and offering more inclusive access than the museums themselves. The British Museum, England's premier national collection, was founded by Act of Parliament in 1753 on the basis of a cabinet owned by Royal Society laureate Sir Hans Sloane.[37] *General Contents of the British Museum*, a visitors' guide published in London in 1761, reinforces the collection's elite and intimate point of origin by calling the museum a *Noble Cabinet* in its subtitle. Yet the guide seeks to close the gap between the privileged few who have had early and frequent access to the "Noble Cabinet" and the many others, especially the many women, who have only now been to the Museum for the first time: "The judicious Reader will observe, that I have endeavoured to be as intelligible as possible; making use of very few Words but what are generally understood: I therefore flatter myself, that my Readers among the Ladies will be very numerous; *many of them having, in my Company, lamented the want of something of this kind, to direct their Observations, and give them a general Idea of the Contents of this wonderful Collection.*"[38] The intellectual bridge the *Noble Cabinet* provides is not a complete one, however. Packaged as a sort of *British Museum for Dummies*, the guide offers a few basic principles to its multitude of readers—especially "the Ladies"—while explicitly leaving the finer points for the experts who have had more direct and frequent encounters with this and other collections.

Simon Shapin has shown that, in the seventeenth and eighteenth centuries, natural philosophers understood the limits of their own axiomatic suspicion of tradition and authority. Notwithstanding empirical injunctions to value direct experience above all, to "be skeptical of what others say, and wander the fields alone with your eyes open," modern practitioners recognized that you couldn't figure everything out on your own: to make advances in science, a good deal of knowledge had to be "acquired at second hand."[39] The top of the social hierarchy was deemed the most trustworthy source for scientific knowledge as well, because of ongoing attention to civility and honor among the nobility, as Shapin explains:

The imputed constancy, steadfastness, and reliability of an authentic gentleman was a master-figure of the traditional honor culture of medieval Europe, a trope by which the official interpreters of feudal society identified and justified its hierarchical order. Yet while conceptions of gentility changed, and while the honor culture underwent substantial alterations in early modern Europe, the description and injunction of gentlemanly constancy, reliability, and truthfulness continued, recruiting and assimilating new resources all the while. The justifications changed, but the outcome was recognizably the same: the distribution of imputed credit and reliability followed the contours of authority and power.[40]

So while publishers of textual collections of knowledge sometimes explicitly embrace proto-democratic notions of collective discovery, at the same time they tacitly authorize traditional architectural closets and cabinets as ideal points of origin for the information and ideas most worthy of sharing. In his *Rich Cabinet,* John White artfully navigates this double orientation, establishing that his own learning has depended on private learning and collecting while also expressing concern that this learning now should serve "the publick ... good": "No man (I think) should be born onely to himself, and hide his Talent," he clarifies. "And therefore these few Receits which I have Collected with divers of mine own (gentle Reader) I dedicate freely to thy use."

Other textual cabinets imagine the passage of knowledge from elite and private to more accessible textual venues as a form of inheritance. The publisher of *England's Choice Cabinet of Rarities* (1700) claims to print "Many Curious Physical Receipts for Curing the most Dangerous Diseases and Grievance incident to Men, Women, and Children" as a means to preserve the lifelong intellectual yields of Mr. Wadham, its author: "Age growing on him (he knowing he was but Mortal, and must dye) he thought fit to leave in Writing such things as might benifit after his Death, and be a living Monument of what he had formerly done: and ... [this] may be accounted his Golden Legacy to the World as being the last he Writ before his Death."[41] The rationale for publication in *Mother Bunch's Closet Newly Broke Open* (1760) also centers on the prospect of immortalizing a private collection of insights. After an elderly midwife spreads the word that she wants to leave to posterity her "stock of knowledge," she has to corral the crowd of women who come begging for love spells, each one clamoring so insistently for the midwife's attention "that they made the old woman deaf with their great noise." "My dear daughters," Mother Bunch cautions, "sit you down and be quiet ... I'll sit in the midst of you and ... give you a large account of some extraordinary curiosities here in my closet newly broke open; declaring it as my opinion, that the things which are profitable for one maid, are so for another."[42] Mother Bunch's "large," or more general, "account" will allow her to address the needs of many more people than she has time to diagnose and heal one-on-one. While this framing narrative depicts the midwife exchanging her usual intimate mode of address for a lecture—a more

abstract but still oral approach—the text itself represents a further mod-
ification of her usual style. By first recording then later printing her generalizations, Mother Bunch can project an unlimited future audience for
her wisdom. However, as a virtual and collective space of knowledge
transmission, the published textual zone of the *Closet Newly Broke Open*
will require readers to adapt knowledge presented in broad terms to the
particularities of their own cases.

Thus, even when the printed closet or cabinet is pictured as a mechanism for preserving a legacy, the analogy also makes readers aware of
the dislocation that, from the perspective of traditional manuscript and
closet culture, was the necessary and necessarily inferior condition of all
print learning. That is, by comparing published texts to closets and cabinets, authors and editors also reinforced ordinary readers' sense of their
exclusion from originary acts of knowledge transmission that had already taken place. Readers were presumed not to be participating in actual closet circles but to have access only to these virtual cabinets, where
they could consume knowledge that had already been encountered, engaged, processed, and preserved by and for others. Sometimes purveyors of print were upfront about the stratified social dynamic of their
productions. The author of *Wit's Cabinet: A Companion to Gentlemen and
Ladies* (1715), for instance, begins by asserting the importance of travel to
the art of conversation, then offers his book as a substitute for those who
lack the breeding, connections, money, or time to gain this skill through
experience: "Since every one's Stars have not been so lucky as to let them
obtain it [wit] by their Observation of Men and Manners abroad, by
travelling into Foreign Countries, it is Pity that such should not be as-
sisted by Books, proper for their Instruction at Home, which is both the
easiest and the cheapest Way: And to accomodate such, is the Design of
this Book."[43] Similarly, the author of *Curiosities. Or The Cabinet of Nature* (1637) echoes but corrects Francis Bacon's claim that "true sons of
learning" can accompany him through Nature's "inner chambers." In
fact, only scholars are admitted to "the ever-vernant and private walkes
of Naturall Philosophie." While the author offers his book as a surro-
gate for such familiarity, he nevertheless lords his advantage over readers
(figure 22). An accompanying poem reinforces the sexualized image of
privilege on the frontispiece:

The Goddesse[,] like her selfe so plac't on high,
So open brested, freely doth descry
Her love, which heretofore shee long conceal'd

Wisely, to make thee love what's here reveal'd
She opens here her closet, richly set
With high priz'd gemmes, her richest Cabinet.

The author explains that he "[entered] the very bowels (as I may say) of [Nature's] secresies, not without infinite pleasure I penetrated her *Arcana*, and opening her *Cabinet*, finding her full of Curiosities, and having free-licence to take what I thought fit, selected none, but what I thought, might not only content my selfe, but generally recreate all."[44] Despite his inclusive concluding caveat, the author clearly distinguishes between his own immediate, hands-on form of learning and his readers' secondary and passive one. Adam Smyth argues that seventeenth-century printed miscellanies, by "opening up the exclusive to anyone," "were treading a fine line between cultivating a sense of the socially eminent and debasing that eminence."[45] The metaphor of the opened closet or cabinet in many printed collections of the period manifested this fine line. The metaphor represents booksellers' shared hope that the knowledge of the closet and cabinet could retain its intrinsic social capital after having been dislodged and mechanically reproduced for profit. But it also produces an image of print readers yearning to learn yet caught in a (Groucho) Marxian paradox of social inclusion: either opened closets and cabinets and their contents were no longer in any real sense elite and exclusive or ordinary readers weren't really entitled to see them.

HAVE YOU EVER BEEN EXPERIENCED?: PEEPING IN THE CABINET OF LOVE

The uneasy affects of print readership were sexualized, dramatized, and partially resolved in the shifting figure of the peeping Tom in printed cabinets of love. Like other textual closets and cabinets, printed cabinets of love had real-life referents. A cabinet of love was a place where passions were pursued or recorded in secret. It might be a decorated wooden receptacle for locking away souvenirs, such as the box in *Memoirs of Count Grammont* that lands in the hands of the Duchess of York after a lover of one of her young maids of honor has died. Opening it up in her closet, the Duchess finds all manner of "love trinkets" in it, including pictures, "hair of all descriptions, wrought into bracelets, lockets, and into a thousand other devices wonderful to see" as well as "three or four packets of letters" that especially pique her curiosity.[46] When *cabinet of love* referred

FIG. 22. Classical philosophers Pliny and Plutarch stand in front of Nature, a four-breasted goddess, who entices votaries to enter into the closet beneath her legs. (Frontispiece from Robert Basset, *Curiosities, or the Cabinet of Nature* [London: N. & I. Okes, 1637]. Reproduced by permission of the British Library, London, UK © British Library Board. All Rights Reserved/Bridgeman Images.)

to a whole room, it might be a closet designed for use as a dressing room, or a theatrical dressing room or green room, or what the French called a *boudoir*.[47] Noting that its atmosphere was expected to make seduction nearly effortless, Diane Berrett Brown translates a description of a boudoir from an eighteenth-century French novel called *The Sopha*: "Everything radiated sensuality: the adornments, the furniture, the scent of the exquisite perfume that was always burning. Everything brought sensuality to the eye, everything transported it to the soul. This cabinet could have been taken for the temple of voluptuousness, for the indisputable seat of pleasure."[48] At a time when love was a handle for any sort of passion, and law and religion condoned only married sex, *cabinet of love* could also refer more broadly to the capacity of a closet to provide a cover for illicit sexual activity of all kinds, including the mutual embraces of a patroness and her favorite, the grabbing and groping in which Pepys specialized, or looking, unseen, at others enjoying their privacy.

Accordingly, publishers of printed cabinets of love aimed at once to inform and arouse readers by making available poems, letters, anecdotes, ballads, lists, written descriptions, or illustrations of the arts of courtship, sex, or seduction. An early instance of this subgenre is a graphic guide to human reproduction translated from Latin called *Rare Verities: The cabinet of Venus unlocked, and her secrets laid open* (1658). The work's central metaphor combines the protoscientific orientation of cabinets of curiosities with the sensual pleasures of the boudoir: "Sinibaldus," the putative author of the text, "lay[s] open the mysteries of generation and its concomitants" under headings like "What is Copulation" or "Through what part is love at first received in," while also promising "Amorous Readers" that his "little store-house" will "augment [their] pleasing fires."[49] Other examples include *Love's Perpetual Almanack . . . From a Manuscript found in Cupid's Cabinet* (1681), which provides, among other things, a handbook on the Turkish and continental sex trades (the "Fairs of Love"), and *The Portal to the Cabinet of Love* (1807), which supplements translations of the "Nineteen kisses of Johannes Secundus" with other lyric poems on the same subject. The subgenre continued into the late nineteenth century with *Cabinet of Venus* (1896), an anthology of pornographic drawings, whose publisher's name, the "Erotica-bibliomaniac Society," reflects the affinity between collectors, especially book collectors, and pornographers that defined this whole group of texts.[50] Since classical times, to know someone has been a euphemism for sex. As Eve Sedgwick remarks, "Cognition itself, sexuality itself, and transgression itself have always been ready in Western culture to be magnetized into an unyielding though not an unfissured alignment with one another."[51] Barbara Benedict finds that, in the eighteenth century, the British discourse of curiosity put new pressures on this longstanding alignment.[52] Since all printed closets and cabinets both generated and promised to satisfy desires for secret knowledge, it isn't really surprising that sex, historically deemed the archetypal object of untamed curiosity, became a regular focal point for such collections.

The representative status of printed cabinets of love within the larger category of the printed closet and cabinet is also suggested by two further connotations of the word *cabinet* in this context. As Brown points out, eighteenth-century French writers felt that new designs for privacy were not merely well-suited for seduction but arousing in themselves. For example, Louis-Sébastien Mercier claimed that "[French] architecture is no less licentious than our erotic poetry": with its "secret passages and hidden stairways," the eighteenth-century building "anticipates and fulfills all the aims of debauchery and libertinage."[53] The imaginative links between architectural and bodily openings spurred suggestive literary imagery, Brown notes, such as when, in *Les Liaisons dangéreuses*, the rake Valmont, who has acquired a key, insists that the ingénue Cécile "oil the lock and hinges of her bedroom door so that he can enter with ease."[54] After it came into English from French in the sixteenth century, the word *cabinet* and the lock used to secure it on the one hand, and the key that unfastened it on the other, became common code for female and male genitals respectively. In John Harington's early seventeenth-century poem, "Of a Ladyes Cabinet," a gentleman glimpses his wife "sitting in a muse" in her closet with her legs parted.[55] When he chides, "Wife, awake, your Cabinet stands open," her comeback is a come-on that also reminds him that the privacy of her room, her sexuality, and the whole of her person are in fact his responsibilities: "[Then] locke it if you list," she says, "you keep the key." Whereas in William Wycherley's Restoration comedy *The Country Wife*, the patriarchal Mr. Pinchwife insists that "wives, like their writings, are never safe but in our closets under lock and key," Harington, by having the wife deliver the message that her cabinet belongs to her husband after all, makes room for female mental autonomy and wit, notwithstanding women's legal status as male property.[56] Oversaturated with meaning, the titles of printed cabinets of love referred to built sites for indulging in secret passions, the bodily zones of sexual penetration and pleasure especially implicated in these passions, and also, most complexly, to themselves as erotic texts in which bodily passions were represented in order, ideally, to generate similar passions in their readers. In this way, the subgenre of the cabinet of love provided an especially lavish ground for investigating the capacity for imaginary intimacy—for pleasure and engagement at a distance. Insofar as the voyeurs in textual cabinets of love experiment with the peculiarly flexible imaginative power of vision, they exemplify a central principle of Joseph Addison's theory of the "Pleasures of the Imagination": "OUR Sight is the most perfect and most delightful of all our Senses. It fills the Mind with the largest Variety of Ideas, converses with its Objects at the greatest Distance, and continues the longest in Action without being tired or satiated with its proper Enjoyments."[57] Insofar as they are archetypes of print culture, however, voyeurs shed light on important distinctions between textual and embodied, authorized and unauthorized, forms of visual intimacy.[58]

Benedict considers how the word *peep* evolved over the course of the eighteenth century from the idea of seeing something novel by a chance occurrence to a more active one-way mode of observing another person:

> [Samuel] Johnson's *Dictionary* initially defines "peep" as "first appearance," the sudden presentation of a new sight, like a bird, to the observer's eye, but subsequently explains it as "curious looking." Finding no etymology for it, Johnson derives it from either the Dutch "to lift up" or the Latin for "spy." Eighteenth-century meanings of the word burgeon to designate a looking-glass, an eye, and a one-eyed person; "Peeping Tom" acquired its meaning as "an inquisitive person" at mid-century.... The rebelliousness of curiosity is correlated with the lust of the eyes.[59]

First merely a passing desire to spy, with the epithet *Peeping Tom*, peeping eventually came to designate an enduring proclivity for transgressive looking. The imaginary intimacies represented in three eighteenth-century textual cabinets of love map the growing cultural coherence of this form of illicit spectatorship. Significantly, however, even as peeping becomes a distinct fetish, the gendered psychodynamics that characterize Harington's "Ladyes Cabinet" persist. Whenever a private setting appears in these erotic cabinets, there's a woman alone in it losing her inhibitions and a man within viewing distance, enjoying watching her while feeling acutely that he is not entitled to this pleasure.

In a poem called "The Discovery," falsely attributed to Rochester in the period's most frequently republished *Cabinet of Love* (1714), the first-person speaker steals into Sylvia's chamber just as she is getting out of bed in the morning.[60] He has dared to intrude, though he knows that he's not welcome. He hides and looks at her, sliding his gaze from her breasts, which are "white as Snow," down to "something ... , which was but thinly hair'd, / ... not too bushy, nor too bald." The stolen glances have an immediate effect:

> Oh! there I thought I could for ever dwell,
> Partaking Bliss beyond what Tongue can tell;
> The Sight would nourish me ten thousand Years,
> Give solid Joys, which are unmix'd with Fears.
> I bless'd my Eyes, and would not change my Seat
> For all the pompous Riches of the Great.

The mere "Sight" of Sylvia "nourish[es]" the speaker with "solid Joys" and he immediately assesses this pleasure as better than physical contact with her, which would be "mix'd with Fears," presumably of her explicit nonconsent and/or getting caught by her father or some other patriarchal protector. His joy increases "to an Extasy" when he learns that, conveniently enough, she too is aroused:

> She turn'd her round, then sate upon the Bed;
> Her Lilly Hand pull'd open her Maiden-head.
> She strove to view what I more plain could see,
> Which rais'd my Passion to an Extasy.
> The Sight alone soon made me shed my ——,
> And spill that —— of which she stood in Need.

At first the speaker views the girl's actions through his own voyeuristic lens, believing she "[strives] to view" herself. As both Benedict and Tita Chico note—with reference to a mid-century novella called *A Court Lady's Curiosity; or, the Virgin Undress'd. Curiously surveying herself in her Glass, with one leg upon her Toilet*—women in private were sometimes represented as both sexual curios for a male viewer and self-exhibitionists or autovoyeurs.[61] But it turns out that Sylvia seeks additional stimulation:

> Then from the Table she her Garment took,
> Where, in her Pocket, was a Baudy Book;
> Which she remov'd, and thence drew out a Tool.
> Much like to that with which Men Women rule;
> She it apply'd where I'm asham'd to tell,
> And acted what I could have done full well.

Sylvia's "Baudy Book" and especially her dildo, both of which have been tucked away, afford her a form of gratification that the speaker understands to be a poor substitute for sex with him. She "acted what I could have done full well," he complains. When he nevertheless grows aroused again, his pleasure is shot through with anxiety and rage. The phallic "Tool" is "Much like to that with which Men Women rule," and Sylvia has rendered his own arousal redundant by using it. Referring to his own penis in the third person, as though it too, by virtue of all of this virtuality, has become a simulacrum of itself, the speaker pictures his own climax as an act of vengeance: "in Revenge, he now again lets fly, / And spewing, fell down in an Agony." After Sylvia finishes then leaves, the speaker emerges from his hiding spot, picks up her dildo, and "quits the Room" too—"to pass at Home my humble Captive's Doom." Though the nature of the punishment is unclear, the speaker's military language for his own genitals and this other phallic object suggests that it's his own sexual ego that has been most affected—at once damaged and inflated—by his curiously parallel and passively violent experience.

The plot and erotic structure of "On Florinda, Seen while she was bathing" from a midcentury *Lover's Cabinet* (1755) follows that of "The Discovery," although the later poem, taking place in an outdoor grotto, is more sentimental in its diction and tone. Hiding in the bushes to observe Florinda washing in a river, the first-person speaker also begins with a blazon:

> Her Hair bound backward in spiral Wreath
>   Her upper Beauties to my Sight betray'd;
> The happy Stream concealing those beneath,
>   Around her Waist with circling Waters play'd:
> Who, while the Fair One on his Bosom sported,
>   Her dainty Limbs with liquid Kisses courted.[62]

Relative to Sylvia with her book and toy, Florinda is sexually inert. But watching her splash around is enough to spark the speaker's libidinal imagination. Like in "The Discovery," the voyeur's arousal seems especially to hinge on the projection of a rival counterpart who makes the direct physical contact he desires: the anthropomorphized "happy Stream" enjoys "circling" and "courting" Florinda "with liquid Kisses." Like in "The Discovery," this sexual jealousy is nearly as depressing as it is arousing for the voyeur himself:

> while the tempting Scene so near I view'd,
> A fierce Impatience throb'd in every Vein,
>   Discretion fled, and Reason lay subdu'd;
> My Blood beat high, and with its trembling made
>   A strange Commotion in the rustling Shade.

Though beginning in "fierce Impatience," the speaker's climax ultimately makes him feel stupid and out of control, not least because his "trembling" body makes a "strange Commotion" that threatens to betray him. Nevertheless his desire returns almost immediately, and the closing couplet suggests that a self-defeating cycle has now begun: "O Venus! give me more, or let me drink / Of Lethe's Fountain, and forget to think."

In the early seventeenth-century poem by John Harington, a husband just happens to catch a glimpse of his wife in her closet. By the middle of the eighteenth century, this mild curiosity is a full-fledged fixation with its own attendant rituals and thrills—the buzz of transgression and possible exposure as well as the play of perspectives it invites, as the voyeur projects himself into the mind and body of the woman he watches as well as the inanimate things that touch her. As writers become increasingly conscious of spectatorship as a substitute for other kinds of sexual contact, so too, it seems, do they give fuller vent to exhibition as a conscious sexual role. Compare Sylvia and Florinda, whose desirability seems to turn in part on their lack of awareness of being watched, to Molly, in "Miss in her Teens: A Tale," a poem attributed to "Mr. H——l" in a 1792 *Cabinet of Love*, who knowingly plays hide and seek with her cousin. Since peeping into her closet has become an obsession for him, Molly, living up to her practical no-nonsense name, resigns herself to accommodating his gaze:

> Whenever Molly was impounded,
>   She left [a] hole for Dick to peep.
> She knew there was no keeping
>   Her cousin, Dick, from peeping:
> For sure as ever you're alive,
>   Either with gimblet or skewer,
> Her cousin Richard would contrive
>   To bore a hole, somewhere, to view her.[63]

Significantly, no one in the poem appears to be confused or conflicted by Dick's frantic need to look at Molly in private. The aggressive images of Dick's desire to penetrate her privacy "either with gimblet or skewer" and Molly's sense that he would never bother to seek her consent suggest both that, if Molly "leaves a hole," this is in the hopes of preventing a physical violation, and that, at least symbolically, this visual violation is a rape. Yet the brutality of Dick's drive "to view" Molly is presented in playful rhythmical language. More like the pragmatic Molly than the neurotic male speakers in the earlier cabinets of love, the narrator treats Dick's compulsive looking and Molly's coerced exhibitionism as routine, and amusing, facets of gendered sexual psychology.

Parables of the Virtual

As this and previous chapters have shown, seventeenth- and eighteenth-century literary representations of elite closet intimacies modeled and inflected relationships between authors and readers in an emerging print culture. The parasitic closet intimacies associated with the peeping Tom had their own part to play in this new media rhetoric. Peeping was compelling enough as an illicit form of extrafamilial closet intimacy. However, given that the cabinets of love in which peeping Toms appear explicitly refer to the physical and imaginary space of the text, the resemblances between these figures and readers of print made them especially provocative. More so than the favorite or client, the figure of voyeur invited reflection on the capacity to feel a connection in the absence of reciprocity. If looking at a person could produce a visceral sense of closeness regardless of whether one's gaze was returned, what were the possibilities for closeness when the mind's eye was doing the looking? In raising this question, authors and editors were implicitly exploring the peculiar appeal of print as a medium for both meeting and fueling a new demand for experiences of shared privacy—both erotic and otherwise—especially among people with few chances of actually entering elite closets.

To understand the value of the printed cabinet of love as an early theory of print relations as such, it is useful briefly to consider the imaginative centrality of one of its generic descendants, Internet porn, within our own hypermediated moment. Each of the abstract concepts of voyeurism, virtuality, and pornography has a general definition that points to a major feature of current media culture. *Voyeurism*, especially when qualified as "mediated" or "trait" voyeurism, refers to a now widely acknowledged and shared desire to access others' privacy without sacrificing one's own.[64] *Virtuality* denotes the capacity of any medium—now particularly those that have been computer generated or electronically enhanced—to produce a simulated or imaginary realm distinct from the material plane where we typically encounter one another as bodies.[65] *Pornography* includes texts in any medium made with the intention of sexually arousing the audience. These three catagories closely converge around the forms of one-way erotic looking at others' bodies that today are not just legally condoned (so long as the people on view are of age and have consented to exhibit themselves) but readily satisfied by the preponderance of personal screens that can display close-up images across an impermeable boundary.[66] Yet because it provides visceral rewards and justifications for encountering others' privacy in parallel and invented worlds, Internet porn is both a specific cultural and aesthetic medium *and* a powerfully representative one. Demonstrating and fueling our capacity to enjoy all kinds of virtual encounters, it primes us not just as consumers of more porn—and of other forms, such as celebrity magazines, reality TV, and Twitter posts, that similarly allow us to witness and vicariously participate in private acts and experiences—but for any and all media.

Likewise, when seventeenth- and eighteenth-century writers and booksellers turned to cabinets of love, they were examining the complicated dynamics of intimacy at a distance on which the success of their medium as a whole depended. In an absolute sense, all writing, and indeed all language, are mediation: tools made by and for human beings to represent and understand ourselves and to communicate indirectly with one another. Yet, as writers and booksellers of the period intuitively understood, a printed text *feels* less immediate, less continuous with everyday lived experience, than a handwritten, hand-exchanged manuscript because the former, made using moveable metal type and sold under the conditions of anonymity, bears fewer obvious traces of the particularities of the people involved in its production and circulation.[67] Serving a partly ironic, partly compensatory function with regard to the apparent disembodiment and social dislocations of the mass medium, the scenes of peeping in cabinets of love are like primal scenes for the genre of the published collection and for print as such. On the one hand, representations of voyeurism tend to reinforce the idea that mutual physical contact is superior to the simulacrum of such an experience that erotic spying (or reading) makes possible.[68] Throughout the seventeenth and eighteenth centuries, popular tracts like *Onania; or, The Heinous Sin of Self Pollution* condemned masturbation as a compulsive, degenerate, and self-depleting form of pleasure.[69] The poetry of voyeurism discussed above characterizes one-way visual arousal in much the same way. On the other hand, however, in the context of the growing print-cultural discourse of closets and cabinets unlocked, the cabinet of love also opened up positive lines of readerly identification with sexual spectators as virtual lovers and as lovers of the virtual. After all, the readers of these erotic cabinets were themselves, ideally, aroused by mental pictures of the arousal of the fictional voyeurs, just as the fictional voyeurs were quite evidently aroused by the real or imagined prospect of the arousal of the person they were looking at (even if they weren't necessarily happy about it). Providing visceral proof that one-way relationships could substitute for interpersonal exchanges to which one was not socially or otherwise entitled, cabinets of love instructed readers to make imaginative use of other people's privacy wherever they glimpsed it and to depend on print to regularly deliver such glimpses.

How the closet intruder stood in for the dissociation and excitement of all eighteenth-century readers of print is nicely encapsulated in *Miss C——y's Cabinet of Curiosities; or, The Green-Room Broke Open*. Published in 1765, at the height of popularity of Laurence Sterne's first mock-autobiographical novel, *The Life and Opinions of Tristram Shandy*, *Miss C——y's Cabinet of Curiosities*, claiming "Tristram Shandy, Gent." as its author, is a mostly affectionate takedown of Sterne's own authorial sensibility and motives. The limited action of the forty-six-page novella involves the theft of an actress's secret box of documents from the green room at Smock Alley Theater, Dublin, where she is rehearsing the male lead in John Gay's *Beggar's Opera*. The novella's title almost certainly refers to the actress and singer Anne Catley, who was cast as Macheath "during the keen competition among theaters in Dublin at midcentury," and whose memoirs were sold in London as *A Brief Narrative of the Life, of the Celebrated Miss C*tl*y, containing the Adventures of that Lady in her Public Character of a Singer, and Private one of a Courtezan ... Taken into Keeping by Sir F.B.D.*, with a long subtitle that hints at the identities of fifteen other lovers, among them a colonel, a captain, a lawyer, a gambler, and a wine merchant, "and several more of the Nobility and Gentry of Distinction."[70] Since Shandy's *Miss C——y's Cabinet of Curiosities* describes events leading to the publication of Catley's memoir, it is effectively a secret history of this secret history, though one that delivers only innuendo and no actual sexual secrets. Marcie Frank has characterized the eighteenth-century emergence of literary criticism as a negotiation of "transitions" not just "from court-centered to public-oriented literary production" but also "from theatre to reading audience."[71] In his metaliterary text, Shandy is acutely aware of both his debts to and distance from the court and the theater alike. Like his fictional namesake, the author stalls and spins rather than propels his plot, musing suggestively and digressing, while continually projecting a near-future moment of virtual contact with his own audience.[72] As the next chapter will discuss in detail, Sterne perfected a technique of teasing readers by maximizing the textual, conceptual, and material—especially the erotic—resonances of certain keywords.[73] In this parody, the cabinet is well nigh exhausted as a trope of the burgeoning print market.

"The Cabinet that had been stolen from the Green Room belonged to Miss C——y. She had been in Possession of it ever since her Birth—It was a might pretty one—fringed about with curling Ornaments," Shandy begins Chapter X. "——A Cabinet that the greatest Monarchs would have been delighted to have laid their Hands on, and which had been enjoyed by Numbers of the greatest personages in both Kingdoms,—— though they had always Honour and Generosity enough to leave it with its fair Possessor, after they had viewed, handled, and enjoyed it sufficiently."[74] Though he is aware of the impressive circle of admirers of Miss C——y's bodily cabinet, to his chagrin, Shandy cannot count himself among the "great Personages" who actually view, handle, and enjoy it. But Miss C——y is nevertheless very present to him as a sexual fantasy. As the woman who came to be known as Roxolana in Hamilton's *Memoirs* had learned too late, in this period female players were generally viewed as sexually available and sexually suspicious.[75] In the role of Gay's libertine highwayman, Miss C——y has become hypervisible. Men's form-fitting clothing revealed the contours of women's bodies, not least of all their legs, which were otherwise almost never seen in public.[76] Though Shandy doesn't discuss C——y's performance—doesn't, in fact, appear to have watched it—he fully grasps the appeal of her breeches part.

Specifying that Miss C——y's cabinet has been taken from her green room adds another dimension to the visual fantasy. The name *green room* for the playhouse retiring or tiring room, perhaps painted green, where actors spent time before and after performing, dates to the late seventeenth century. An evocative liminal zone in the Restoration and eighteenth-century theater, it served as a storage space, wardrobe, dressing area, and passageway to the stage itself. Felicity Nussbaum finds that many eighteenth-century actresses propelled their careers by authorizing memoirs, thereby eliciting from their fans a quality and quantity of interest, sexual and otherwise, that had been "formerly reserved for the royal court and other elite personages."[77] Like their memoirs, the green rooms of "rival queens," as Nussbaum calls the most celebrated female players, promised to reveal the flesh-and-blood human beings who worked hard to create the aesthetic pleasures of the stage, just as royal closets revealed the fallible bodies and minds at the center of the formal spectacle of the court. But the social protocols of the green room were an inversion of those of the courtly closet since the players occupying them generally didn't own them or any part of the theater. Elite male theater patrons, especially those sponsoring the current play or the playhouse itself, assumed that the privileges of proximity in this space were theirs to determine. (In fact, prerogative was so uncertain and the demand so high that tiring room access was legally restricted in 1664 and again in 1668.[78]) In Tita Chico's words, "The tiring-room stood as a figurative doorway into the actresses' 'private' lives that so fascinated their public."[79] Though Shandy has no entrée to intimacy with Miss C——y, his curiosity is unhindered.

Shandy narrates the origins of his own book in Chapter XIII, picking up where he had left off in Chapter X: "The other Cabinet Miss C——y had, and which coming in to my Hands I broke open, was very curious; but I had much rather have broke open the Cabinet I before described, and which she always carried about her——The Cabinet coming, I say, into my Hands,——how, matters not,——when, is alike indifferent——I turned the various Papers in it over and over, and determined to publish such as were the most to my Liking."[80] His conspicuous evasiveness makes it clear that, like the voyeur-speaker in "The Discovery," who, as angry as he is aroused by his irrelevance, takes Sylvia's dildo "captive" at the end of that poem, and like the Parliamentarian who publishes Charles I's stolen letters in *The Kings Cabinet opened*, Shandy has acquired Miss C——y's "other Cabinet" by illegitimate means, probably stolen it himself. Among the contents of Miss C——y's textual cabinet, a manuscript has particularly "attracted [his] Eyes": "ten Sheets, closely written, and in a very small Hand" bearing the title "Genuine and Authentic MEMOIRS OF MISS C——Y ... By a GENTELMAN of QUALITY." "Oh, ho! ... I have found a Treasure.——This is a Mine that will supply me with Gold enough.——All the World are mad for Miss C——Y; and the Devil's in't, if they don't buy her Memoirs," Shandy cries as he scans the loose pages, and then "immediately set to considering, how much I could gain by the Publication of so curious a Work." He dreams big, predicting that the sale will make him as rich as the publishers of *The Memoirs of a Woman of Pleasure*, *Onania*, or *Lord Rochester's Works*, the period's bestselling erotic books.

For all his excitement about this goldmine, however, Shandy has little enthusiasm for the people to whom this publication will connect him most directly. He worries that, unlike Miss C——y's bodily cabinet, which is treated with "Honor and Generosity" by "the greatest personages" in Ireland and England, this textual cabinet will circulate far beyond the limited group actually capable of recognizing its worth: "'Tis not improbable, that out of the ten thousand People that will read this Cabinet not above ten shall be able to form a proper Judgment of the Merit or Demerit of any literary Production at all;" he predicts, "though every Dunce will now-a-Days pretend to determine the precise Value of every Book he looks into." Nor is the original author of the "Genuine and Authentic MEMOIRS" to be admired: "I could not, for the Life of me, put it out of my Head, but that it was the vamped up Work of some mercenary Bookseller, or hungry Devil of an Author, who thought to gull the credulous Public, by a striking Title alone, without any Performance of the mighty Promises made there." Bringing to a head the social contradictions of the first mass medium, Shandy writes off not only the actress's memoirist and his own future/current anonymous readers—whose greed for intimate details far surpasses their ability to evaluate what they buy—but even, implicitly, himself, just another "hungry Devil," who, to console himself for the social impossibility of direct physical access, is prepared to exploit ten thousand other people sharing his desire for Miss Cunny.

Moving closets

"My mind is mightily of late upon a coach," Pepys remarks in April 1667.[1] But this is hardly a passing phase. Throughout the diary, Pepys's obsession with closets competes and overlaps with his obsession with horse-drawn carriages. To get where they want to go, he and Elizabeth must hire coaches or share rides almost every day, often several times a day. Even after they get a vehicle of their own in November 1668, the coach remains a central object of aspiration and anxiety.

Insofar as they are intimate spaces, coaches are like closets. Indeed, many of Pepys's coach conversations are warm-ups or postscripts to private meetings at court and, like them, reward his attention and caution with all kinds of inside intelligence. On a ride back to London from a failed mission to greet the Duke of York in Harwich, Pepys is rapt by Sir John Mennes's account of the secret "passages" that James I and Charles I had used to access their favorites' bedchambers late at night, which, he later reflects, "I was mightily pleased to hear for information, though the pride of some persons and vice of most was but a sad story ... that brought the whole kingdom and King to ruine."[2] En route to White-hall with one of the King's bedchambermen, Pepys gets the backstory on Monsieur Dupuy, a new favorite of the duke—that he is "a knave and by quality but a tailor."[3] Traveling together to the Royal Exchange for business, Mr. Moore, Lord Sandwich's lawyer, gives Pepys disturbing news about his patron's "carelessnesse" in both naval and family matters.[4]

As in the courtly closet, proximity and the exchange of confidences tend to intensify the feelings between coach companions. Pepys describes how he and Mr. Gawden, on their way to the Duke of Albemarle, "contracted a great friendship" in "the freedom of [their] discourse" about the king's mismanagement of navy money and the knavery of Sir William Penn.[5] Yet there does seem to be a disproportionate number of bad trips.

Listening to Penn drone on as they ride to Whitehall, Pepys secretly looks forward to a day when his own improved "condition" will allow him openly "to slight" his more established colleague "and his simple talk."[6] Travelling to Westminster with John Colville, Pepys decides that his banker, who "finds fault with our great Ministers of State" and "blabs … what hath passed between other people and him," is too loose-lipped to trust with anything but pleasantries.[7] Having laughed at Captain Cocke's heated opinions about the Dutch war over dinner in Erith, Pepys and Lord Brouncker travel back to London with him "hardly having a word all the way, he being so vexed at our not yielding to his persuasion."[8] Pepys is thoroughly unimpressed when he rides to Dagenham with Carteret in July 1665, "But Lord, what silly discourse we had by the way as to … love-matters, he being the most awkerd man I ever met withal in my life as to that business." On a later journey the courtier manages to serve up some useful personal advice for Pepys—about keeping distance from Brouncker, "who hath said some odd speeches against me"—alongside a sharp account of the navy finances "and the state of the Kingdom too."[9]

Especially if they have been temporarily hired, shared coaches can lead to more neutral conversations, like those Pepys has with the most regular visitors to his own closets. The navy housekeeper William Griffith gives him advice about where to build a stable as they travel to an accounts meeting a few miles from Seething Lane, and also tells him "pretty" facts about the Great Fire, such as that it has left standing as many taverns as churches.[10] After a tour of his friend's gardens, Pepys and John Evelyn ride to Greenwich, "all the way having fine discourse of Trees and the nature of vegetables."[11] On the rare occasions that Pepys shares a hackney coach with a stranger, he resists the draw to social and emotional engagement. On leaving Whitehall one day, he gets a lift from "a Frenchman with one eye that was going my way." Pepys remarks that "this fellow, without [my] asking, did tell me all what he was, and how he hath run away from his father and come into England to serve the King, and now going back again," and finds this unsolicited frankness "strange."[12] After attending a ship launch on a "very cold and fowle day" in the spring of 1664, an "ordinary woman" "prayed me to give her room to London." Pepys lets her in, but won't acknowledge her: "I … spoke not to her all the way, but read as long as I could see my book."[13]

Pepys exploits his sense of sexual entitlement in coaches in much the same way as he does in closets. The very close quarters and lack of fixity of hired coaches seem to make him feel, if anything, even less concerned to control himself than elsewhere. One night, when "in pain," as he puts it, about damages to the coach that he has borrowed from William Penn, he comforts himself by groping his bookseller's daughter-in-law: "But to ease myself therein, Betty Michell did sit at the same end with me, and there con su mano under my manteau, I did pull off her cheirotheca and did tocar mi cosa con su mano through my chemise.... Being very much pleased with this, we at last came home; and so to supper." A few months later, he demands a repeat performance. Claiming the need to protect his mysteriously bruised right testicle, "I did ask my wife [to] shift sides with me, and I did come to sit avec Betty Michell, and there had her mano, which ella did give me very frankly now, and did hazer whatever I voudrais avec la, which did plazer me grandement."[14] Pepys accosts at least two other Elizabeths in coaches, neither one his wife. Of Knepp, the actress, he reports, "I ... got her upon my knee (the coach being full) and played with her breasts and sung" and of Burrows, the widow of a navy lieutenant, "I ... sent her away by agreement, and presently I by coach after ..., and so into the fields Uxbridge way ... all the way most excellent pretty company. I had her lips as much as I would."[15]

When Mary Mercer, his wife's companion, rejects one of his coach advances, Pepys affirms his own innocence: "This evening coming home I did put my hand under [her] coats ... and did touch her thigh, but then she did put by my hand and no hurt done, but talked and sang and was merry."[16] However, in his affair with the family maid, Deb Willet, he sometimes consciously overrides her lack of consent, taking advantage of the fact that she is trapped with him. "This day yo did first with my hand tocar la cosa de our Deb in the coach—ella being troubled at it—but yet did give way to it," he reports in August 1668. A few months later, after Elizabeth has discovered the relationship and Deb has been fired, Pepys sneaks off at night to look for her: "She come into the coach to me, and yo did besar her and tocar her thing, but ella was against it and laboured with much earnestness, such as I believed to be real; and yet at last yo did make her tener mi cosa in her mano, while mi mano was sobra her pectus, and so did hazar with grand delight."[17] But when the tables are turned, he's contemptuous. Eliding sex work and female worthlessness, Pepys calls a woman who fondles him in a hired coach "a wench that was naught." He chooses not to accompany her back to her lodgings as she proposes, but "yo did donner her a shilling and hazer her tocar mi cosa and left her, and home."[18]

When Samuel and Elizabeth ride alone together, the coach serves as a closet-like extension of their domestic privacy, and thus becomes the setting and subject of some of their most heated disputes. She tells him off for "checking her ... in the coach" when she had hoped to entertain

fellow passengers with an account of the intricate plot of a French romance, and for ignoring her "in the company of Pierce—Knipp—or
other women that I love."[19] When she accompanies him to an event at
Whitehall with blond hair extensions through her dark hair, he gives her
the silent treatment all the way. She returns the favor on the way home
after he rages about the "false locks," "swearing by God, several times . . .
and bending my fist, that I would not endure it."[20] A momentous time
for the couple in other respects, May Day 1669 is a wash for Pepys's li-
bido. He's first disappointed that his cousin's daughter doesn't show up
as arranged, then irritated when Elizabeth won't let him sit next to her,
then "sullen all day almost, and little complaisant" after he is "against
[his] will . . . forced" to allow his wife's friend Henry Sheeres to join them
instead.[21]

Owning a coach is appealing for a number of practical reasons. Pepys
complains of having been "forced to walk a most dirty walk" after failing
to hail a hackney when he needs one, and of a "great pain in his back"
inflicted during a particularly fast, rough ride in a colleague's vehicle.[22]
He likes being able to read and sing en route when he's traveling alone.
Autonomy must secretly be part of the draw for Elizabeth, too, who, not
long after they get their coach, goes to gather dewdrops at dawn, unaccompanied by her husband.[23] And Pepys claims that finances are a major
factor: as the prospect grows clearer, he determines that owning a family
coach rather than hackneys "will save us money."[24]

Yet he can hardly be sure this is true, given that a coach owner had
to budget for the initial outlay for the vehicle, horses, coach house, and
stable as well as the ongoing costs of their maintenance and a driver. A
couple of years into the journal, Samuel and Elizabeth had excitedly
planned to cut back on smaller pleasures so that they could grow the
nest egg of two thousand pounds that Pepys had then estimated as necessary to "be a knight, and keep my coach."[25] Though the association
between having a title and having a coach is colloquial rather than lit-
eral, it registers the couple's understanding that, practical or not, having
a handsome coach of their own will be a boon to their social position, or
what Pepys sometimes refers to as their "condition." And it's telling that,
after underscoring the economic advantages of having a coach in May
1667, Pepys adds, "and I am a little dishonoured by going in" hackneys.[26]
Looking good—which is to say, pride—is the strongest draw.

Whereas the inside of any coach can function like an intimate closet
in which formal hierarchical relations are acknowledged but intention-
ally suspended, fancy coach exteriors, elevating and framing elite passengers as if on a moving stage, reinforce the traditional opposition between

those entitled to make a spectacle of themselves and those whose lower birth positions them as spectators. Especially early in the diary, Pepys takes pleasure in looking. On the road back to London after a business trip, Pepys is delighted to pass the philosopher and poet Margaret Cavendish, Lady Newcastle, loose haired and patched, in "a black just-au-corps" and "velvet cap," with her coach and footmen all decked in velvet, and immediately plans to catch a better view of her at the May Day coach parade at Hyde Park.[27] When the day comes, other vehicles and clouds of "horrid dust" crowd her coach, but Pepys does take in Cavendish's stark color scheme and silver adornments, and likes what he sees.[28]

Pepys, like other Londoners, also likes looking at the elite look at one another. During another Hyde Park parade, he observes that, though the king and Lady Castlemaine ride in separate coaches, they are unabashed about "greeting one another at every tour."[29] Glass-coaches, in which the openings had been covered with translucent panes rather than the usual leathers and textiles, facilitated such mutual acknowledgement. An anecdote about Lady Peterborough's difficult adjustment to the new trend amuses Pepys: "Seeing a lady pass by in a coach whom she would salute, the glass was so clear, that she thought it had been open, and so ran her head through the glass, and cut all her forehead."[30]

But Pepys is even happier when he can be part of the coach spectacle himself. Not even the company of "Madam Williams" can diminish his excitement in traveling to Sandwich's house in Covent-Garden in Brouncker's coach with four horses, "But Lord, what staring to see a nobleman's coach come to town—and porters every where bow to us and such begging of beggars."[31] A return trip to Windsor with three noble women also leaves him breathless with pleasure:

> Took coach with so much love and kindness from my Lady Carteret, Lady Jemimah, and Lady Slaning, that it joys my heart (and when I consider the manner of my going hither, with a coach and four horses and servants and a woman with us, and coming hither being so much made of, and used with that state, and then going to Windsor and being shown all that we were there, and had wherewith to give everybody something for their pains, and then going home, and all in fine weather and no fears nor cares upon me, I do think myself obliged to think myself happy ...).

Significantly, Pepys directs himself to feel grateful in the journal, consciously suppressing—and yet recording—the ambition that propels his thoughts toward a later and better version of this experience, in a coach of his own: "Whereas we take pains in expectation of future comfort and ease, I have taught myself to reflect upon myself at present as happy, and enjoy myself in that consideration, and not only please myself with thoughts of future wealth and forget the pleasure we at present enjoy."[32]

Early in the spring of 1669, Samuel and Elizabeth are finally able show off their own vehicle in Hyde Park: "With mighty pride rode up and down, and many coaches there; and I thought our horses and coach as pretty as any there, and observed so to be by others."[33] Presumably, both direct compliments and the reactions of passersby augment their "mighty pride." During an evening tour of the coach ring about a month later, "Sir W. Coventry did first see me and my wife in a coach of our own; and so did also this night the Duke of York, who did eye my wife mightily."[34] When May Day comes around again, Mr. and Mrs. Pepys go to some lengths to ensure they will stand out. Two years before, Elizabeth had attended the celebrations "in a hackney coach incognito," with the intention only to witness the spectacle.[35] This time, the vehicle is fully decked out, with our "new liveries of serge, and the horses' manes and tails tied with red ribbons, and the standards there gilt with varnish, and all clean, and green refines"—and so are Elizabeth, in a freshly laced "flowered tabby gown," and Samuel, having changed out of his second-best stuff suit at Elizabeth's insistence, in a matching "flowered tabby vest, and coloured camelott tunique ... with the gold lace at the hands." "People did mightily look upon us," he beams, "the truth is, I did not see any coach more pretty ... than ours, all the day."[36]

But riding high on London streets also brings the risk of overexposure. Pepys intuits this upper threshold of visibility while watching Penn's daughter and daughter-in-law in Hyde Park on May Day 1667. The young women, "both patched and very fine," ride in a new family vehicle that is, Pepys writes, "much the finest coach in the park, and I think that ever I did see ... for neatness and richness in gold, and everything that is noble." The Penns' coach is more ornate than the king's, and therein lies the problem. The vehicle misrepresents not only the quality of the family's blood (Penn was born to a seafaring family and knighted for service to the Cromwells in 1658), but also the material state in which they generally live—that is, the quality of their furniture. "Lord, to have them have this, and nothing else that is correspondent, is to me one of the most ridiculous sights that ever I did see ... [Peg's] present dress was well enough; but to live in the condition they do at home, and be abroad in this coach, astonishes me."[37] The flashy vehicle partly triggers Pepys's anxieties about his own peripheral status at court. Though Pepys works and socializes often with William Penn and his family, assaults his daughter, accepts rides and shares drinks in his "fine new coach," and even borrows it from time to time, he is repulsed, over and over again, by the transparency of his neighbors' social ambitions. Sir Penn "imitates" the original design of Elizabeth's closet chimney-piece and boasts about a fine country house that he wants to buy.[38] After blocking Penn's efforts to appropriate some of the collective navy office space for another small chamber of his own, Pepys claims to be relieved that the relationship has broken down: "No friendship or intimacy since our late difference about his closet, nor do I desire to have any."[39]

But he is at least not a hypocrite with regard to his own standards of coach discretion. The balance of his own priorities have been guided by his understanding that a vehicle should represent, if not actual nobility, then at least its owners' secure place within the courtly culture of the closet, on the one hand, and the luxury of their household and closets in particular, on the other. While Pepys still feels that they have farther to go on both fronts, the closet must take precedence over the coach. In the spring of 1668—and despite the fact that they already have three times more in savings than he had initially predicted they would need, Pepys notes that, "In lieu of a Coach this year, I have got my wife to be contented with her closet being made up ... , and going into the country this summer for a month or two."[40] In the autumn of the same year, just as the dream "of a coach and coachman and horses, &c" is on the verge of coming true, he and Elizabeth again get "mighty busy laying out money in dressing up our best chamber."[41]

And his concern is hardly misplaced. Sir William Warren's first comment to Pepys about his coach is that he hopes "that the owner might not contract envy by it."[42] Beforehand, Pepys has suspected that "my being so much seen in my own coach at this time, may be observed to my prejudice." Shortly thereafter, he finds out from Creed and Povey that courtiers are indeed sneering about "how fine [his] horses and coach are" and his gold-lace sleeves. Pepys is only briefly "vexed." As soon as his colleagues leave, he goes straight to the tailor to have the trim taken off his favorite suit.[43]

5

Parson Yorick's Vis-à-vis

We will try to show later that intimacy is in fact greater in
interocular experience than in sexual intercourse per se.

—Silvan Tomkins[1]

What if we saw [intimacy] emerge from much more
mobile processes of attachment?

—Lauren Berlant[2]

It would have been better ... in a *Vis a Vis*.

—Laurence Sterne[3]

SENTIMENTAL CLOSETS

All kinds of intimate spaces were on Laurence Sterne's mind when he
began writing *A Sentimental Journey* alone at home in the summer of 1767.
With his wife and daughter away in France, he was improving the family's Yorkshire cottage, and entertaining fantasies of domestic bliss with
Eliza Draper, a young woman whom he had met in London several months
before while soliciting subscriptions for his second novel: "I have this
week finish'd a sweet little apartment which all the time it was doing, I
flatter'd the most delicious of Ideas, in thinking I was making it for you—,"
he writes in his *Bramine's Journal*, addressed to Eliza as she travelled to
back to her husband in Bombay.[4] "Tis a neat little simple elegant room,
overlook'd only by the Sun—."[5] Three weeks later, the apartment fantasy
was growing: "I ... am projecting a good Bed-chamber adjoining [the
sitting room], with a pretty dressing room for You, which connects them
together—. The Sleeping room will be very large. The dressing room,
thru wch You pass into yr Temple, will be little— ... but if ever it holds
You & I, my Eliza—the Room will not be too little for us—but we shall
be *too big* for the Room."[6] Around the same time, Sterne acquired a small

second-hand carriage, the first of his own. In a letter to a friend, he adores it unequivocally: "When I say my Lord's prayer, I always think of it," he jokes.[7] But in his *Journal*, the coach, like the dressing room, fills him with yearning. "This day, set up my Carriage—new Subject of heartache, That Eliza is not here to share it with me," he observes, and then two months later, "I have a thousand things to remark & say as I roll along—but I want You to say them to—I could sometimes be wise—& often Witty—."[8] Where Sterne imagines togetherness in the dressing room as a static experience of uncontainable pleasure, the carriage brings in the sense of motion and of time passing, of change and the desire for verbal exchange. As if keeping pace with the vehicle, his mind speeds up as he "roll[s] along," and he longs for a wide-ranging conversation with his lover.[9]

This chapter argues that Sterne's sense that the carriage fostered an especially dynamic and versatile kind of intimacy is at the heart of his concurrent exploration of interpersonal relations in *A Sentimental Journey*. Like closets, carriages had originated at court. And, although comparisons were sometimes drawn, in general, the courtly and absolutist protocols were suppressed and transformed more quickly and thoroughly in carriages than in closets. Indeed, a survey of key scenes from seventeenth- and eighteenth-century writing shows that shared coaches were typically pictured as freewheeling sites of conflict, where acute consciousness of social differences, unless it was rerouted into sexual desire, would not lead to pleasurable forms of interpersonal intimacy, as was expected in the closet, but rather to cruelty or even violence. Sterne takes a more decidedly upbeat view of shared vehicles than previous authors had done, however. Implicitly attributing the provisional reciprocity of traditional closets to carriages, he invites readers to appreciate vehicles as much for the feelings of interdependence that they can very quickly ignite as for the geographical distances they can cover. The model known as the vis-à-vis, in particular, shores up the novel's fantasy of its own international public as an entirely approachable sphere in which an English parson may communicate breezily yet meaningfully with anyone, from a beggar on the street to a duke at Versailles.[10]

Sterne's unusually optimistic attitude toward intimacy with French strangers in *A Sentimental Journey* was undoubtedly informed by his own unabashed pursuit of literary celebrity on both sides of the English Channel. Significantly, Sterne felt much more comfortable with his own desire for a large, international, and socially diverse audience than the previous authors in this study, including Shandy, his imitator.[11] Yet, notwithstanding its continued growth, the print commerce that Sterne now embraced still held vestiges of the elitism that Anthony Hamilton had simply expected and that Swift had come to hate. In particular, the increasingly common practice of seeking sponsors in advance of publication was, as Dustin Griffin emphasizes, "a kind of democratized patronage."[12] Subscribers paid authors half the publication price up front for the privilege of appearing on a list that would be circulated by the author, posted in the booksellers' shop, and eventually published in the first edition of the book. On the one hand, subscription served commercial ends: the lists were marketing tools and the author appreciated the advance. On the other hand, subscription appealed to a traditional concern over the social networks of textual circulation. Unlike formal patronage, where the patron's status mattered most, here adequate cash was the only requirement. Yet untitled merchants, professionals, and manufacturers liked imitating, and in fact joining, the nobility or royalty in publicly aligning themselves with their favorite authors. With a subscription list, authors were liberated from the whims of a single noble patron, but nevertheless had a means of signaling who their supporters were. Sterne had risen to fame and notoriety for *Tristram Shandy*. Having appeared in installments between 1759 and 1767, Sterne's first novel was quickly translated into several European languages, selling particularly well in France.[13] Capitalizing on this success, he immediately sought advance support for his next projects and had gathered a list of 334 subscribers for the first two volumes of *A Sentimental Journey* by the time they appeared, two weeks before his death, in 1768.[14]

Sterne's awareness of his wish to sell well seems to have made him feel deeply attached to his readers. In *Tristram Shandy*, he explored the emotional ups and downs of author-reader relations through the frequent use of direct address, beginning within a few pages of the first volume:

> My dear friend and companion, if you should think me somewhat sparing of my narrative on my first setting out,—bear with me,—and let me go on, and tell my story my own way:—or if I should seem now and then to trifle upon the road,—or should sometime put on a fool's cap with a bell to it, for a moment or two as we pass along,—don't fly off,—but rather courteously give me credit for a little more wisdom than appears upon my outside;—and as we jogg on, either laugh with me, or at me, or in short, do any thing,—only keep your temper.[15]

An equivalent passage in Swift's *Tale of a Tub*, an important source for Sterne, requests "one concluding favour ... of the reader": "that he will not expect to be equally diverted and informed by every line or every page of this discourse, but give some allowance to the author's spleen and short fits or intervals of dullness, as well as his own."[16] Whereas Swift, for whom dependence generally felt like a prison, had invented a narrator who assumes his readers are as grumpy as him, Sterne emphasizes the capacity for generosity on both sides. Continuing to experiment in his second novel, Sterne drops the direct address and instead generates a metafictional context for the whole of the work by naming his narrator-diarist for his own alter ego, Yorick, the Anglican clergyman living in York who had briefly appeared in *Tristram Shandy* (and was named after the character who had appeared, posthumously, and more briefly, in *Hamlet*). Sterne had already identified himself with this posthumous character by publishing his own sermons as *The Sermons of Mr. Yorick* in 1760. The lines between fiction and nonfiction are also thematically blurred by the fact that Yorick is beginning the same tour through Europe that Tristram is taking at the end of Sterne's first novel and which Sterne himself had just completed.[17] Thus, the roads between Calais, Paris, and the Moulins that provide the infrastructure for Yorick's journey are those along which Sterne/Yorick, Tristram, and *Tristram Shandy* had traveled, and along which, Sterne hoped, the new narrative he was composing would soon often travel in turn. Focusing especially on his encounters with strangers, Yorick's semifictional travelogue allowed the author at once to contemplate the various in-person and virtual dialogues in which he had already extensively participated and, indirectly, to continue them.

A Sentimental Journey's engagements with and contributions to eighteenth-century social theory have long been recognized. The literature and philosophy of sympathy, also variously known as sentimentalism and sensibility, when it emerged in the mid-eighteenth century, offered by far the most explicit, expansive, and influential justification for a horizontal social imaginary to date. In his *Theory of Moral Sentiments*, published less than ten years before Sterne's second novel, Adam Smith had outlined the innate mental processes that would become central to the discourse of sympathy: "As we have no immediate experience of what other men feel, we can form no idea of the manner in which they are affected, but by conceiving what we ourselves should feel in the like situation."[18] That is, as Jonathan Lamb has recently summed it up, sympathy names "the actual affective and imaginative experience of feeling what it is like to be someone or something other than one's self."[19] Significantly, sympathy uncovered a redoubled and affirming quality in all social emotions, acknowledging the enjoyment that comes with feeling what other people are feeling, even where that primary feeling is not in itself enjoyable. As Smith observes, "We run not only to congratulate the successful, but to condole with the afflicted; and the pleasure which we find in the conversation of one whom in all the passions of his heart we can entirely sympathize with, seems to do more than compensate the painfulness of that sorrow with which the view of his situation affects us."[20] Insisting that projecting and then entering into others' inner experiences was an intuitive moral impulse, sympathy provided the conceptual foundations for the abolition of slavery, the education of women, and universal human rights well into the nineteenth century.[21] The emphasis placed on the social imagination in theories of sympathy also opened up new perspectives on apparently more mundane experiences, like talking to strangers or getting lost in a book. Not an overtly political author, Sterne was especially eager to investigate how the virtual nature of all social feeling could help to explain the robust emotional attachments between authors and readers, and to expose the illogic of the fear that the bonds generated by books sold for profit and circulating among socially inferior people, or both, were somehow illegitimate or second best.

Several literary scholars of the period have considered the importance of the coach to Sterne's exploration of sympathy and fictionality. Most recently, tracing a prehistory for *A Sentimental Journey* and for sympathy in general, James Chandler focuses on the influence of the "vehicular hypothesis," which the seventeenth-century Platonic philosopher Henry More proposed to explain how, in his view, the inner body—or what he referred to as the spiritual vehicle—both literally and figuratively transports the soul. "Sterne's groundbreaking book was, in an important sense, actually precipitated out of the vehicular discourse," Chandler argues: "Yorick's itinerary is guided by affection. His movements respond to his being moved, and they express his capacity to go beyond himself. Part of Sterne's great genius—and his special brand of sentimental wit—was to create a textual exercise where these two dimensions could not finally be told apart."[22] Maintaining *The Closet*'s focus on the material history of extrafamilial intimacy, this chapter sheds a different light on the emergence of sympathy by considering how the carriages and closets in *A Sentimental Journey* build on and differ from earlier representations of these everyday settings of status consciousness.

Looking Up and Looking Down

From the advent of coaches in Elizabeth I's court until the later eighteenth century when driving came into fashion, the honored place in the carriage was that of the passenger, not the driver. Coaches were more comfortable than carts because of their built-in covers and suspension systems—the use of straps and braces, and later springs, between the axle and carriage body. In May 1665, Pepys had gone with a group of men that included Robert Hooke, the Royal Society's curator of experiments, to participate in "pretty" tests with levers to make coaches "easy." He had determined the most comfortable one to be one in which "the whole body ... lies upon one long spring" and predicted that "it is ... likely to take."[23] Yet the primary role of these vehicles at the time of their arrival in England was pageantry, as it had been on the continent. Ornate gilded exteriors framed royal and noble occupants like living tableaux or portraits of themselves. In this sense, in their original moment, coaches made the traditional public role of an elite family visible to a wider range of people than did the addition or redecoration of a closet or two or, indeed, than any other household improvements. However, like closets, faster, horse-drawn vehicles did not remain exclusive for long. Beginning in the seventeenth century, the gentry, merchants, and bureaucrats like Pepys could afford to buy equipages. And people with very little money—who had never set foot in a fancy closet or noble carriage—had opportunities for short trips in hackneys or stagecoaches. Questions about the limits of traditional codes of obligation and deference that had been raised by the proliferation of closets in this period were also raised by this growing parade of vehicles. But because the range of people directly affected by coaches was greater, the proposed answers were different. In general, aristocratic values were more enduring within the bounds of fixed domestic space than beyond them.

Two early seventeenth-century anticoach tracts are framed as contests between modes of transport whose relative entitlement to the road can no longer be established at a glance. The authors of both *The World Runnes on Wheeles; or, Odds between Carts and Coaches* and *Coach and Sedan Pleasantly Disputing for Place and Precedence* puzzle and rage over the effects of the new accessibility of English equipages. The author of the first of these is John Taylor, who worked throughout his life as a boatman on the Thames and called himself the Water Poet. In his transportation tract, Taylor celebrates the openness of not the boat but the cart, restraining his disgust at the pretensions of the coach for just long enough to exempt the aristocracy: "Princes, Nobilities, and Gentlemen of worth, Offices & Quality, have herein their priviledge ... [and] may ride as their occasions or pleasures shall indite them, as most meete they should, but," he goes on, "when every Gill Turntripe, Mrs. Fumkins, Madame Polecat, and my Lady Trash, Froth the Tapster, Bill the Taylor, Lavender the Bro-

ker, Whiff the Tobacco Seller, with their companion [Thugs], must be
Coach'd ... I say upon my hallidome, it is a burning shame."[24] Though
visibility on public streets befits the elite, when ordinary people raise
themselves above the crowd it dangerously inflates them. The impostors
Taylor describes at length include "two Leash of Oyster-wives" and the
author himself. The oyster wives hired a coach to take them to a fair and,
en route, were "so be-Madam'd, be-Mistrist, and Lady-fide [by Beggars
on the street], that [they] began to swell with a proud supposition or
Imaginary greatnesse, and gave all their money to the mendicating Can-
ters."[25] Taylor once traveled "from Whitehall to the Tower in my Maister
Sire William Waades Coach." He recalls, "Before I had beene drawne
twentie yard such a Timpany of pride puft me up, that I was ready to
burst with the winde Chollick of vaine glory. In what state I would leane
over the Boote, and looke, and pry if I saw any of my acquaintance, and
then I would stand up, vayling my Bonnet, kissing my right clawe, extending my armes as I had been swimming, with God save your Lord-
ship, Worship, or how doest thou honest neighbour?" Taylor mocks his
own clumsy gesturing but ultimately blames the coach, as "it made me
think my selfe better [than] my betters that went on foote, and that I
was but little inferiour to Tamberlaine."[26] Transgressive publicness in
the coach is a kind of intoxication or vertigo reinforced by the visceral, defamiliarizing effects of the vehicle's motion, height, and luxurious frame. Under ordinary circumstances, Taylor and the oyster-wives
know their place—know that they are fit only to be onlookers. But in the
coach, it seems, they can't help but feel superior, and spectators like the
beggars who ingratiate themselves to the oyster-wives exploit their altered state.

Henry Peachum's tract gentrifies the form and content of Taylor's
rant. Part morality play, part philosophical dialogue, *Coach and Sedan*
appeared in 1636 along with the first set of Parliamentary laws forbid-
ding the use of hackney coaches within three miles of the city.[27] As a
debate about traffic decorum between a sedan chair and a coach erupts
on a street on the outskirts of London, various passersby, including Wa-
terman, Carman, Beer-Cart, a clergyman, and the civic-minded narrator,
join in to voice their own concerns over the omnipresence of coaches and
the declining value of their heraldry amid this surplus. Sedan tells the
narrator: "The occasion of our difference was this; Whether an emptie
Coach, that had a Lords dead painted Coate and Crest ... upon it without, might take the wall of a Sedan that had a Knight alive within it."[28]
The dispute turns right of way into a riddle. The sedan chair, which was

a newer, less costly, and less dignified means of transportation than the coach, required the labor of footmen rather than horses. In this case, the sedan carries a knight in the flesh. Though the coach bears the emblem of a superior noble, the fact that it is empty may indicate that it is available for hire. As Ralph Straus explains, early hackney coaches were "old and disused carriages [once] belonging to the quality. Many of them still bore noble arms, and, indeed, it would seem that when the hackneys were no longer disused noblemen's carriages, the proprietors found it advisable to pretend that they were."[29] So which should take precedence, Peachum asks, a real knight or the heraldry of a lord? Like the perceived need for a legal bill to restrict the use of coaches by nonelite travelers, the conundrum itself suggests that the courtliness of the vehicle is no longer self-evident.

The narrator affirms that riding in coaches is still the prerogative of the elite: "I condemne not ... the lawfull use of Coaches, in persons of ranke and qualities." But, as he develops his rationale, expediency threatens to override the aristocratic values of privilege and spectacle:

> yea and in cases of necessitie ... , they defend from all injurie of the skie, Snow, Raine, Haile, Wind, &c. by them is made a publique difference, between Nobilitie, and the Multitude, whereby their Armories without speaking for them, they are known and have that respect done to them; as is due to them: they are seates of Honour for the sound, beds of ease for the lame, sick and impotent, the moving closets of brave Ladies, and beautifull virgins, who in common sence are unfit to walke the streets, to be justled to the kennell, by a sturdie Porter, or breathed upon by every base Bisogno: they are the cradles of young children, to be convei'd with their Nurses, too, or from their parents into the Citie or Countrie.[30]

The first justification of the coach's dominance seems traditional enough: "the Armories without" speak for their noble passengers to "the Multitude," demanding their respect. However, Peachum's narrator's concern with "cases of necessitie" leads to a description of the coach as a shelter from the elements and the various dangers of the streets, making it unclear whether he approves the use of a coach by anyone in need of a safe haven on the road or whether necessity for him is in itself an exclusive privilege of the nobility. While the first two examples of appropriate carriage use, as "seats of Honour for the sound" and "beds of ease for the lame, sick and impotent," seem to represent "nobilitie" and "necessitie" as discrete, even contrasting, conditions, the latter two examples satisfy both at once. Children may need coaches to travel between city and country houses, while "brave Ladies" and "beautifull virgins" may use them like "moving closets" to avoid the harassment of the rabble. Either way, bringing utility into the discussion of coach legitimacy weakens the initial claim that heraldry in and of itself makes a "publique difference."

The even greater number of coaches in the second half of the seventeenth century continued to unsettle visual relations on the street. When Pepys is libeled in an anonymous pamphlet in 1679, the images on his coach are especially derided:

> First you had upon ye Forepart of your chariott tempestuous waves & wrecks of Ships ... And now really consider with your self, That you are but ye Sonne of a Taylor & wipe out all this presumptious painting & new paynt it with these things which are agreeable to your quality. In the first place paint upon the Forepart as hansom a Taylor's shop Board as you please, wth the old Gentleman your Father at worke upon it and his Journy men sitting about him, each man with his pint of Ale & Halfepenny Loafe before him, And the good old Matron your mother, and your selfe, & the rest of your Brothrs & Sisters Standing by. This will be agreeable to your qualities. Then behind your Coach Paint all ye Evil deeds of P[epys] & H[arbord] in particular.[31]

The original heraldry that Pepys had commissioned for his family vehicle depicted Neptune, the demanding ruler of the oceans in Roman mythology, in order to underscore his senior role within the Royal Navy as the basis of his elevation. According to the traditional exclusive social logic, the people riding in coaches inevitably merit eye-catching décor. But, given his background, Pepys's chosen design is "presumptious." The libeler proposes a new theme for the coach exterior, a kind of antiheraldry that advertises Pepys's commonness as well as his greed for bribes, which he shares with his coconspirator, H., the MP Sir Charles Harbord.

In Rochester's poem "Tunbridge Wells," there is nothing at all appealing about equipages: they indicate and occasion only ugly extravagances of effort at being seen and getting around. The speaker, "mounting steed," makes an early-morning visit to the suburban spa to purge himself after several days of debauchery.[32] But when he arrives at this "rendezvous of fools, buffoons, and praters, / Cuckolds, whores, citizens, their wives and daughters," he "spew[s]" prematurely at the "sudden cursèd view" of a man alighting:[33]

> From coach and six a thing unwieldy rolled,
> Whose lumber, cart more decently would hold.
> As wise as calf it looked, as big as bully,
> But handled, proves a mere Sir Nicholas Cully ...
> ...
> Though he alone were dismal sight enough,
> His train contributed to set him off,
> All of his shape, all of the selfsame stuff.[34]

A "thing unwieldy," the adult male passenger seems to the speaker to possess all the dumb materiality both of the conveyance itself—he "roll[s]" and is "lumber"—and of a "calf" or bull, animals bred to be eaten or breed, and "more decently" carried in carts. The play on bully/bull continues when the speaker notes that all of Sir Nicholas Cully's "train" of spawn replicates his stupid look. Midwives have it that "these wells will make a barren / Woman as fruitful as a cony warren."[35] What's sickening about the coach and six is not simply the incongruity between its former dignity and its current freight, but also the way it puts the speaker in mind of the rumored fertility of the Tunbridge waters themselves. Through the image of the coach, Rochester conflates reproduction with the try-hard visibility and upward mobility of the family-oriented town. A half century earlier, John Taylor had pictured coaches themselves as a grotesque proliferation, joking that the vehicles must be "male and female, and use the act of generation or begetting, or else their procreation could never [have] so over-spread our Nation."[36]

Looking in to Look Down

In the early eighteenth century, anxiety about the popularity of coaches sometimes found a positive channel in the counter-perspective of the pedestrian. In Richard Steele's essay 144 from the early periodical the *Tatler* and John Gay's poem *Trivia; Or, the Art of Walking the Streets of London*, aristocratic prerogative is never positively invoked. Rather, in both texts, the merit lost to coaches accrues to the ordinary people who go on foot. Unlike the shame-ridden voyeurs of the previous chapter, pedestrians take up their position as outsiders with pride, claiming a moral advantage that they define in contradistinction to the presumed visual and social entitlement of carriage owners.

Steele's narrator is a self-appointed censor bent on reforming "the general expense and affectation in equipage."[37] The demise of sumptuary laws is to blame for these excesses, he says, since now "every man may be dressed, attended, and carried, in what manner he pleases" so long as he can pay for it. The censor proposes a coach tax and, as he justifies it, engages in a kind of pedestrian consciousness raising. First, he stirs up a sense of injustice over the limited space left for ordinary street-goers:

> We, the greater number of the queen's loyal subjects, for no reason in the world but because we want money, do not share alike in the division of her majesty's high road. The horses and slaves of the rich take up the whole street; while we peripatetics are very glad to watch an opportunity to whisk cross a passage, very thankful that we are not run over for interrupting the machine that carries in it a person neither more handsome, wise, or valiant, than the meanest of us.... It is to me most miraculous, so unreasonable a usurpation as this I am speaking of, should so long have been tolerated. We hang a fellow for taking any trifle from us on the road, and bear with the rich for robbing us of the road itself.

With "the rich" rather than the nobility dominating "her majesty's high road," there is no basis for the marginalization of humble "peripatetics." The chaos and crush of vehicles is another form of highway robbery. Moreover, the censor notes that carriages encroach not only on pedestrians' space but on their attention as well. "I cannot but admire," he writes, expressing doubt rather than reverence, "how persons, conscious to themselves of no manner of superiority above others, can, out of mere pride or laziness, expose themselves at this rate to public view, and put us all upon pronouncing those three terrible syllables, 'Who is that?'" Though the social supremacy of vehicles has eroded, the traditional ritual of looking up at them continues. But the censor has a strategy for taking control of this compulsion. Even from below, looking can serve judgment as well as deference, he explains: "When it comes to that question ['Who is that?'], our method is, to consider the mien and air of the passenger, and comfort ourselves for being dirty to the ankles, by laughing at his figure and appearance who overlooks us." Whereas Rochester's speaker's aristocracy is the basis of his instant distaste for the suburban coach and six in "Tunbridge Wells," this kind of critical looking has become a widely shared skill in the *Tatler* essay. Any pedestrian who considers "the mien and air of the [coach] passenger" will, like the censor, begin "laughing at his figure and appearance." Directing a judgmental gaze at pretentious strangers can be entertaining as well: "I must confess, were it not for the solid injustice of the thing, there is nothing could afford a discerning eye greater occasion for mirth, than this licentious huddle of qualities and characters in the equipages about this town." English coach display had originated in the age of the court masque, dramatizing the centrality of the monarch for all of her subjects. Steele invites early eighteenth-century spectators to take charge of their gaze and invent their own comedies and satires as they walk down the street.

The walker-speaker of John Gay's *Trivia* does as the *Tatler* suggests. As he recounts scandalous secret histories for each of six passing carriages, he affirms his own moral high ground:

> See yon bright chariot on its braces swing,
> With Flanders mares, and on an arched spring;
> That wretch, to gain an equipage and place,
> Betray'd his sister to a lewd embrace.
> This coach, that with the blazon'd 'scutcheon glows,
> Vain of his unknown race, the coxcomb shows.
> Here the brib'd lawyer, sunk in velvet, sleeps;
> There flames a fool, begirst with tinsell'd slaves,
> Who wastes the watch of a whole race of knaves.
> That other, with a clustring train behind,
> Owes his new honours to a sordid mind.
> This next in court-fidelity excells,
> The publick rifles, and his country sells.
> May the proud chariot never be my fate,
> If purchas'd at so mean, so dear a rate.
> O rather give me sweet content on foot,
> Wrapt in my virtue, and a good Surtout![38]

When Taylor and Peachum try to reinstate the coach's symbolic authority, their emphasis on the vehicle's illegitimate and practical uses implicitly undermines it. But Gay's walker explicitly challenges the coach's symbolic authority by inverting the relationship between its spectacular grandeur and passengers' merit. "[A]n arched spring" (the newly invented C-spring), footmen's "tinsell'd" uniforms, and a "blazon'd 'scutcheon" (a shield bearing a traditional coat of arms)—all forms of coach display intended to impress passersby—cue his inventory of shameful secrets: the first of these belongs to a man who pimped his own sister, the next to a spendthrift, the third to a self-important commoner. In particular, the "blazon'd 'scutcheon" recalls Steele's censor's promise to "the coach-makers and coach-painters in town" to collaborate with them to compile and decode all of the arms, devices, and cyphers that decorate coaches and thereby form "a collection which shall let us into the nature, if not the history, of mankind, more usefully than all the curiosities of any medalist in Europe."[39] Gay contrasts the glittering things on the coach to the walker's useful, wearable arms against the elements, including his "good Surtout" (overcoat) and, elsewhere in the poem, platform shoes called pattens and an umbrella.

In Peachum's tract, one of the passersby who joins the debate blames the proliferation of coaches for the lack of familiar faces on the street: "Whereas heretofore, I could walke in some one streete, and meete with a dozen of my acquaintance, I can now walk in a dozen streets and not meete one."[40] Conversely, in *Trivia*, the experience of anonymity is something to celebrate. All those who cultivate a public reputation through coach display have become infamous, while walkers—who, by the speaker's definition, are not public figures—tend also to be unknown to one another. Deliberately choosing less traveled paths, the walker "silent wander[s] in the close abodes / Where wheels ne'er shake the ground" and enjoys a feeling of detached curiosity: "Here I remark each walker's diff'rent face, / And in their look their various bus'ness trace."[41] When he chances upon people in need, he responds as he should: "Charity still moves the walker's mind, / His lib'ral purse relieves the lame and blind."[42] He takes special pleasure, moreover, in the creative possibilities of anonymity: watching a shoeshine boy launches an epic flight of imagination.

Whereas walking seems naturally to stir compassion in Gay's poem, coach travel curtails it in part by confusing distinctions between bodies and machines, and between the senses, as when "Proud coaches pass, regardless of the moan / Of infant orphans, and the widow's groan."[43] Conflating travelers with vehicles, and sight with hearing, this couplet implies that their superior speed, height, and comfort blocks occupants' capacity to feel anything at all for the people down on the street.[44] The oyster wives in Taylor's tract indiscriminately give away their money through the windows of their hired coach. In Gay's later point of view, however, as in Steele's, upstart arrogance has supplanted the coach traveler's traditional generosity and benevolence: "In sawcy state the griping broker sits, / And laughs at honesty, and trudging wits."[45] The walker recognizes that the expansion of passengers' visual field has paradoxical effects. The elevation of the coach allows them to see without being seen, and to see further than pedestrians do. Yet sitting in "sawcy state" effectively diminishes the range of interpersonal feelings of which coach travelers are capable. Particularly disgusted by a haughty man in an equipage, the walker imagines poetic justice: "I've seen a beau ... / When o'er the stones choak'd kennels swell the show'r / In gilded chariot loll, he with disdain / Views spatter'd passengers [passersby] all drench'd in rain," he begins.[46] Though bad weather first increases the physical and perceptual discrepancies between the coach and the street, it eventually leads to the man's come-uppance:

> [The dustman's] pond'rous spokes thy painted wheel engage,
> Crush'd is thy pride, down fall the shrieking beau,
> The slabby pavement crystal fragments strow
> Black floods of mire th'embroider'd coat disgrace,
> And mud enwraps the honours of his face.[47]

When a cart full of waste catches and topples the "gilded chariot," the "crystal fragments" strewn across the pavement signal the fragility of the beau's cocoon and its failure, finally, to protect him from the "floods of mire" on the street, or from the walker's judgmental gaze.[48]

LOOKING ACROSS

The second half of the seventeenth century had brought not just glass windows but more substantial structural changes to the coach interior as well. Originally, most coaches had heightened passengers' visibility by orienting them toward the street. The coach "makes people imitate Sea Crabs, in being drawne side-wayes," John Taylor had complained (figure 23).[49] But in the mid-seventeenth century, a barge-like structure was superseded by a more compact one, in which travelers faced one another, a change that transportation historians surmise was probably "suggested by the shape of the sedan chair"—though closet sociability must have helped as well.[50] The reorientation retained the crucial exterior visual axes. With the curtains raised passengers could still see outside, and see and be seen by passersby if they wanted or needed to be, though most often just in profile. However, the interior focus now allowed for mutual observation and conversation among passengers. Not only did couples,

FIG. 23. Prioritizing the street spectacle, early coaches sat passengers back to back and facing the street. (Engraving of front-facing coach from T. F. Tout, *A First Book of British History* [London: Longmans, 1903], 159. Reproduced by permission. Hilary Morgan / Alamy Stock Photo.)

families, and small groups of friends and acquaintances have occasion for a new kind of proximity on the road, so too did strangers.

Wolfgang Schivelbusch remarks on the historical coincidence of the coach shape with the flourishing of social exchange beyond the court: "The creation of this curious arrangement during the same period that saw the rise of other bourgeois institutions of communication, such as coffee-houses, clubs, newspapers, and theaters, indicates that the coach must be seen as part of that larger configuration."[51] To support his view of the significance of the coach's face-to-face orientation, Schivelbusch points to the early sociologist Georg Simmel's proposition that "before the development of buses, trains and streetcars in the nineteenth century, people were quite unable to look at each other for minutes or hours at a time, or to be forced to do so, without talking to each other."[52] Scenes of coach travel by Delarivier Manley, Richard Steele, Henry Fielding, and Samuel Johnson generally corroborate the idea that the redesign of coach interiors played a part in the development of modern sociability. However, they especially reveal the incipient nature of coach civility implied in Schivelbusch's remark and the resistance to communication implied in Simmel's double negative ("unable to look ... without talking"). That is, eighteenth-century prose writers tend to view the shared coach less as a place of inevitable mutual engagement than as a laboratory for investigating the conditions of possibility of sociability as such.

Whether the random people crossing the city or the country together would find something to talk about was a dilemma to be worked out anew in every case. Unlike the diverse groups that were beginning to mingle in cafes, clubs, pleasure gardens, and masquerades, people in hired carriages didn't have coffee, alcohol, or diversions to smooth the edges of their temporary relationships. Their incidental encounters also differed significantly from those associated with the traditional courtly closet, where feelings of closeness came from the royal owner's politically motivated suspension of codes of distance and deference. On the other hand, especially because of the physical proximity, the experience of sharing a coach with a stranger might be something like that of going into a closet belonging to someone whose position relative to yours was unclear. That is, it could be intimate precisely because the social confusion was so palpable, like when Pepys finds himself alone with Abigail Williams. Where to look, and for how long? To whom to talk, and about what? How might differences of birth or wealth shape this transitory relationship? And how could you even be sure that other people were who they looked or claimed to be? Close encounters in coaches particularly endowed clothing, gestures, manners, and facial expressions as signs of social status that could be analyzed in advance of any conversation (figure 24).

At the start of her *Stagecoach Journey to Exeter*, Delarivier Manley is so certain of her superiority, and so depressed about the unspecified circumstances that have led to her departure from the city and her lover, that she contrives not to acknowledge any fellow passengers.[53] She looks out the window: "The green inviting Grass (upon which I promised to pass many pleasing solitary Hours) seems not at all entertaining: The Trees, with all their blooming, spreading Beauties, appear the worst sort of canopy; because where I am going, they can offer their Shade to none but solitary me."[54] Manley knows that her impressions of the countryside are colored by melancholy: "I am got ... sixteen Miles from you and London; but I can't help fancying 'tis so many Degrees. Tho' Midsummer to all besides, in my Breast there's nothing but frozen Imaginations."[55] Yet when she finally takes in her coachmates, she's not in the least self-conscious about her dismissive snap judgments. She scoffs that

FIG. 24. The strangeness of strangers lay not only in the random and unverifiable things they said and did, but their bodily presence as well. (William Hogarth, *A Country Inn Yard at Election Time: The Stage Coach*, 1747. Reproduced by permission of Sarah Campbell Blaffer Foundation, Houston.)

the lowest women aboard "were never so promoted before, and hugely delighted, with what they are pleas'd to call Riding in State."[56] She nicknames a merchant's wife "Mrs. Mayoress of Tatness." The only other passenger of quality, a baronet's son whom she dubs "Beaux," preoccupies Manley the most. [57] After they stop at an inn, she sees that he expects his new coat and vest will impress her. "The Way I took to mortifie his Foppery was, not to speak a Word of the Change; which made him extream uneasie," she laughs. When the group does finally start to talk to one another, they tell tales of lost love. Though she never shares what she is running from, the fact that everyone in the little group is heartbroken suggests there may be a greater commonality among them than the narrator cares to recognize. She transcribes several of the narratives into her letters, but some are deliberately left out. "She entertain'd us all the Morning with a sorry Love-business about her second Husband; Stuff so impertinent, I remember nothing of it," Manley writes of the merchant's wife, reasserting, through her refusal even to take in the story, the social boundaries that the "Mayoress of Tatness" has violated.[58]

Several later coach scenes direct their sharpest satire not at common people as such but at bad manners on the stagecoach. In *Spectator* number 132, Richard Steele as Mr. Spectator gives an account of his travels from the countryside back to London. Accompanied by an heiress, her widowed mother, their Quaker guardian, and a recruiting officer, the start of the trip is tense: "We ... sat with that Dislike which People not too good-natured usually conceive of each other at first Sight." On the basis of their facial expressions alone, Mr. Spectator understands that he and his fellow travelers are not predisposed to friendly chitchat. But after they have traveled two miles, the "Coach jumbled us insensibly into some sort of Familiarity," Mr. Spectator observes. Though the motion of the vehicle seems to compel a conversation, the passengers' mutual discomfort endures until, finally, "the Widow asked the Captain what Success he had in his Recruiting." The officer sees an opening: "I have suffered much by Desertion, therefore should be glad to end my Warfare in the Service of you or your fair Daughter." But the women's guardian cuts him short:

> Friend, Friend, we have hired this Coach in Partnership with thee, to carry us to the great City; we cannot go any other Way ... [I]f thou wert a Man of Understanding, thou wouldst not take Advantage of thy courageous Countenance to abash us Children of Peace. Thou art, thou sayest, a Soldier; give Quarter to us, who cannot resist thee.... To speak indiscreetly what we are obliged to hear, by being hasped up with thee in this publick Vehicle, is in some Degree assaulting on the high Road.

The officer's double proposition has impinged on the basic equanimity of the women and also, less directly, on all of those "hasped up" with him in the "publick Vehicle." But the Quaker knows how to speak the soldier's language, and peace prevails. At the end of the journey, the Quaker remarks on the men's complementary interests: "When two such as thee and I meet ... , thou should's't rejoice to see my peaceable Demeanour and I should be glad to see thy Strength and Ability to protect me in it." While the soldier's crudeness is clearly objectionable, with a milder irony, Steele also mocks the Quaker's naive efforts to discipline him. Ultimately, the narrative silently endorses only the disinterested, nonverbal form of stranger sociability modeled by Mr. Spectator, who listens attentively to everyone but never says a word.[59]

The Quaker characterizes the officer's proposition as a verbal assault, but it's a physical assault by highwaymen that leads to one of the century's best-known comic coach scenes in *Joseph Andrews*. Like Steele, Henry Fielding rigs his gig—fills it, that is, with disparate flat characters— then takes pleasure in the discord that ensues. After having been cast out by his mistress, Joseph Andrews is attacked on the road, left naked and bleeding in a ditch. The postillion in a passing stagecoach offers to lend him a hand and, when Joseph accepts, each of the travelers react according to type. The coachman worries about the delay that picking him up will cause; the lady is afraid for her reputation; the gentleman suspects he's a thief. Fortunately for Joseph, the lawyer fears "some Mischief happening to himself if the Wretch was left behind in that Condition."[60] It's only the postillion, the person with the least to lose, who has a modicum of compassion and gives Joseph a coat to cover himself.[61] Even after the same highwaymen catch up with and rob the stagecoach, there's no serenity in the temporary leveling of this crew. As soon as they're gone, the gentleman and the lawyer immediately reassert their dominance, making suggestive jokes at Joseph's and the lady's expense.

How innate competition undermines relationships between passengers is the explicit didactic concern of a letter from "Viator" in Samuel Johnson's *Adventurer*. Because stagecoach passengers don't know one another, and generally don't expect to meet again after the journey, "one should therefore imagine," Viator begins, "that it was of little importance to any of them, what conjectures the rest should form concerning him. Yet so it is, that as all think themselves secure from detection, all assume that character of which they are most desirous, and on no occasion is the general ambition of superiority more apparently indulged."[62] Passengers view the people they meet en route as separate from the rest of their lives, implicated only in the moments that they share with them. With no further ends in view, they nevertheless seize the opportunity to see themselves as better than they are in others' eyes. As in Mr. Spectator's stagecoach, bad tempers set the tone at the start of Viator's journey. But the consciousness underlying this grumpiness is more sophisticated and also more visible here since, rather than merely stare at one another "with ... Dislike," the passengers in Viator's coach actively seek out flattering reflections of themselves: "It was easy to observe the affected elevation of mien with which every one entered," Viator recalls. "We sat silent for a long time, all employed in collecting importance into our faces, and endeavouring to strike reverence and submission into our companions."[63] More so than in any of the previous examples, the performance of superiority in Johnson's stagecoach involves the face as both a surface and an index of social significance. Eyes in particular serve double duty, since they have not only to suggest "importance" but also to gather evidence of the "reverence and submission" that the passengers hope to elicit in one another. Though Viator doesn't claim any moral superiority over the group, his eyes, in particular, are further engaged in penetrating the layers of pretense in others' comportment—internally calling their bluff.

Viator's commitment to this special way of reading others is what finally leads to him to identify an ideal of stagecoach sociability in one passenger who is apparently entirely lacking in social ambition: "Of one of the women only I could make no disadvantageous detection, because she had assumed no character, but accommodated herself to the scene before her, without any struggle for distinction or superiority."[64] Most of the stagecoach passengers scrutinize others in order to determine the degree to which their wish for recognition has been fulfilled. At least in Viator's eyes, the woman has rejected—or perhaps has never internalized—this social competition. Her apparent lack of "character" and her blank expression indicate that she doesn't seek to position herself above others, but rather "accommodate[s] herself to the scene before her." While exposing the staginess of stagecoach passengers, Johnson's essay also promises that a different form of connection between strangers can emerge if the space is approached as a neutral ground of anonymous sociability, that is, if self-interest and status consciousness are visibly set aside. For Johnson, then, the shared coach is a hall of mirrors—generally a hellish one, but not, finally, necessarily so. Sterne puts a decidedly confident spin on this site of social potential.

THE DESOBLIGEANT, THE PREFACE, AND THE CLOSET FOR ONE

At the start of his *Sentimental Journey*, Yorick lacks both a mode of transportation and a clear sense of purpose for his travels, the written record of which will be the novel itself. During the early modern period, spending months or even years traveling around Europe had been de rigueur for young noblemen. As the Grand Tour became common for all Englishmen of means in the eighteenth century, this practice, like the collection of curiosities that touring encouraged and facilitated, was increasingly justified with reference to the empirical ideal of the direct encounter: "If knowledge is rooted in experience and nowhere else, travel instantly gains in importance and desirability.... Merely reading about conditions elsewhere was not enough. Those who could travel, should."[65] Travelers were expected "to see certain sites, acquire certain knowledge, and return home improved," as Lisa Coletta sums it up.[66] The first of many practical considerations that English travelers had to confront was how to get around.[67] Yorick has chosen to travel in his own carriage rather than hiring or sharing vehicles as he goes along. Throughout the long opening episode, during which his protagonist shops for a chaise, Sterne weaves together the promise of self-improvement through travel, the trope of the awkward coach encounter, and the print-cultural and philosophical rhetoric of the closet and cabinet to suggest that Yorick's vehicle will also provide the moral and social frame for his journey.

When Yorick walks out to the coach yard beside his hotel soon after his arrival in Calais, he's feeling unsettled. He has just refused the petition of an old Franciscan monk, having "predetermined"—at first sight— "not to give him a single sous" (7). As he climbs into a tiny ramshackle carriage of the sort known, he tells us, as a *Desobligeant*, it occurs to Yorick to compose a preface, then and there, in which he will explain "the efficient as well as the final causes of travelling" (13). But with paper and pen in hand, his thinking loops and strains: each new idea confronts some limitation in his mind. He starts by identifying three distinct "motives" for travel, none of which sounds particularly inspired: "Infirmity of body," "Imbecility of mind," and "Inevitable necessity." Then, though ostensibly anxious "to observe the greatest precision and nicety," he muddies his own argument by distinguishing "Simple Travellers" from the rest, arbitrarily switching from motive to type as the key term of comparison (14). Struggling for control over his increasingly unwieldy scheme, he next announces that "the whole circle of travellers may be reduced to the following *Heads*." However, what follows actually increases the number of categories of travelers from four to eleven. The logical failings of this construction are reinforced by the odd presentation on the page of the final of these eleven types, along with his confused, and incongruously informal, explanation:

And last of all (if you please) The
Sentimental Traveller (meaning thereby myself) who have travell'd, and of which I am now sitting down to give an account, as much out of Necessity, and the besoin de Voyager, as any one in the class. (15)

Yorick's decision to make a new category for himself appears in this context as impetuous and absurd as his line break after "The" and the redundant translation of "out of Necessity." Not only is he inadequately distinguishing this new class from the previous "Travellers of Necessity," but he also misrepresents his current state of inexperience, adopting the stance of the future Yorick who will "have travell'd" only by the time his book makes its way into readers' hands. From his English servant's wry question in the opening lines—"You have been in France?" (3)—it's clear that, up to this point, Yorick's time across the Channel consists only in the few minutes he has spent in Calais.

Yorick brackets this useless attempt to systematize travellers' motives with speculations on the many obstacles to communication that he and others must face when they leave home. He complains that, "from the want of languages, connections, and dependencies, and from the difference in education, customs and habits, we lie under so many impediments in communicating our sensations out of our own sphere, as often amount to a total impossibility" (13). A short while later, he convinces himself that, given the role played by chance in learning, travel is as unlikely to pay off as gambling: "Knowledge and improvements are to be got by sailing and posting for that purpose; but whether useful knowledge and real improvements, is all a lottery.... I am of the opinion, That a man would act as wisely, if he could prevail upon himself, to live contented without foreign knowledge or foreign improvements" (16), a maxim that, if taken seriously, would end his Grand Tour before it has even begun.

Significantly, Yorick has been using the tiny carriage like a gentleman's study, closing its taffeta curtains against distractions so that he can think and write alone. Immediately upon leaving, Yorick attributes the failures of his preface to the place where he's composed it, assuring himself, along with two Englishmen who've been watching the tiny parked vehicle rattle and shake while he writes, "It would have been better ... in a *Vis a Vis*" (17).[68] In Britain, a single-seat horse-drawn vehicle had generally been known as a Solitaire (and later a Sulky).[69] Sterne was the first British author to refer to it by its ironic French name. By associating Yorick's futile, masturbatory attempt at learned privacy with the desobligeant in particular, Sterne evokes the period's most negative closet and cabinet symbolism.[70] As this book has shown, a growing desire among nonelite people for access to knowledge was at once reinforced and challenged by the many closets and cabinets represented in print in the seventeenth and eighteenth centuries. Chapter 4 especially focused on the transitional qualities of this print-cultural rhetoric, arguing that while textual closets and cabinets "broken open" or "unlocked" served as obliging conceptual links between old/elite and new/accessible media, they also gave vent to the uncertainty and disorientation accompanying this shift. With the desobligeant as writing room, Sterne alludes to the radical branch of this print-cultural closet rhetoric, in which private space encapsulates the most stifling qualities of traditional manuscript culture.

Such tropes had been in circulation since at least 1700. Probably the best-known instance is when Joseph Addison's Mr. Spectator declares, "I shall be ambitious to have it said of me, that I have brought Philosophy out of Closets."[71] Searching for an image to convey the lively virtual conversation that he hoped to cultivate, Addison gives the familiar symbol of media shift a sharper-than-usual edge by making the closet stand in for an outmoded, pedantic way of doing philosophy—passively, alone, and out of touch—then defining his own interactive educational project in opposition to it. The association between closets, philosophy, and mental isolation draws and builds on metaphors that seventeenth-century philosophers of knowledge had used to describe the processes and qualities of human understanding. In rationalist epistemology, the beam of light at the center of the camera obscura had become an image of the clarity that distinguishes ideas that depend exclusively on one's own mind—like the knowledge of one's own existence affirmed in René Descartes famous "I think therefore I am"—from ideas that are less coherent or less trustworthy (figure 25).[72] In empirical philosophy, in keeping with the emphasis on how understanding develops in relation to the exterior world, the opening of the camera obscura was also of symbolic interest. Locke compares sense impressions and ideas entering the mind to light pouring through the window of an empty closet. Yet the empiricist, attending to the shapes and glimmers that propel her mental processes, is no less isolated by consciousness than the rationalist.[73] Addison's pointedly negative philosophical trope of the closet registers suspicion of these alignments of thinking and solitude, countering that the best ideas will be sociable in spirit from the very moment of conception.[74]

Significantly, Locke had himself used a negative closet trope in a discussion of the importance of social contexts for moral development in his *Thoughts Concerning Education*: "It is not possible now (as perhaps formerly it was) to keep a young gentleman from vice by a total ignorance of it, unless you will all his life mew him up in a closet, and never let him go into company. The longer he is kept thus hoodwink'd, the less he will see when he comes abroad into open daylight."[75] Though the closet keeps the gentleman-scholar pure, it cannot equip him for the ethical complexity of

FIG. 25. As a philosophical image of consciousness at work, the camera obscura also reinforced broader cultural associations between closets and solitude. (Reprinted from Athana-
sius Kircher, *Ars Magna Lucis et Umbrae* [Rome: Sumptibus H. Scheus, 1646], Fig. 3, Fol. 812.
Courtesy of the Department of Special Collections, Stanford University Libraries.)

"company." Similarly, in "Of the Study of History," David Hume as-
cribes the stultifying abstraction of most philosophical writings to their
authors' remoteness, which seems destined to produce mental as much
as physical claustrophobia: "When a philosopher contemplates characters and manners in his closet, ... the sentiments of nature have no room
to play, and he scarce feels the difference between vice and virtue."[76] In
other uses of this trope, the closet stands for misguided intellectual isolation more generally. In *The Dunciad*, Alexander Pope uses fussy language
to mock an antiquarian scholar so absorbed by his own abstruse thoughts
that he doesn't notice the walls of his room crumbling about him: "in
closet close y-pent, / Of sober face, with learned dust besprent."[77] At
once a critic and expert navigator of the print marketplace, Pope has no
patience for this self-important obscurity. Samuel Johnson, one of the
first English writers wholeheartedly to embrace commercial authorship,
also correlates learned privacy with choking narrow-mindedness when he
cautions in his *Preface to Shakespeare*, "He that will understand Shakespeare, must not be content to study him in the closet, he must look for
his meaning sometimes among the sports of the field, and sometimes
among the manufactures of the shop."[78] Here the closet is the site of

incomplete analysis and interpretation—of poor reading—rather than deficient modes of reflection or composition. Johnson finds that Shakespeare may be a model author for the age of print because of his extensive grasp of human nature, but only "discloseted" readers, that is, those whose imaginations willingly extend beyond their own experience, can fully appreciate this about him.

When Sterne sets Yorick's first writing experience in the desobligeant, this pro-print trope, which associates contemplative solitude with a limited, cold perspective, is adapted to the context of travel. A preface is designed to welcome and orient readers but is generally composed only after the rest of the book is done. When Yorick calls the system- and axiom-making he attempts in the desobligeant a preface, he is taking the word and its conventional placement too literally, misconstruing it as the starting point for the author as well. Given his negligible experience at this point, what can he possibly say about traveling? The setting in which Yorick tries to pen his opening pages seems to allow him to evade the temporal paradox behind his misperception.[79] Without particulars, Yorick can nevertheless reach for some important-sounding generalizations: he can play the philosopher. In this way, the desobligeant reveals just how much Yorick has still to learn about the purpose of his journey. If his Grand Tour is meant above all to expand the range of Yorick's experience, then hiding himself away obviously represents a false start.

Lust in Transit

Though vis-à-vis was not yet in regular English use as an adverb or preposition, the carriage in which two, or sometimes three or four, passengers sat opposite one another had been called by its French name in Britain for several decades by the time Sterne wrote A Sentimental Journey (figures 26 and 27). Like the desobligeant, the very name vis-à-vis calls attention to the issue of stranger relations that authors had been considering in coach scenes for at least a century. Sharing roots with vision and visage (face), vis-à-vis provides a compact symbol against which Yorick's unsatisfying preface (pre-face) and his solitude in the run-down carriage can be lumped together in retrospect. Both the place and the moment of writing precede and preclude significant contact of any sort with other people, foreign or otherwise.[80] Shortly after leaving it, Yorick declares that he has written himself "out of conceit with the Desobligeant" (18). When he begins his second attempt at selecting a vehicle, he spies but

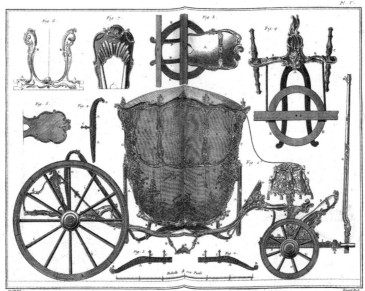

Sellier-Carossier, Berline ou vis-à-vis à panneaux arrasés.

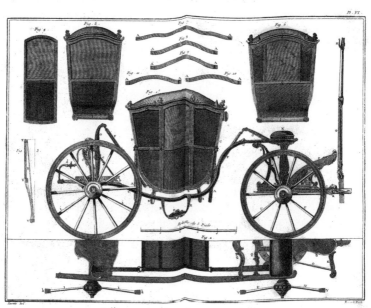

Sellier-Carossier, Berline de Campagne à Cul de Singe.

FIGS. 26 AND 27. These plates from Diderot and D'Alembert's *Encyclopédie* show two vis-à-vis carriages, an ornamental one for town use and a plainer model, of the type Monsieur Dessein sold, for distances. (Reprinted from *Encyclopédie*, eds. Denis Diderot and Jean le Rond d'Alembert. University of Chicago: ARTFL Encyclopédie Project [Autumn 2017 Edition], Robert Morrissey and Glenn Roe, eds. Sellier-Carrossier, Planches V and VI.)

immediately rejects "another tatter'd *Desobligeant*." Now he knows better: "Notwithstanding it was the exact picture of that which had hit my fancy so much in the coach-yard but an hour before—the very sight of it stirr'd up a disagreeable sensation within me now; and I thought 'twas a churlish beast into whose heart the idea could first enter, to construct such a machine" (32).

The novel never again refers directly to either of these two French coach names. Yet, significantly, the next vehicle Yorick tries—the one he will eventually buy—is the setting of his first foreign flirtation.[81] The artful Monsieur Dessein leads a woman whom Yorick has just met into another chaise with him, one just big enough to seat them both face to face. Jonathan Lamb proposes that the first interchange in this carriage is the definitive one in the novel: "A situational sentiment at its best, where what is meant is what is being done, and what is being done is what is being said." Yorick doesn't succumb to extremes of any kind here, doesn't ravish the woman with embraces or declarations as he believes a Frenchman would (33). Instead, he offers a "course of small, quiet, attentions, not so pointed as to alarm,—nor so vague as to be misunderstood,—with now and then a look of kindness, and little or nothing said upon it" (34). Yorick finds that understatement communicates best as he observes the woman, whom Monsieur Dessein has introduced as Madame de L***, starting to enjoy the moment as well. She blushes, "I solemnly declare you have been making love to me all this while" (34). Rather than determining his identity as a traveler in advance, the more sociable chaise allows Yorick to improvise an exchange in which he attends and responds to specific words and gestures—to another person—in all their nuance.

This second chaise also recalls an explicitly erotic aspect in the evolution of carriage sociability. Even prior to its interior reorientation in the mid-seventeenth century, male commentators had found coaches well disposed to accommodate, and produce, sexual desire. As Pepys's *Diary* makes abundantly clear, men in shared coaches often cornered young, unaccompanied, and nonelite women, such as domestic servants. An association with the sex trade was especially strong for hackney coaches, and linguistically overdetermined: *hackney*, derived from the Old French *haquenée*, meant "for hire" or "common" but was also the name of the London borough where there were many brothels. John Taylor layered these meanings, depicting coaches as go-betweens: "Many times a hired Coachman ... may man, a brace of ... [Hackney women] to their places of recreation, and so save them the charge of maintaining a Sir Pandarus or an Apple-squire."[82] Peter Anthony Motteux's opening song for *The*

WHITSUNTIDE HOLIDAYS.

FIG. 28. A woman in the crowd atop a stagecoach grins as she is groped. (Carington Bowles, *Whitsuntide Holidays*, 1783. London Metropolitan Archives. Reproduced by permission of the London Metropolitan Archives/Art Collage London.)

Stagecoach, the farce he cowrote with George Farquhar, adds the fantasy, reiterated in an engraving entitled *Whitsuntide Holidays*, that the erratic shaking of moving vehicles makes female passengers especially receptive to men's advances (figure 28):

> Here chance kindly mixes,
>   All Sorts and all Sexes,
>   More Females than Men;
>   We squeeze them, we ease them,
>   The Jolting does please them;
>   Drive jollily then.[83]

Other erotic associations targeted the strangely invisible publicness of the coach. Taylor worries about what people hiding inside a coach might get up to, stressing the difference between the coach and its low-brow cousin: "The Cart is an open transparent Engine, that any man may perceive the plaine honesty of it; there is no part of it within or without, but it is in the continuall view of all men: On the contrary, the Coach is a close hipocrite, for it hath a cover for any Knavery."[84] Furthermore, the coach "is never unfurnished of a bed and curtaines, with shop windowes of leather to buckle Bawdry up as close in the midst of the street as it were in the Stewes."[85] When Elizabeth Pepys accuses Samuel of having been "seen in a hackney-coach with the glasses up with Deb [Willet]," the nature of his offense doesn't have to be spelled out.[86]

Stagecoach passengers of any sex might self-consciously perform themselves and scrutinize others' reactions in order to reinforce real or illusory status distinctions. Yet the erotics of looking in the coach could complicate or derail this quest for social superiority. Some travelers, especially men, might instead experience a mutual visual relationship as a form of communion with the object of desire. For instance, the Italian adventurer and autobiographer Giacomo Casanova, though proudest of a conquest in a carriage during a thunderstorm, also enjoys sitting opposite Henriette and her boyfriend: "My eyes saw her without my having to turn my head to give them that pleasure, which is certainly the greatest a lover can have among those which he cannot be denied."[87] As Delarivier Manley demonstrates in her *Stagecoach Journey*, this kind of male interest represented a major liability of female mobility. In her second letter, Manley complains of Beaux, "I think none was ever so plagu'd with dying Eyes; his are [so] continually in that posture, and my Opposites, that I am forc'd to take a good deal of pains to avoid 'em." When Beaux provokes her, "I vow, this Indifferency does not look natural to you; your eyes promise us much more Fire," Manley thinks, "I'll shut 'em ... for ever rather than such a Fop shall find any thing to like them for." But stuck in the stagecoach, she can't elude this sexual entrapment for long: "What! no answer, Madam ... ; I perceive your Attention by your Silence."[88] On the other hand, when desire was reciprocated in a coach, the results were sometimes understood to be especially electric. German satirist Georg Lichtenberg presents British stagecoach journeys as frenzies of opportunity for "a dangerous exchange of glances but often also for a scandalous entanglement of legs causing a giggling in both parties and a confusion of souls and thought, so that eventually many an honest young man who only [wants] to travel from London to Oxford [goes] straight to the devil instead—"[89] In this late eighteenth-century example, visual pleasures between strangers induce cognitive meltdown, which leads in turn to conversation of the most embodied sort.

Sterne's novel dwells in that possibility, but never fully embraces it. Yorick and Madame de L***'s lovemaking delicately engages the coach's notorious reputation. Yorick is planning to ask Madame de L*** to accompany him to Amiens. The thought has first occurred to him soon after meeting her: "Now where would be the harm ... if I was to beg of this distressed lady to accept of half my chaise?—and what mighty mischief could ensue?" (28) But upon articulating the question, Yorick inevitably begins to posit an answer. The words produce the idea of lust and a physiological response: "Every dirty passion, and bad propensity in my nature, took the alarm, as I stated the proposition" (28). When Yorick is in the post-chaise with Madame de L***, Monsieur Dessein approaches to announce that the widow's brother has arrived to escort her home. The turn of events is "fatal" to Yorick's as-yet unstated proposal, but elicits from Madame de L*** parting words that demonstrate that the thought has nevertheless been conveyed. "I think, said she, looking in my face, I had no evil to apprehend—and ... had determined to accept [a place in your carriage]—If I had—(she stopped a moment)—I believe your good will would have drawn a story from me, which would have made pity the only dangerous thing in the journey" (35). This connection between Yorick and Madame de L**** hinges on their setting. The foreclosed possibility of navigating the carriage's erotic reputation together is still palpable in Madame de L***'s extended pause. The sound and appearance of the name of the vis-à-vis mimics their connection, as looking at one another and listening to one another, they intuit one another's thoughts.

So whereas the desobligeant leaves Yorick alone to speculate, classify, and generalize, the second chaise invites a more fluid relationship to communication and to form. In the desobligeant, Yorick has predicted that his "travels and his observations will be altogether of a different cast from any of my fore-runners" (15). He wants to define this difference but he decides he had better wait "till [he has] some better grounds for it, than the mere *Novelty of my Vehicle*" (15, original emphasis). In this first phase, his book is just a husk, an idea of an idea of a journey and a sketch of a textual structure. In the post-chaise for two, however, Yorick begins to clarify his direction as he talks to a foreign woman he has just met. He now understands that he must avoid the perceptual limitations of self-involved travel writers like Smelfungus, whose diseases had "discoloured or distorted" everything he saw, or Mundungus, who "made the whole tour ... without one generous connection or pleasurable anecdote to tell of; but he had travell'd straight on looking neither to his right hand or his left, lest Love or Pity should seduce him out of his road" (37–38). Yorick immediately buys the double chaise—"I never finished a twelve-guinea bargain so expeditiously in my life" (36), he puns—and confirms that the substance of his journey and thus of his journal will be his encounters with others: "I declare, said I, clapping my hands chearily together, that was I in a desart, I would find out wherewith in it to call forth my affections—" (36).

Vis-à-vis Intimacy

The witty contrast between the desobligeant and the vis-à-vis thus structures both Sterne's objections to solitary, elitist styles of perceiving, traveling, and writing as well as their interactive, accessible reinvention throughout *A Sentimental Journey*. Sterne emphasizes that Yorick will literally not get anywhere, either as a writer or a traveler, until he finds alternatives to the outdated values of the solitary closet. An idealized symbol of the sentimental traveler as best-selling novelist, the vis-à-vis embodies the belief that learning and thinking, and writing and reading, must be dynamic, spontaneous, and reciprocal processes. In effect, Yorick advocates for this chosen vehicle throughout the novel by showing in each self-aware yet gregarious entry how well his encounters on the road are equipping him to explore the grand questions of the age in accessible terms, to own his desire to reach every one of the men and women who would or could constitute the book's own public.

After the flirtation with Madame de L***, Yorick shares his own carriage only one other time. Yet actual coaches do set the terms of several interpersonal encounters in *A Sentimental Journey*. In each other's way at the entrance of a Milan concert hall, Yorick falls into a pas-de-deux with the Marquesina de F*** before he thinks to stop moving to let her pass (77). He follows to apologize and offers to escort her to her coach. "Upon my word, Madame, I made six different efforts to let you go out," Yorick says as he hands the lady in. "And I made six different efforts ... to let you enter," she replies, making room for him to join her (78). The coach abets this sort of flirtation again in a later incident. La Fleur asks Yorick for time off *"pour faire le galant vis-à-vis sa maîtresse,"* and Yorick observes, "it was the very thing I intended to do myself *vis-à-vis* Madame de R***, I had retain'd the remise [coach] on purpose for it" (132). He relates to La Fleur's desire to *"faire le galant,"* and the repetition of the relational preposition reminds Yorick of the utility of the coach itself to this aim. On the other hand, the coach sometimes shores up Yorick's antisocial impulses, such as when he tries to cultivate compassion for a German man mourning his dead ass on the road to Amiens. A crowd of sympathetic spectators gather around him, but Yorick doesn't join them, choosing to maintain his lofty position instead: "As I continued sitting in the post-chaise, I could see and hear over their heads" (53). Yorick soon moves on, and though he remains "as candidly disposed to make the best of the worst, as ever wight was" (56), the indifferent, impatient postillion and the jolting of the coach thwart his attempts to share in the strangers' grief. The vis-à-vis thus remains largely a metaphysical structure throughout *A Sentimental Journey*. The vehicle compels, though it cannot assure, Yorick's openness to the moment, to movement, and to passing connections rather than fixed attachments. Providing a template for Yorick's serially sociable aims as, one by one, he moves toward the people who catch his eye and encourages them to return his attention, words, and sometimes his touch, the vis-à-vis functions as a kind of reciprocal zoom whose very intensity and exclusivity seem to ensure that it won't last.

Though Yorick has many encounters with women, it's fitting to conclude by noticing how the vis-à-vis paradigm shapes several of his memorable meetings with men in the novel.[90] Yorick's conversation with an old French army officer while waiting for a performance at the Opéra comique, for instance, beautifully illustrates his vis-à-vis notion of sympathy. When Yorick first sees him, the French man is reading the program notes through a large pair of glasses, but he puts them in his pocket as soon as he notices Yorick looking at him. For Yorick, the gesture is utterly transparent: "Translate this into any civilized language in the world, the sense is this: ... 'Here's a poor stranger come into the box—he seems as if he knew no body; and is never likely, was he to be seven years in Paris, if every man he comes near keeps his spectacles upon his nose—'tis shutting the door of conversation absolutely in his face'" (76). The English parson shows his appreciation with a bow, and when the two men finally speak to one another they simply reiterate the reciprocal respect that they've already communicated very effectively by nonverbal means. To Yorick's delight, the officer ends their chat by summing up what he has learned: "The advantage of travel ... [is] by seeing a great deal both of men and of manners; it [teaches] us mutual toleration; and mutual toleration ... [teaches] us mutual love" (84). Yorick can't quite identify the cause of his pleasure on hearing this maxim: "I thought I loved the man; but I fear I mistook the object—'twas my own way of thinking, the difference was I could not have expressed it half so well" (84). Is his own sense of the importance of mutual respect affecting Yorick? Or is it the words the French officer has used to express this view? Or the presence of the man himself? The difficulty in locating its source is both the index and consequence of his profound feeling of communion in the exchange.

As transportation, carriages were undoubtedly helping to expand social and intellectual horizons, facilitating the greater and faster circulation of people and books and ideas through Britain, Europe, and beyond. In *A Sentimental Journey*, Sterne insists that carriages also simultaneously help to concentrate and align different perspectives, offsetting the social, intercultural, and epistemological tensions that all of this movement was also producing. Whereas in the early episode in the desobligeant, the traditional writing closet, presumed to be fixed and solitary, serves as a point of contrast for the novel's vis-à-vis ideal, in two later encounters involving noblemen, Sterne affirms that the courtly closet has in fact played a part in generating this ideal too. Throughout *A Sentimental Journey*, the structure of Yorick's brief, discrete (if sometimes indiscreet) close encounters mimics the seriality of a secret history, the classic genre of courtly closet intimacy, and his habit of redacting the family names of the people featured in these intimate episodes, even where their rank (not to mention their fictionality) doesn't seem to warrant anonymity, underscores his debts to this form. As Eve Sedgwick has argued, Sterne's status consciousness is "not only bourgeois-centered, but based on … an expropriation of the aristocracy, too, for the cognitive needs of elements of the middle class."[91] Thus, when Yorick finds himself in need of elite favor near the end of the novel, a barely repressed setting and set of absolutist practices at last breaks into the plot and Sterne's—if not Yorick's—awareness.

After a Paris hotelier asks to see his passport, Yorick is quite desperate to meet with the Duc de C***, the courtier responsible for such documents, in his cabinet at Versailles. Yorick had "left London with so much precipitation, that it never enter'd [his] mind that we were at war with France" and that the formal recognition of his national identity would be required.[92] Having barely begun his Tour and duly afraid of the Bastille, Yorick prepares himself for the meeting by focusing on the skills in intuiting and matching others' moods that he has already begun to master:

See Monsieur le Duc's face first—observe what character is written in it; take notice in what posture he stands to hear you—mark the turns and expressions of his body and limbs—And for the tone—the first sound which comes from his lips will give it you—: and from all these together you'll compound an address at once upon the spot, which cannot disgust the Duke—the ingredients are his own, and most likely

> to go down ... as if man to man was not equal throughout the whole
> surface of the globe; and if in the field—why not face to face in the
> cabinet too? (101)

Yorick is not oblivious to the fact that the courtly closet is a place where
nobility may share in the concerns of their inferiors, at least for a couple
of minutes. Yet, in comparing the pursuit of patronage to a battle or duel
between equals, he disavows the arbitrary and hierarchical basis of such
relationships. Yorick's radically progressive account reduces favor to a
largely mechanical mode of attachment that depends not on the duke's
aristocratic prerogative but rather on Yorick's own capacity as petitioner
to appeal to the Frenchman's narcissism by observing and then effectively reproducing his facial expressions, tone, and gestures—all the elements of his conversation. When Yorick asks "Why not face to face in the
cabinet too?" his missing term is vis-à-vis, which names both the vehicle
where diverse strangers often encounter one another and the equalizing
mode of perceiving and responding that Yorick and his fellow travelers
have begun to associate with it.

As Yorick's scene of imagined intimacy with a duke gives way to an
actual encounter with a count, Sterne gently corrects Yorick's misrepre-
sentation of closet relations, however. When Yorick arrives at Versailles,
there are already so many other people waiting for a private word with
the Duc de C*** that he decides to try his luck in the meantime with a
lower-ranking courtier who lives not far from the palace. Admitting that
he "has come without any one to present me," Yorick capitalizes on the
Comte de B***'s evident love of "my countryman the great Shakespeare,"
whose works are sitting on a table in his apartment. Inviting Yorick to
settle into an armchair, the count takes the lead in a friendly conversation "of indifferent things;—of books and politicks, and men—and then
of women." When eventually asked to introduce himself, Yorick points
to the fifth act of *Hamlet* and says "*Me Voici!*" after which the Comte goes
immediately to Versailles. Yorick has not yet read to the end of the third
act of *Much Ado About Nothing* when the Comte is back with the passport:
"Mons le Duc de C***, said the Count, is as good a prophet, I dare say, as
he is a statesman—*Un homme qui rit*, said the duke, *ne sera jamais dangereuz.*
—Had it been for any one but the king's jester, added the Count, I could
not have got it these two hours.—" Yorick wonders as he leaves whether
he has taken advantage of these men. If the duke and the count have
confused him with the fictional (and dead) character, is he entitled to the
document he now holds in his hands? But Sterne's narration of this epi-

sode makes it clear that, although Yorick can't see it, these courtiers' sense that *noblesse oblige* has in fact created the social conditions under which the various agreeable projections take hold. The Comte de B***'s remark exposes the hierarchical—patronizing—dynamics of closet intimacy that Yorick has tried to override when he narrates the hypothetical encounter with the Duc de C***. While Parson Yorick's unprecedented excitement about stranger relations in general, and author-reader relations in particular, has hinged on a reductive contrast between the solipsism of closet solitude and the social potential of the carriage, Sterne nevertheless acknowledges here his debts to the courtly closet as the original breeding ground of extrafamilial intimacy and as a gateway to modern conceptions and experiences of sympathy, face to face and virtual alike.

CODA

Coming Out

Ten years later, Patrick had become more open about
his sexuality, but he had yet to make it, in his words,
"Facebook official."

—Carrie Nelson[1]

Coming out, to me, just seems so '90s, you know?

—Josh Thomas[2]

so we are out of the closet, but into what?

—Judith Butler[3]

Coming Out in the Stone Age

The speech that Jodie Foster gave when accepting a lifetime achievement
award at the 2013 Golden Globes ceremony and the responses it elicited
show just how central the media have become to the notion of queer
visibility. "So while I'm here being all confessional, I guess I have a sudden urge to say something that I've never really been able to air in public," Foster began. "But I'm just going to put it out there, right? Loud
and proud, right? So I'm going to need your support on this. I am single."[4] Then, pointing to the expectations that she was purposely subvert-
ing, Foster effectively told the audience off: "[This is not going to] be a
big coming-out speech tonight because I already did my coming out
about a thousand years ago back in the Stone Age, in those very quaint
days when a fragile young girl would open up to trusted friends and
family and co-workers and then gradually, proudly, to everyone who
knew her, to everyone she actually met." Characterizing her youth as a
time when people faced much less pressure to discuss their sexuality
with strangers, Foster acknowledged but refused the assumption that the
rehearsed speech that she was now delivering on television was more con-

sequential than the many in-person conversations that she had been having with family, friends, and acquaintances at least since the early 1990s. Reiterating the definition of coming out that GLAAD, the queer media monitoring organization, continues to provide, Foster represented the acknowledgment and exposure of her sexual identity as an incremental but bounded process, in which she spoke first to the people with whom she felt safest and knew best, and then to a more expansive social circle, though one that, significantly, extended only as far as "everyone she actually met."[5] In the "very quaint" days of her youth, Foster recalled, in-person proximity was an essential condition of coming out. A few minutes later, the actor thanked Cydney Bernard by name, describing her as "one of the deepest loves of my life, my heroic co-parent, my ex-partner in love but righteous soul sister in life, my confessor, ski buddy, *consigliere*, most beloved BFF of 20 years." In this televised speech, Foster was not going to deny her lesbianism but neither would she be revealing it exactly. "I am not Honey Boo Boo Child," she said, referring to the reality show star. Making a big pronouncement about her sexuality on TV would be a spectacle as vulgar as the dysfunctional family life of a precocious preschooler: Foster was not going to degrade herself like that, nor should viewers want her to.

Among the many online and print responses to the speech, one of very few that accepted the way Foster privileged face-to-face over widely broadcast modes of self-revelation was a piece in the UK paper the *Independent*, which credited Foster, notwithstanding the medium of her message, with successfully "affirm[ing] her right to only come out to her friends and family, not publicly."[6] The vast majority of comments deemed that since she had referred to her lesbianism on television for the first time, Foster had finally come out to her fans. Some in this group of commentators, ignoring or overlooking Foster's effort to oppose a genuine, unmediated process of identification to a lesser, mediated one, celebrated Foster's use of the award-ceremony platform as a step forward for queer liberation. In the *New York Times*, Steven Petrow defended Foster's bravery and worried that others' scrutiny of Foster's speech would affect "all of those still closeted—whether 15 or 50—who may find yet another reason not to come out, lest their way might not be the 'right' way."[7] For others the speech seemed redundant: "[W]ho DIDN'T KNOW Jodie Foster was gay? This is not news."[8] Yet others faulted her for coming dangerously close to squandering her special opportunity to role model queer pride on a grand scale. In an email to *ABC News*, culture columnist Michael Musto wrote: "A straightforward coming out would have been preferable to the route she took—and by the way, I think she should have done it many years ago. But parts of her speech were very moving and now she is out, so I think we should just throw her a party."[9] Thus, both directly and indirectly, through their own online and printed engagements with her speech, viewers confirmed Foster's insight that coming out is now widely understood as a process that must include the media. At the same time, they almost universally rejected her effort to oppose this change.

Mentioning that she had recently turned fifty years old, Foster suggested that the new centering of the media in queer life has happened over the past two or three decades, in the period between her youth and middle age. Foster's historicization is undoubtedly apt, considering that the basic conditions of visibility, awareness, and community for sexual minorities—as for pretty much everyone—have been dramatically transformed by the rapid growth in widely accessible electronic media in the late twentieth and early twenty-first centuries. As Ellis Hansen puts it in his "History of Digital Desire," "Queer is the new normal. It thrives with capitalism online."[10] However, the closet rhetoric that has been explored throughout this book gives a longer view of the new synergy between sexual minorities and the mass media that Hansen observes and Foster was trying to challenge. This older history reveals the extent to which the language of the closet continues to structure conflicts over our desires not just for self-knowledge and self-definition, but also for intimacy, both in the flesh and virtually, and over how best to distinguish between them. The ideal conversational form of queer disclosure, as Foster describes it, sounds just like what often happens *inside* architectural closets of all kinds in the seventeenth and eighteenth centuries—more like bringing someone into your closet than leaving it yourself. Yet the passion for virtual intimacy, which Foster fears devalues personal privacy (and perhaps implicitly face-to-face encounters as well), was also central to the rhetoric of the closet, and especially the in/out opposition, throughout this period.

The Etymology of the (Queer) Closet

Jeffrey Masten has celebrated etymology as a surprisingly generative method for opening up the present moment: "Not only a backward-looking *history*, etymology as a practice looks forward to remind us that words that seem identical and familiar to modern eyes and tongues we might better see as false cognates ('false friends,' as we used to say in French class)—words that only *pass* as 'the same' as ours ... when pressed, release whole new contexts, while also holding within themselves the genealogical seeds of their eventual direction."[11] Aspiring to defamiliarize the closet in this way, this book has pursued the word's rich resonances in seventeenth- and eighteenth-century English writing, focusing on the myriad extrafamilial relationships, desires, and anxieties that, though frequently channeled through the eighteenth-century discourse and practices of the closet, have rarely been centered in our histories and theories of this space or in our histories and theories of intimacy. While the social and sexual transformations stirred up or spurred on by the growth of print commerce have been of particular interest, queerness as such has been handled with caution. Closets often accommodated homosocial and homoerotic bonds, not least because royals and nobles almost always chose favorites of their own sex to serve them in their most private rooms. But it has been important to this argument to disguish the stakes and dynamics of historical modes of attachment from those of our own time, and not to draw connections between historical closets and the current metaphor for the invisibility of queer and trans people too hastily. Indeed, as chapter 2 emphasizes, the apparent similarity between early modern architectural and contemporary metaphorical closets as spaces of homosexual secrecy is actually a bit of a red herring, historically speaking, since, in keeping with the political and cultural status of exclusive knowledge under absolutism, same-sex favorites at court had tremendous influence and were proud of their intimacy with power. So how did one of the most desirable rooms in early modern domestic architecture become a metaphor for the experiences of invisibility, shame, and fear of sexual minorities, experiences that are, for most people who now use the metaphor, troubling and patently undesirable?

As is generally the case with oppositions that stick, the conceptual elegance of the eighteenth-century distinction between closeted and out came at the cost of subtlety and qualifications. As discussed in chapter 5, when writers like Addison, Pope, Hume, and Johnson made the closet stand in for an outmoded intellectual culture in which knowledge was considered to be only as valuable as the social status of its source, they displaced the provisional forms of intimate interdependence across the ranks traditionally associated with this room.[12] The closeted thinker was both alone and lonely on the inside—reactionary, selfish, and snobbish. Out of the closet, on the other hand, roughly corresponded to what English writers sometimes called the world, the sum total of places beyond the home where new people and perspectives could be encountered directly. A maxim in Chesterfield's *Letters to his Son* makes this correspondence explicit: "The knowledge of the world is only to be acquired in the world, and not in the Closet," he advises.[13] However, the eighteenth-century drive to come out is perhaps best defined with reference to the context under which the metonymy most often crossed into pure metaphor. Beyond the closet was the metatopical locus of the many new opportunities for knowledge exchange facilitated by print, a ground of and spur to social mobility and an increasingly mobile form of sociability. Getting there thus entailed a shift in thinking and feeling achieved not necessarily by way of actual interactions with strangers, though these might help, but by making mental room for ideas, experiences, and interests other than one's own. This lively, flexible, generous frame of mind was in fact modelled on the interdependence attributed to the closet itself in multiple contexts. But the new opposition appropriated the traditional, provisional, emotional and intellectual reciprocity of the closet, resituating it in the unbounded imaginary zone of mediated publicness beyond it; thereby a structure of feeling that had primarily been a model of dyadic connection was transformed into one that could unite large, even theoretically infinite, groups.

Of course, the coming out metaphor was utopian insofar as it covered over both the many ways eighteenth-century intellectual life, including print, continued to privilege people with status, leisure, and property as well as the many ongoing obstacles to literacy that most women, non-white, and poor people faced in the period. As Michael Warner, Nancy Fraser, and many others maintain, most of the discourses and forms of address that characterized eighteenth-century print publics remained in crucial respects exclusive.[14] In fact, injunctions to come out of the closet such as Johnson's and Chesterfield's, which assume that readers have rooms of their own that they can leave at will, expose the paradoxical limits of the democratic, egalitarian vision promoted by this trope. During this transitional period, it was obviously easier, even for people with an upbeat or radical view of print's potential, to picture only people who had personal closets in their homes having the capacity to come out of them, to think and feel with others. Habermas himself notes that the apparently inclusive conversations of eighteenth-century print culture were crucially grounded on *"the fictitious identity of ... the role of property owners and the role of human beings pure and simple."*[15] Sterne's attention to the carriage in *A Sentimental Journey* is in part an effort to overcome social and economic inequities inherent in the print-cultural rhetoric of the closet.

The negative, antisocial valences that the closet accrued in the context of the shift from manuscript to print culture marked and precipitated a decline in the cultural value of this space that was reflected in the ongoing development of the word. Thus, in the nineteenth century, the closet's principal architectural referent could change from the generic private room to the recess for clothes and personal effects built into a bedroom or hallway. Previously, some windowless, or dark, closets had served exclusively as storage rooms. But when households began to fill up with consumer goods in the late eighteenth century, that storage capacity became urgent. In a letter written in 1799, Jane Austen bemoans the semantic reduction that followed from this new obsession with things: "A Closet full of shelves ... should ... be called a Cupboard rather than a Closet."[16] In *Pride and Prejudice*, Austen mocks both Mr. Collins and Lady Catherine at once when she plays up the delight that the clergyman takes in his patroness's suggestion that he add "some shelves to the closet upstairs."[17] Though houses on both sides of the Atlantic were making more room for stuff, modern closet designs were finessed in the United States. Henry Urbach explains, "The closet we know today was invented as a new spatial type in America around 1840 ... for the first time, a wall cavity was produced for household storage. Briskly disseminated among all the classes, the closet effectively outmoded wardrobe, armoire, and chest."[18] The overlap between the closet's negative associations in eighteenth-century print culture and its later spatial designation is evident in the nineteenth-century coinage *skeleton in the closet*. Giving hidden storage a creepy, gothic aura, the expression connotes archaic notions of the closet as a site of collection and a claustrophobic room. (Today this expression also calls to mind the trans experience of deadnaming, which reimposes a previous gender identity that never fit.)

However, it wasn't until the 1960s that the closet came to serve as the dominant English term for shameful queer and trans withdrawal. In the early twentieth century, *closet case* was first used colloquially for any "unattractive or embarrassing person, a social outcast." The *Washington Post* helpfully explained, "Unattractive girls are 'strictly closet cases,' meaning they should be in the closet when men are around." The *Oxford English Dictionary*'s first example of *closet* as referent for sexual minorities comes from a 1967 study called *Homosexual Behavior among Males: A Cross-Cultural and Cross-Species Investigation*: "The 'closet queen' or so-called latent homosexual becomes a menace ... to the entire community." Like the female closet cases, the metaphorical closets that hide "queens" are presumed to keep something untoward from view. However, the different forms of hatred that constitute misogyny and homophobia are reflected in the two citations' contrasting views of concealment—as something desired in the first instance and something to be feared in the second: whereas men expect and hope not to have to see unappealing women, it is the conscious or semiconscious secrecy of homosexuals, their "so-called latency," that frightens the author of *Homosexual Behavior among Males*, presumably because it means that he and others cannot prepare to defend themselves from the threat of queer contagion.

By the time *Homosexual Behavior among Males* was published, gay and lesbian activists were already beginning to appropriate and transform this language of bigotry to describe their own painful experiences of invisibility and self-hatred and, conversely, to promote the pursuit of acceptance by coming out of the closet. The *Oxford English Dictionary*'s first example of *coming out* in reference to homosexuality comes from an article in the *Globe and Mail* magazine in 1968 about a new gay collective: "Several [of the men] I spoke to referred to the difficulties they experienced in 'coming out'—realizing they *were* homosexuals." Here, the implied closet represents a psychological obstacle to self-understanding, an inner censor that protects people from awareness of the uncomfortable truth about their own queer desires. When the gay and lesbian liberation movements flourished in the wake of the Stonewall Inn Riots in New York City in 1969, the in/out opposition was widely taken up. The opening lines of the first issue of *Come Out!*, the earliest publication of the Gay Liberation Front, enjoin sexual minorities to "COME OUT OF THE CLOSET BEFORE THE DOOR IS NAILED SHUT!" The allusion to a coffin highlights the imminent danger of social death for those individuals who don't join the movement, and implicitly for the movement itself if it doesn't continue to grow (figure 29). While the possibility of hiding from oneself was (and still is) suggested by the closet metaphor, in the hands of queer activists the importance of leaving the closet

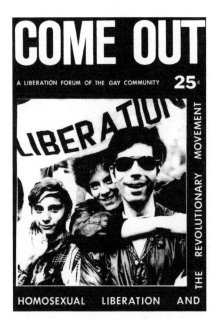

FIG. 29. The men on the cover of the first edition of *Come Out!* manifest the social condition that the magazine explicitly fights for. (Photograph from *Come Out!*, the newspaper of the New York Gay Liberation Front, with permission of the editors of *Come Out!* vol. 1, no. 2, January 10, 1970. Photographer: Diana Davies.)

was framed as a quest less for self-acceptance than for recognition and rights from others. By the end of the twentieth century, the common use of closeted versus out to contrast an undesirable/antisocial state of privacy to a desirable/sociable public orientation reinvigorated the opposition originally used to promote the first mass medium.

DECONSTRUCTING THE QUEER CLOSET

Following Stonewall, as the interdisciplinary study of sexuality gained traction, the closeted/out binary became an object of critical analysis. Queer theorists were, from the start, appreciative of the activism that the opposition helped to justify and advance, and suspicious of its deceptive simplicity. Notably, for Eve Sedgwick, Judith Butler, and Michael Warner, the basic assumption of the coming out myth—that sexual minorities can and should, individually, seek a special sort of recognition of their difference—is questionable because it rests on and perpetuates the cultural inflation of personal agency, identity, and subjectivity. Sedgwick shows how post-Enlightenment faith in the power of knowledge, including self-knowledge, to defeat homophobia has made it hard to see the profound damages wrought by willful silence, ignorance, and denial.[19] Butler objects to the way the concreteness of the closet reinforces the idea that sexual identities are fixed and transparent, asking, "Could it be that the subjection that subjectivates the gay and lesbian subject in some ways continues to oppress, or oppresses most insidiously, once 'outness' is claimed?"[20] Grounding his intellectual and political investments in public discourse, Warner addresses problems arising from the belief that "the personal is political"—that is, the belief that personal experiences provide the best focus for political action—finding a dangerous corollary between the emphasis in coming out discourse on self-awareness and self-expression and the notion that queer people alone are responsible for their invisibility.[21] For all three theorists, the binary logic of the closet metaphor as it is generally used serves to exaggerate the effect of individual acts of self-recognition and disclosure, as if, one by one, queer and trans people could easily defeat intolerance, if only enough of us were brave and honest enough with ourselves and others.

In this influential criticism of the in/out opposition, as in contemporary culture at large, figurative closets—and archaic architectural closets, on the rare occasions they are considered—are understood to be necessarily and fundamentally solitary spaces.[22] This sense of the closet's connotations has concentrated critical attention on how crucial, and problematic, this metaphor has been in delimiting the relationships between sexuality, personal identity, and barriers to inclusion. This emphasis is shared by queer criticism that draws on the in/out opposition to make sense of the popular media. For instance, Lynne Joyrich's "Epistemology of the Console" extends Sedgwick's seminal argument by considering how several ostensibly ground-breaking TV shows in fact reinforce homophobic ignorance and denial, while Amy Villarejo finds that televisual forms have in turn framed individual acts of queer disclosure: "In most of our [experiences] of coming out, I would say it involves shuttling ... between a sitcom and a soap opera (or between comedy and melodrama).... Its temporality is also televisual: a cross between a repetition (serial) and an event." [23] In the early twenty-first century, queer cultural studies have been especially interested in the surprising compatibility between representations of sexual minorities and the hypercapitalist agenda of popular media.[24] Reflecting on the implicitly racist turn in primetime network television in the 1990s, during which queers took the place of African Americans as the model minority, Ron Becker argues that the surge of coming out narratives on TV was in fact driven by an effort to appeal to straight, white, socially liberal, urban or urban-minded eighteen to forty-nine year olds, the demographic known to be the biggest and most experimental consumers.[25] Katherine Sender discovers that, in the hopes of growing a specifically queer middle-class demographic, many advertisers have begun producing "sexy not sleazy" images of gayness, a stylistic limitation that she calls "the closeting of queer sex."[26] Thus critical analysis focused on the new market appeal of queerness also tends to approach the in/out opposition as a knotty cultural tool that serves to reinforce individual identities, styles, and desires, though not exclusively those of people who identify as queer.

Yet, as this book has demonstrated, historically closets were not just personal rooms but also shared spaces, and myriad concerns over the intimate navigation of difference were woven into closet rhetoric long before the advent of sexual identities, of photography, TV, film, or digital and social media, or global conglomerates and megamonopolies. Keeping an eye on the closet's sociable past expands our vantage on coming out today. The fuller etymology reveals links between this current moment and a distant period of change, when media expansion first became an urgent concern. If, as Masten says, words contain "the genealogical seeds of their eventual direction," then the recent trend toward mediated queerness has, for better or for worse, been in the works ever since outness was defined in relation to print in the eighteenth century.

WWW.COMINGOUT.SPACE

The massive media shift accompanying the turn of the millennium has undoubtedly placed intense new pressures on the rhetoric of the closet. When the gay main character in the Australian TV comedy-drama *Please Like Me* dismisses coming out as "so '90s," it's no coincidence that his date for the sea change in the conditions of queer visibility lines up with the one that both Jodie Foster and Ellis Hansen have proposed.[27] This period has seen the rise of electronic media and, along with it, the "poly-media environment," a recent coinage to capture the many ways that the proliferation and intersection of various media and digital technologies have affected the forms, styles, and protocols of all interpersonal communication.[28] The electronic media seem to "rhizomatically disperse" social life into endless numbers and kinds of apparently disposable or endlessly renewable connections, as Hansen observes: "Online, one can experience countless possible permutations of friendings, ratings, hits, chats, pokes, thumbs-up, glances, flirtations, cruisings, hookups, and invitations from places one has never otherwise been and from people one would never otherwise meet, but one might find oneself paradoxically anchored to a keyboard or webcam, in solitude, in a room somewhere, for hours on end."[29] In recent arguments about the important role that Tumblr has played in cohering trans and asexual self-representations and communities online, the closet and coming out aren't even mentioned, suggesting that in certain contexts this binary language of public self-definition has already lost its explanatory force.[30]

Yet the in/out opposition is still in wide use, and not just by people who, like Foster, long to return to a time when the superiority of in-person conversations over virtual ones could simply be assumed. The final endeavor of this coda is to propose that the fantasies and fears of mediated intimacy across difference that were embedded in the closeted/out opposition three hundred years ago have acquired a paradoxical new urgency in widely shared twenty-first-century coming out narratives. In keeping with the change to the dominant associations of the closet trope, from status hierarchy to sexual difference, heteronormativity has taken the place that elitism once held in the liberal closeted/out binary, as the debilitating bias that the mass media are best equipped to transcend. The closet's long history as a conceptual tool for navigating public intimacy helps to explain how and why the accommodation and appreciation of sexual diversity should recently have become one of the most representative neoliberal ideals. In the second half of the twentieth century, gay and lesbian activists developed their movements by addressing one another, queer to queer, through alternative media. Reflecting on the significance of this phenomenon at the turn of the twenty-first century, Warner remarked that though, in theory, "no one is in the closet" in a virtual queer space—like *Come Out!* magazine, for example—in fact, "the individual struggle with stigma is transposed, as it were, to the conflict between modes of publicness." [31] While shedding light on the significant political impact of queer counterpublics, Warner did not want to understate their relative invisiblity or the ongoing obstacles to speaking publicly as a sexual minority. Yet the new millennium has seen queer counterpublic styles and modes of address come flooding into the most widely circulating, commercial, and lucrative of media, bringing with them the promise to transform our excesses of virtual publicness, however temporarily, into scenes of social cohesion and fun.

Consider Absolut Vodka's retort to the poster that pop artist Keith Haring designed for the first National Coming Out Day (figure 30). In the "advertising and awareness" campaign that Absolut launched exactly fifteen years later, the personal risks of disclosure give way to the easy pleasures of an urbane community in which many things can go without saying. The Absolut Out campaign, which also included billboards and postcards, centered around a four-page print ad in the *New York Times Magazine* whose audience was invited to "Come Out" by pulling tabs on the centerfold (figure 31).[32] Nine closet doors slide open, revealing the clothes, shoes, and accessories of nine queer types, including the drag queen, the butch, and the activist. While borrowing Haring's visual, architectural pun, Absolut Out collapses his distinction between states of closetedness and outness. Instead it posits queerness as a variety of modes of consuming and costuming that, thanks to the proliferation of mediated representations like the ad itself, are instantly recognized, and equally widely enjoyed by all, especially after everyone has had a couple of drinks.

The L Word, the first lesbian-themed serial TV drama, similarly projects and pays tribute to its own appeal to heterogenous viewers by thematizing coming out as a joyful community-building exercise that the commercial media are most capable of managing. In her season one trajectory, the character Dana Fairbanks, a tennis player, wins a lucrative endorsement contract with Subaru. Though her agent has advised her to "be a lez later," she soon discovers how outdated his marketing instincts are. It turns out that the Subaru campaign pivots around a photograph of her mid-swing, under the caption, "Get out. And stay out."[33] Since appearing in the ad is Dana's most decisive act of sexual self-exposure to date, the slogan in fact performs what it ostensibly celebrates. In subsequent

FIG. 30. In Keith Haring's poster for the first National Coming Out Day in the United States, a single yellow figure emerges from a black background, goofy and wobbly but shooting off sparks of joy. (Keith Haring, National Coming Out Day, 1988. © Keith Haring Foundation. Reproduced by permission.)

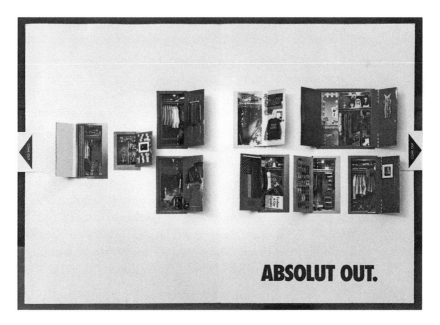

FIG. 31. When you pull the tab on Absolut Out, the open closets form the shape of a vodka bottle on its side. ("Absolut Out" advertisement for Absolut Vodka, October 1, 2003, *New York Times Magazine*.)

episodes, Dana's career takes off as the ad draws the attention and affection of a diverse range of people throughout Los Angeles and the vicinity, including at least one Orange County Republican, most of whom admire Dana less for her talents on the tennis court than for her willingness to become a focal point for their admiration. Instantly casting Dana as a "professional lesbian," as one of her friends puts it, the Subaru endorsement highlights the inefficiency, if not exactly the redundancy, of the old-school face-to-face disclosure.[34] Dana's suburban conservative parents, who willfully misunderstand the ad, seem to be the only people in California who need Dana to discloset herself in the direct and vulnerable way that Haring depicted (figure 32).[35]

The Enlightenment value of universal access and the newer liberal values of queer pride and visibility come together especially seamlessly at www.comingout.space. This nonprofit, open source website presents itself as the tool by which anyone can launch her own coming out campaign, or engage with someone else's, surging instantly into outness while avoiding some of the pain, anxiety, or tedium of serial disclosures. Visitors may "search stories by keywords and categories" or "submit [their] own." In many respects, the site riffs off the It Gets Better web campaign that media pundit Dan Savage started with his partner Terry Miller in October 2010, with the explicit mission to give comfort and support to the isolated queer and trans youth who are most vulnerable to depression and suicide. As Savage explained, the idea for that website came when it occurred to him that, though digitial communication has undoubtedly provided new forums for cruelty and harassment, it has also provided the ideal means of countering the taboo on intergenerational discussions of queer and trans experience: "In the era of social media—in a world with YouTube and Twitter and Facebook—I could speak directly to LGBT kids right now. I didn't need permission from parents or an invitation from the school. I could look into a camera, share my story."[36] Whereas It Gets Better tries to give young people the out-and-proud role models and sense of hope for the future that the adults whom they actually know have been unwilling or unable to provide, Coming Out Space is the venue where this same youth may announce their sexual minority status, without needing to directly address their parents or indeed any specific people.

However, Coming Out Space finesses the self-referentiality of the older project through its pointed use of the language of the closet. Aiming to become "a leading resource for coming out education by building a massive, diverse library that is easy to navigate so anyone can find relatable stories," it evokes the desires for both curatorial completeness and

FIG. 32. In the last frame of her short graphic narrative, Alison Wilgus pictures herself emerging from a Haring-style closet and immediately being welcomed by a group that at once seems to represent her own queer friends and the diverse audience that the story aims to reach online. (Reproduced by permission from Alison Wilgus, "I Came Out Late in Life and That's Okay," *The Nib*, April 26, 2019.) With thanks to Emily Wilson for passing this along.

infinite appeal that were filtered through textual closets without walls in the eighteenth century. As a kind of digital cabinet of love in particular, Coming Out Space registers the special capacities of the electronic media to continually expand the numbers and kinds of difference they register. Contributors can classify their experiences according to the many sub-categories suggested by drop-down menus under location, age, race, religion, and gender identities (including heterosexual and ally)—though class is notably missing—or they can add their own. Thus the site features accounts from a "Gay + Male / 17 and Under + 18–22 Christian + Muslim," who lost his medical school scholarship and went into exile after facing criminal charges for his homosexuality in Gambia; from a "Female + Pansexual / 17 and Under / Hispanic or Latinx Athiest" in Happy Valley, Oregon, who experienced her first girl-crush during a basketball game; from a "Heterosexual + Queer + Trans man / 18–22 + 23–29 / Hispanic or Latinx," who has found inhabiting a straight male identity to be the most awkward of all; from a "Gay / 23–29 / Middle Eastern Other," now the leader of an activist organization called IraQueer, whose family in Iraq learned he was gay from a interview with him published the *Huffington Post*; as well as from a "Heterosexual + Male / 18–22 / White Christian" who admires his gay brother, among many others. Yet all these particularities become most meaningful here in relation to the greater value the site places on assimilation—on its own capacity to hold, and ultimately transcend, the many variations it registers. Like It Gets Better, which proudly declares that people of "all ages, races, religions, nationalities, gender identities and sexual orientations" come together via the site, Coming Out announces, "Today, we reach 10s of thousands of people a month in more than 150 countries and we're still growing!" The emphasis on "coming out education" on the newer website in particular seems designed to foreclose the possibility that any global visitor will view these personal stories from afar or with anything other than delight, recognition, or concern. Where eighteenth-century closet rhetoric tackled the unstable hierarchical foundations of and ongoing obstacles to virtual public feeling, the latest coming out narratives are adamant that there are no conditions to such feeling at all: anyone who wants to can share in it.

ACKNOWLEDGMENTS

In the stateroom scene in the Marx Brothers' *Night at the Opera*, a tiny ship cabin fills with people over the course of a couple of minutes. Every few seconds there's another knock on the door, and Groucho opens it and lets someone else in, just as happily every time. "Did you want a manicure?" "No, come on in." Materializing this book has taken a little bit longer than that scene, but I picture it now, giddily, when I think of all the people who have helped me and joined me along the way.

For their fantastic research and administrative skills, I thank Jordan Crosthwaithe, Desirée de Jesus, Graeme Desrosiers, Lars Horn, Julie McIsaac, Alexei Perry-Cox, Sara Press, Shannon Tien, Krystale Tremblay-Moll, and Colin Young. I thank Brianne Colon and Emily Wilson for contributions of insight, ingenuity, and energy that have gone far beyond assistance. For the funding to hire them and to travel to the British Library, I thank Concordia University and the Fonds Québécois de la Recherche sur la Société et la Culture. For offering fellowships, I thank the Huntington and Clark Libraries.

I thank Jonathan Kramnick, Michael McKeon, Paula McDowell, and Joan Scott, my dissertation committee, for their brilliant scholarship, fantastic courses, and generous mentorship over many years. I thank the Graduate School and the English Department at Rutgers University for various forms of doctoral funding and for excellent admissions decisions that allowed me to live and learn in the company of Saladin Ahmed, Margaret Anderson, Kristin Girten, Melanie Holm, Tina Lupton, Regina Masiello, Nick Monk, James Mulholland, Susie Nakley, Bronwen PerLee, John Mark Rogers, Michal Shapira, Alison Shonkwiler, Alexandra Socarides, Richard Squibbs, Sunny Stalter, Kathryn Steele, Kirsten Tranter, and Madhvi Zutshi, among many other fine people.

I thank Emory University, Martine Brownley, the Fox Center for Humanistic Inquiry, and the 2010–2011 Fox fellows, especially Ross Melnick, for a stimulating and fruitful postdoctoral year. For other opportunities to present and discuss parts of this book as it developed, I thank Heather Meek and the Université de Montréal, Concordia's CISSC Early Modern Working Group, and Elizabeth Elbourne, Brian Lewis, and the Montreal British History Seminar. I also thank the American and Canadian Societies for Eighteenth-Century Studies and the Queer People Conference for opportunities to cross paths with so many inspiring scholars. I'm particularly grateful to Harriette Andreadis, Katherine Binhammer, Helen Deutsch, Bridget Donnelly, Joseph Drury, Katherine Ellison, Noelle Gallagher, Caroline Gonda, Paul Kelleher, Sara Landreth, Wendy Anne Lee, Sandra Macpherson, Mary Helen McMurran, Chris Mounsey, Holly Faith Nelson, Julie Park, Brad Pasanek, Jeffrey Ravel, Kristen Saxton, Betty Schellenberg, Vanessa Smith, Diana Solomon, Kristina Straub, Kyoko Takanashi, Rebecca Tierney-Hynes, Sarah Tyndall Kareem, Cynthia Wall, Linda Zionkowski, and Eugenia Zuroski for conversations, suggestions, and encouragement that have contributed immeasurably to this project.

I thank my colleagues and friends in the English Department and around Concordia who commented on work in progress or offered moral support, including Jessica Bardill, Nathan Brown, Susan Cahill, Jason Camlot, Bonnie-Jean Campbell, Ronjaunee Chatterjee, Beth Crevier, Jill Didur, Mary Esteve, Meredith Evans, Sharon Frank, Bina Friewald, Andre Furlani, Judith Herz, Darragh Languay, Gada Mahrouse, Omri Moses, Nicola Nixon, Kevin Pask, Manish Sharma, Theresa Ventura, and especially my dazzling coaches, Jonathan Sachs and Anya Zilberstein, who have held my hand through the whole process of making this book. My debts to Marcie Frank, who introduced me to the eighteenth century, encouraged me to keep studying, and has remained a rigorous and supportive interlocutor for twenty-five years, can never be repaid. I'm also deeply indebted to the many students at Concordia and Emory who've been game to puzzle out eighteenth-century closets with me, and to try to help me understand what matters now.

Very special thanks to Anne Savarese and my three anonymous readers for believing in and helping to shape this book. I'm also grateful to Jenny Tan, Bob Bettendorf, Annalise Zox-Weaver, Natalie Baan, Eileen Allen, and everyone at Princeton University Press. I thank Jerry Singerman for sage advice. I thank Sue Nicholson for her vital additions to the preludes, and Phil Gyford and all of the other online Pepys peeps for my daily (annotated!) *Diary* fix.

Parts of this book have appeared as essays. Chapter 2 expands on "Female Favouritism, Orientalism, and the Bathing Closet in *Memoirs of*

Count Grammont," published in *Eighteenth-Century Fiction* 24, no. 1 (2011): 1–30. Both chapter 4 and the coda draw on "Coming Out: Closet Rhetoric and Media Publics," published in *History of the Present* 5, no. 1 (2015): 31–64. Chapter 5 expands on "Carriages, Conversation, and *A Sentimental Journey*," published in *Studies in Eighteenth-Century Culture* 35 (2006): 243–66. An earlier version of the appendix was published in "The Literature and Culture of the Closet: A Pedagogical Resource" in *Digital Defoe: Studies in Defoe and His Contemporaries* 6, no. 1 (2014): 70–94. For their help in developing this project and permission to include these revisions, I thank these journals and their editors.

With lots of love, I thank my patient family, Ann, Ron, Adam, Hannah, and Sadie Bobker, and Nadine D'Aguiar, and the many others who've always been there (or feel like they have been): Kristie Allen, David Baumflek, Rachel Berger, Tracy Bohan, Joseph Chaves, Mary Chinni, Nitika Dosaj, Gillian Graham, Alyson Grant, Nat Hurley, Angela-Ruth Idelson, Zohar Kfir, Kathy Lubey, Susanna Luhmann, Lisa Lynch, Nancy Lyons, Anne Newman, Ara Osterweil, Emer O'Toole, Trish Salah, Theresa Stowe, Margaret Webb, Dahna Weber, Rachel Zellars, and my soul sisters, Andrea Aster and Claudine Crangle. I thank Chava Field-Green and Amber Eckhardt for their expert care. Finally, *Baruch HaShem* for Sina Queyras, my *sine qua non*, and for our children. I used to imagine dedicating this book "To Naomi and Sam, who couldn't care less." One advantage of taking so long is that you can now tell me otherwise. This book is, as I am, for the three of you, forever and always. Cheers, *lachaim*, amen.

APPENDIX

Closets without Walls, 1550–1800

This archive of 205 printed closets and cabinets has been assembled with reference to Early English Books Online, Eighteenth-Century Collections Online, and the British Library catalog. Where closet or cabinet is in bold, the word refers to the space of the text itself.

1550–1599 (4)

1569   The **closet** of counsells conteining the advice of divers philosophers

1573   The treasurie of commodious conceits and hidden secrets. commonly called, the good huswiues **closet** of prouision, for the health of her houshold

1591   The Christian mans **closet**

1596   Psalmes of confession found in the cabinet of the most excellent King of Portinga

1600–1649 (21)

1608   A **closet** for ladies and gentlewomen

1612   The golden **cabinet** of true treasure: containing the summe of morall philosophie

1616   The rich **cabinet** furnished with varietie of excellent discriptions

1620   Audi filia, or a rich **cabinet** full of spirituall ievvells

1630   The chyrugians **closet**

1632   Two spare keyes to the Jesuites **cabinet**

1637	Curiosities: or, the **cabinet** of nature
1639	The ladies **cabinet** opened
1640	Jocabella, or a **cabinet** of conceit
1641	Cupids **cabinet** unlock't
1642	A true narration of the surprizall of sundry cavaliers being sent from Nottingham to Oxford, as they were lodged at Brackley and also of a cabinet
1644	Ruperts sumpter, and private cabinet rifled
	The kings cabinet-counsell
	The key to the kings cabinet-counsell
1645	The Kings **cabinet** opened
	A key to the Kings **cabinet**
	A satyr, occasioned by the author's survey of a scandalous pamphlet intituled, the King's **cabanet** opened
1646	The Irish **cabinet**: or His Majesties secret papers
	The Lord George Digby's cabinet and Dr Goff's negotiations
	To a vertuous and judicious lady who (for the exercise of her devotion) built a closet
1648	A key to the cabinet of the Parliament, by their remembrancer

1650–1699 (61)

1651	Five treatises of the philosophers stone. Two of Alphonso King of Portugall, as it was written with his own hand, and taken out of his closset
	A **closet** for ladies and gentlewomen
	Approved medicines of little cost, to preserve health and also to cure those that are sick provided for the souldiers knap-sack, and the country mans closet
	Delights for ladies to adorn their persons, tables, closets and distillatories
1652	A rich **closet** of physical secrets
1653	The treasury of hidden secrets commonly called the good huswives **closet** of provision for the health of her houshold
1655	The Queens **closet** opened
	Queen Elizabeths **closset** of physical secrets
	Three sermons preached by the reverend, and learned, Dr. Richard Stuart, Dean of St. Pauls, afterwards Dean of Westminster, and clerk of the closset to the late King Charles

1657 Herbert's devotions, or, a companion for a Christian
containing, meditations & prayers, fitted for all conditions,
persons, times and places either for the church, closet, shop,
chamber, or bed

   The expert doctors dispensatory the whole art of physick
restored to practice: the apothecaries shop and chyrurgions
closet open'd

   Catholique divinity: or, the most solid and sententious
expressions of the primitive doctors of the Church ... by Dr.
Stuart, dean of St. Pauls, afterwards dean of Westminster, and
clerk of the closet to the late K. Charles

1658 A wise virgins lamp burning ... and found in her closet after
her death

   Rare verities, the **cabinet** of Venus unlocked, and her secrets
laid open

   Rich **cabinet** with variety of inventions in several arts and
siences

1660 The two tables, or, the exercise of a good conscience towards
God, ourselves and others, to be hung up in parlors, chambers,
and closets

   A choice banquet of witty jests, rare fancies, and pleasant
novels fitted for all the lovers of wit, mirth and eloquence:
being an addition to Archee's jests, taken out of his closet

   A New-Years-gift for women, being a true looking-glass which
they seldome have in their own closets

1661 Golden remains or three sermons of the most learned and
pious R. Stuart. D.D Dean of Westminster, and clerk of the
closet to his late Majesty King Charles the I

1660 The devils cabinet-councell discovered, or the mistery and
iniquity of the good old cause

1662 A brief rule of life directing how to manage it according to the
principles both of piety & prudence ... which may likewise be
used in the closet by those that want such helps

1665 The privie key of heaven, or, twenty arguments for
closet-prayer

1666 Enter into thy closet

1669 The **closet** of the eminently learned Sir Kenelme Digbie Kt.
opened

   The Jesuites intrigues with the private instructions of that
society to their emissaries: the first, translated out of a book

privately printed at Paris: the second, lately found in
manuscript in a Jesuites closet

Cabinet of choice jewels or, a box of precious ointment

1670 The kings psalter ... also prayers for every day of the week,
beginning with the letters of the name of our soveraign lord
King Charles; and other observable varieties, fit either for the
school, or for the closet

The queen-like **closet**; or, rich **cabinet** stored with all manner
of rare receipts for preserving, candying & cookery

1671 Closet-prayer a Christian-duty

1672 A companion to the temple and closet

The ladies delight: or, a rich **closet** of choice experiments &
curiosities

1674 An introduction to a devout life containing especially, a
prudent method for spiritual closet-exercises

A supplement to the queen-like **closet**

1675 Every woman her own midwife, or, a compleat cabinet opened
for child-bearing women

1680 A true picture of the much honoured & reverend Mr. John ...
for the closets of his friends

1681 The paper which was seized in the E. of Shaftsbury's closet

The two associations one subscribed by CLVI members of the
House of Commons in the year 1643: the other seized in the
closet of the Earl of Shaftsbury

Love's perpetual almanack ... from a manuscript found in
cupid's cabinet

1682 The addresses importing an abhorrence of an association,
pretended to have been seized in the E of Shaftsbury's closet

1684 Dunton's remains, or, the dying pastour's last legacy to his
friends and parishioners comprehending these following
treatises ... closet employment

A brief rule of life being a second part of the guide to heaven ...
which may likewise be used in the closet by those that want
such helps

A guide to scattered flocks, or, a closet companion for such as
want the comfort

1685 A provocation to good works written in an epistle to an old
man of a very cumbersome estate to perswade the easing
himself of part of it by some eminent act of charity ... but
have no better way for it then conveying such a book into their
hands or closets

Modern curiosities of art & nature extracted out of the cabinets
of the most eminent personages of the French court

1686   The accomplish'd sea-mans delight containing : ... The **closset**
of magnetical miracles unlocked

Markham's faithful farrier wherein the depth of his skill is laid
open ... found in the authors closet since his decease

1687   The common-prayer-book the best companion in the house
and closet

The accomplished ladies rich **closet** of rarities

1688   A certain rule, to find out how many honest men there are
in this nation ... proper to be set up in all schools, shops,
parlours, chambers, or closets

An index to the Indian **closset**

A short and plain way to the faith and church composed many
years since by ... Mr. Richard Hudleston ... found in his closet
after his decease

1689   Prayers in the closet for the use of all devout Christians

1690   An address given in to the late King James ... the original
whereof was found in the late King James closet

1691   A discourse of closet (or secret) prayer from Matt. VI 6

1692   Prayers in the closet

The **cabinet** open'd, Or the secret history of the amours of
Madam de Maintenon, with the French King, translated from
the French copy

Closet-devotions to a devout and worthy reception of the
Lord's Supper

1693   Of closet-prayer: a sermon preach'd before the Queen at
White-Hall

1694   The poor man's help and young mans guide containing ...
prayer publick in the congregation, private in the family, secret
in the closet

1695   The duties of the closet

1696   The experience of Gods gracious dealing with Mrs. Elizabeth
White ... found in her closet after her decease

1700–1749 (39)

1700   England's choice **cabinet** of rarities; or the famous Mr.
Wadham's last golden legacy

1701   A **cabinet** of choice jewels

1704   A rich **cabinet** of modern curiosities containing many natural and artificial conclusions

1706   The accomplish'd Lady's Delight beautifying, and cookery containing I. the art of preserving and candying fruits & flowers ..., II. the physical **cabinet**

1707   The phenix volume one ... no where to be found but in the closets of the curious

The second volume of the phenix or, a revival of scarce and valuable pieces no where to be found but in the closets of the curious

1709   The poor man's help, and young man's guide containing ... I. prayer publick in the congregation, private in the family, secret in the closet

1710   The compleat english and french vermin-killer: ... directions for gardiners & the prizes of workmens labour being a rich **cabinet** of modern curiosities

A coppy of verses writt in a common prayer book presented to a lady in 1644 upon her building a closet for her books

1711   Aristotle's last legacy: or, his golden **cabinet** of secrets opened

1714   England's mournful monument: or, the pious, glorious and everlasting example; of our late, good & gracious sovereign Lady Queen Anne: ... likewise her closet devotion, both for her private and publick affairs

Cabinet of love, in the works of the Earls of Rochester, Roscommon, Dorset, &c.

1715   Hocus pocus; or, a rich **cabinet** of legerdemain curiousities, natural and artificial conclusions

Wit's **cabinet**

1718   Ladies **cabinet** broke open, part 1

Letters, poems, and tales: amorous, satirical, and gallant ... found in the cabinet of ... Mrs. Anne Long

The French Momus: or, comical adventures of the Duke of Roquelaure ... found in the closet of Marshal D'Huxells

1719   The Book of Psalms made fit for the closet with collects and prayers

The Christian's plea for his god and saviour Jesus Christ. Found in a gentleman's closet

The British treasury; being cabinet the first of our Greek and Roman antiquities of all sorts. Never before printed: Volume 1

1721   A **closet** piece: the experimental knowledge of the ever-blessed
        God

1724   A manual history of repentance and impenitence ... and a
        penitential form of prayer made fit for the closet

1725   A letter from the man in the moon to Mr. Anodyne Necklace;
        containing an account of a robbery committed in hell, and the
        breaking open the devil's cabinet
        Delights for young men and maids ... Also Cupid's **cabinet**
        open'd ...

1726   The genuine letters of Mary Queen of Scots, to James Earl
        of Bothwell: found in his secretary's closet after his decease

1728   Mist's **closet** broke open
        Christ's famous titles, and a believers golden chain. handled
        in divers sermons. together with a **cabinet** of jewels

1729   A brief history of the restauration: published from original
        letters, and other royal authorities. from the cabinet of the late
        Lord Frederick Howard

1730   The Christian's duty from the sacred scriptures ... part II.
        devotions for the closet; consisting of confessions, praises,
        supplications

1731   A general history of the proceedings and cruelties of the court
        of inquisition in Spain, Portugal &c. consisting chiefly of fact
        well attested intermix'd with many remarkable tryals and
        sufferings ... now only to be found in the closets of the
        curious

1732   Duties of the closet
        Flower-garden display'd ... or furniture for the closet

1733   Gloria Britannorum or, the british worthies. a poem. being
        an essay on the characters of the most illustrious persons in
        camp or cabinet, since the glorious revolution to this present
        time

1739   Religion the most delightful employment ... with devotions
        for the closet and for the family

1740   Incomparable varieties: or, a **cabinet** of secrets unlock'd by the
        key of experience
        Seven conferences held in the King of France's cabinet of
        paintings

1743   The ladies **cabinet**
        A book of rarities: or, **cabinet** of curiosities unlock'd

1746   The Irish **cabinet**

1750–1800 (80)

1750   Cupid's **cabinet** open'd
        M——c L——n's **cabinet** broke open
        The history of Mother Bunch of the west. containing. many
        rarities out of her golden closet of curiosities
        The history of Mother Bunch of the west. containing. many
        rarities out of her golden closet of curiosities. part the second
1752   The gentleman and lady's palladium … the **cabinet** disclos'd;
        an express from the lazy all over the kingdom
1753   Fragment of the chronicles of Zimri the Refiner. found in a
        cabinet of jewels belonging to Nathan Ben Amri
1754   The **cabinet**
1755   The lovers **cabinet**
1757   Apollo's **cabinet** or the muses delight
        A **cabinet** of jewels opened to the curious, by a key of real
        knowledge
1759   The general state of education … inscribed to the Reverend
        Doctor Hales, clerk of the closet to Her Royal Highness the
        Princess of Wales
1760   Mother Bunch's **closet** newly broke open
1762   The British phoenix, a great variety of scarce and valuable
        literary amusements, artfully fetched from the closets of the
        curious
        A **cabinet** of choice jewels
1763   The believer's golden chain … together with the **cabinet** of
        jewels, or a glimpse of Zion's glory
1764   The Christian's New Year's Gift … and a manual of devotions
        for the closet and the family
        The celebrated Mrs. Pilkington's jests: or the **cabinet** of wit and
        humour
1765   The golden **cabinet**
        Miss C——Y's **cabinet** of curiosities; or, the green room broke
        open
1769   A catalogue of the cabinet of birds, and other curiosities
1770   The Christian's **closet**-piece
        The new week's preparation for a worthy receiving of the lords
        supper … to which are added a morning and evening prayer
        for the closet or family
        The spirit of liberty or Junius's loyal address being a key to the
        English **cabinet** or an humble dissertation

1771   The muses **cabinet**

1772   The riches and extent of free grace displayed: in three letters ... found in his cabinet after his death

       The Christian's preparation for the worthy receiving of the holy sacrament of the lord's supper ... devotions adapted to various occasions, both with regard to a family and the closet

1773   The golden **cabinet**

1775   A catalogue of the elegant cabinet of natural and artificial rarities of the late ingenious Henry Baker, Esq.

1776   A thousand notable things, on various subjects. disclosed from the secrets of nature and art ... being a rich **cabinet** of select curiosities and rarities, in one volume

1779   A catalogue of the genuine curious, and valuable, cabinet of British, Saxon, and English, coins and medals

       Instructions for a prince: to which are added, state maxims, and interesting papers; found in the cabinet of the King of Lunaria

1783   The **cabinet** of true attic wit

       The Cyprian **cabinet**

       The modern family physician: being Dr Green's treasure of health: or, **cabinet** of cures unlock'd

1785   Elegant Drawing and Cabinet Pictures

       For the inspection of the curious ... a **cabinet** of royal figures

       Cabinet of jewels opened to the curious, by a key of real knowledge

1786   The laird of Cool's ghost ... found in Mr. Ogilvie's closet after his death

       The **cabinet** of Momus and Caledonian humorist

1787   A catalogue of that superb and well known cabinet of drawings of John Barnard, Esq.

       The **cabinet** of genius

1788   Every lady her own physician or the closet companion

1790   The housekeeper's valuable present: or, lady's closet companion

       The golden **cabinet**

       Copys of several conferences and meetings ... as it was found in Mr. Ogilvie's closet, after his death, which happened very soon after these conferences

1791   The closet companion

1792   The copper-plate magazine, or monthly **cabinet** of picturesque prints

A catalogue of a pleasing assemblage of prints, a small, but well-chosen library of books ... together with about fifty lots of beautiful shells for cabinets

The **cabinet** of love

The royal jester, or prince's **cabinet** of wit

To be seen in Curtius's cabinet of curiosities

1793   Monthly beauties; or the **cabinet** of literary geniius

1794   A **cabinet** of miscellanies

1795   **Cabinet** of curiosities, no. 1

The world's doom: or the **cabinet** of fate unlocked. vol.1

The world's doom: or the **cabinet** of fate unlocked. vol. 2

1796   **Cabinet** *littéraire*; or, A catalogue of a circulating library, Consisting of French books only

Coins and medals, in the cabinets of the Earl of Fife

Gale's **cabinet** of knowledge

1797   The Oxford **cabinet**

Specimens of British minerals selected from the cabinet of Philip Rasleigh

The **cabinet**

The **cabinet** of wit

1798   The children's **cabinet**: or, a key to natural history

A key to natural history, to accompany the children's **cabinet**

Sedwick & Co; or A key to the six per cent **cabinet**

Lineal arithmetic; applied to shew the progress of the commerce and revenue of England during the present century; which is represented and illustrated by thirty-three copper-plate chart. being an useful companion for the cabinet and counting house

Beautiful cabinet pictures

Catalogue of the genuine and entire cabinet of choice and capital drawings, of the late John Duke of Argyll

1799   The naturalist's pocket magazine or compleat **cabinet** of the curiosities and beauties of nature 1

The naturalist's pocket magazine or compleat **cabinet** of the curiosities and beauties of nature 2

The naturalist's pocket magazine or compleat **cabinet** of the curiosities and beauties of nature 3

The naturalist's pocket magazine or compleat **cabinet** of the curiosities and beauties of nature 4

The naturalist's pocket magazine or compleat **cabinet** of the curiosities and beauties of nature 5

The naturalist's pocket magazine or compleat **cabinet** of the
curiosities and beauties of nature 6
Phylaxa medinae. the **cabinet** of physick
Catalogue of the intire cabinet of capital drawings, collected
by the late Greffier Francois Fagel
A **cabinet** of fancy
The **cabinet** of the arts
1800   The **Cabinet** of beasts
Curtius's grand **cabinet** of curiosities

NOTES

PREFACE

1. See definition 1 in the *Oxford English Dictionary*, s.v. "conversation, *n.*"
2. See, for instance, the introduction to the *Routledge Queer Studies Reader*, where the term *queer* stakes a claim to " 'a pluralistic sexual ethics' organized around a concept of 'benign sexual variation' " or "The New Unhistoricism," 22, where Valerie Traub stresses "the analytic capacity of queer to deconstruct sexual identity, to illuminate the lack of coherence or fixity in erotic relations, and to highlight the radical indeterminacy and transitivity of both erotic desire and gender."
3. As Cynthia Wall, *Prose of Things*, 4, observes, eighteenth-century writers tend to take a partial and pragmatic approach to physical space: "Specific interior details appear precisely—and in isolation—when they are needed, rather than being presented as connected visual wholes. Windows, closets, and wainscotings emerge when jumped out of, hidden in, or fainted against, and not a moment sooner; space is created in the act of narrative."
4. Congreve, *Way of the World*, 4.223, 793; and Steele, no. 308, *Spectator* (Vol. 2), 361.

ROOMS FOR IMPROVEMENT

1. Claire Tomalin, *Samuel Pepys*, 119, considers the whole of the Seething Lane property as highly symbolic for Pepys: "The new house was the outward sign of his progress; it became almost the emblem of himself. Even though it was not his own freehold, he was from the start obsessed with altering, decorating and improving the place." In "At Home with Mr and Mrs Pepys," Sue Nicholson finds that the sumptuous dining room in particular—the most public space in the house—"came to symbolize Pepys's meteoric rise in wealth and status during the diary period." Mentioned at least four times more often than dining rooms, closets evidently also have tremendous social and symbolic value for Pepys. Kate Loveman, *Samuel Pepys*, especially chapter 9, 245–74, provides another detailed account of Samuel and Elizabeth's closets, noting that, "After major disruptions such as the plague and the Great Fire, it was specifically the return of his closet to an orderly state that signalled the return of normality to this home and his life in general" (258). Though, as Loveman points out, Pepys also uses *study* and *chamber* to refer to his personal rooms, closet is his preferred term.
2. Pepys, *Diary*, 19 January 1663 (4.17–19). All citations of Pepys's *Diary* give in parentheses the volume and page numbers from the University of California edition and follow its editors' dating practices. Phil Gyford's searchable weblog, www.pepysdiary.com, with its many annotations, has also been invaluable for this research. On 1 September 1663 (4.293–94), Pepys feels a mix of joy and guilt at learning that he can undertake major

renovations at no personal expense: "I got my bill, among others, for my carved work, which I expected to have paid for myself, signed at the table, and hoped to get the money back again—though if the rest had not got it paid by the King, I never entended nor did desire to have him to pay for my vanity." Everyone else in the complex is doing it, so why shouldn't he?

3. 8 September 1662 (3.192–93). See also entries from 15 August 1662 (3.165–66), 10 September 1662 (3.194–95), and 21 October 1662 (3.231–32). In part because of Pepys's neighbors' protests, the installation of railings on the rooftop terrace was delayed for four years. See 11 April 1666 (7.95–96).

4. 21, 22, 24, and 27 August 1663 (7.282–86, 7.289–90).

5. 5 October 1663 (4.324). See also entries from 7, 22, 23, 27, 29, and 30 September and 9, 17, and 31 October 1663 (4.300–301, 314–21, 328, 337, 357–59).

6. 6 May 1664 (5.143), 29 and 30 May 1665 (6.111–12).

7. 18 August 1666 (7.253–54) and 22 August 1666 (7.256–57). Also see 20 and 21 August 1666 (7.255–56).

8. 24 August 1666 (7.258).

9. 27 August 1666 (7.261–62). Shortly thereafter, this brightened closet was repurposed as a private dining room (23 September 1666, 7.293–94). See Tomalin, *Unequalled*, 279–80, on Pepys's unfounded fears that he was going blind.

10. 13 May 1667 (8.213).

11. See 8 November 1667 (8.522).

12. 8 January 1666 (7.7) and 17 November 1668 (9.365).

13. 6 May 1664 (5.143) and 27 August 1666 (7.261–62).

14. 12 January 1666 (7.12–14).

15. 8 September 1662 (3.192–93) describes the Duke of York's decision, which Pepys was glad of, to "renew the old custom for the Admirals to have their principal officers to meet them once a week, to give them an account what they have done that week."

16. See 8 September 1662 (3.192–93) and 1 December 1662 (3.272–73).

17. 20 April 1661 (2.79–81), 9 November 1663 (4.369–77), 26 October 1668 (9.338), and 19 May 1669 (9.557–59).

18. See 21 March 1666 (7.79–80), 20 February 1667 (8.73–75), and 26 October 1668 (9.338–39).

19. 21 March 1666 (7.79).

20. According to Clarendon's *History of the Rebellion* (Vol. 1), 211, this name for the group of the king's closest advisors dates from Charles I's court.

21. 7 October 1666 (7.311–13).

22. See entries from 29 June 1667 (8.303–6), 31 October 1667 (8.511–13), and 26 November 1667 (8.547–50).

23. 18 June 1663 (4.188).

24. 18 July 1664 (5.211–13).

25. 30 April 1665 (6.92–93).

26. 24 January 1667 (8.28–29).

27. 17 July 1663 (4.233–34).

28. 20 September 1666 (7.291–92).

29. 21 January 1665 (6.17–18); 27 November 1665 (6.310–12).

30. 1 November 1660 (1.280–81).

31. 19 January 1663 (4.17–19). According to Latham and Matthews, Povey's "piece of perspective" was probably a painting of a corridor by Samuel van Hoogstraten. See Figure 1 in this book. Pepys admires it again on 29 May 1664 (5.159–62) and 21 September 1664 (5.276).

32. 16 September 1667 (8.438–40).

33. 3 August 1662 (3.153–54).

34. 8 March 1668 (9.108–9.

35. 3 October 1660 (1.257–58).

36. 25 May 1663 (4.154–57) and 17 February 1663 (4.45–49).

37. 24 June 1663 (5.188–89).

38. 27 August 1667 (8.403–4).
39. 16 May 1664 (5.151).
40. 4 July 1668 (9.255) and 6 March 1669 (9.471–72). *The Country Gentleman*, by George Villiers, Duke of Buckingham, and Sir Robert Howard, was banned before performance and never printed.
41. 20 September 1665 (6.234), 23 October 1665 (6.273–74), 1 November 1665 (6.285–86), and 16 March 1666 (7.74).
42. 19 March 1666 (7.76).
43. 6 August 1666 (7.235–38).
44. 22 August 1667 (8.395).
45. 15 May 1668 (9.199–201).
46. 3 October 1660 (1.257–58).
47. 20 April 1661 (2.79–81).
48. 9 December 1663 (4.409) and 18 May 1664 (5.152).
49. See 2 February 1667 (8.40), 17 January 1669 (9.417–18), 26 December 1663 (4.434–35), and 29 May 1665 (6.111). For an account of Pepys's relationships to his books throughout his life, see Loveman, *Books*.
50. 30 April 1667 (8.191–92) and 19 August 1664 (5.247).
51. 30 July 1666 (7.226–28).
52. 23 July 1666 (7.214) and 13 August 1666 (7.243–44).
53. 30 April 1667 (8.191–92).
54. 2 March 1669 (9.463–64).
55. 14 March 1668 (9.116–17).
56. 20 April 1669 (9.527–29).
57. 2 September 1666 (7.267–72).
58. 27 December 1668 (9.401–3).
59. 19 March 1669 (9.487–89).
60. 11 October 1668 (9.325) and 7 October 1667 (8.465–67).
61. 19 June 1667 (8.278–80).
62. 17 October 1660 (1.267–68), 24 November 1660 (1.301–2), 5 March 1662 (3.41), 24 August 1663 (4.285–86), 27 August 1663 (4.289–90), 30 January 1665 (6.25), 12 May 1665 (6.100–101), 11 Sept 1666 (7.284), 20 September 1666 (7.291–92), 18 January 1667 (9.18–20), 16 November 1668 (9.364–65).
63. 20 and 21 September 1666 (7.291–92).
64. 24 June 1667 (8.286–89).
65. 30 July 1667 (8.367–69).
66. 28 November 1666 (7.389), 18 February 1667 (8.71), and 20 June 1667 (8.280–81).
67. 12 March 1669 (9.479–81).
68. 30 June 1662 (3.126) and 9 July 1662 (3.134–35). Here "Griffen's girl" refers to a young woman in the service of William Griffith, the housekeeper and doorkeeper for the navy offices at Seething Lane, whom Pepys sometimes misnames throughout the *Diary*.
69. See 10 August 1662 (2.161–62), 6 March 1664 (5.77), 30 May 1665 (6.111–12), 25 June 1665 (6.138–39), 1 December 1665 (6.315–18), 27 August 1666 (7.261–62), 28 August 1666 (7.262–63), 21 October 1666 (7.335–37), 24 November 1666 (7.381–82), 15 March 1667 (8.113–14), 22 March 1668 (9.126–27), and 9 January 1669 (9.410–11).
70. 10 August 1662 (2.161–62).
71. 2 September 1666 (7.267)

Chapter 1: The Way In

1. Mark Girouard, *Life in the English Country House: A Social and Architectural History* (New Haven, CT: Yale, 1993), 56. Reproduced with permission of Yale Representation Limited through PLS Clear.

2. 19 January 1663 (4.17–19).
3. This is the first of three definitions contributed to *Urban Dictionary,* s.v. "intimate, *adj.*" by suburban scum on 4 June 2005.
4. See definition 1a in *Oxford English Dictionary*, s.v. "drawing-room, *n.1*"; and McKeon, *Secret History of Domesticity*, 228.
5. Stone, *Family, Sex, and Marriage,* 8 and 395.
6. Ware, *Complete Body of Architecture*, 327–28.
7. Quoted in Wall, *Prose of Things*, 89.
8. *Oxford English Dictionary*, s.v. "cabinet, *n.*"
9. Girouard, *Country House*, 174. Throughout this book, *closet* refers to a room and *cabinet* refers to a chest of drawers unless otherwise indicated.
10. Pominan, *Collectors and Curiosities*, 9.
11. Stewart, *On Longing*, 157.
12. Ibid., 162.
13. Mauriès, *Cabinets of Curiosities*, 156.
14. Benedict, *Curiosity*, 10.
15. Brewer, *Pleasures of the Imagination*, 254–55.
16. 15 April 1666 (7.99).
17. Edson, "'A Closet or a Secret Field,'" 22.
18. Rambuss, *Closet Devotions*, 109.
19. Clery, *Feminization Debate*, 134. See also Folkenflik, "A Room of Pamela's Own," 585–96.
20. Girouard, *Country House*, 174.
21. Hackel, "The Countess of Bridgewater's London Library," 142.
22. See, for example, Burroughs, "'Hymen's Monkey Love'"; Raber, *Dramatic Difference*; Saggini, "Eighteenth-Century Actress between Stage and Closet"; and Straznicky, *Women's Closet Drama.*
23. Laqueur, *Solitary Sex*, 343.
24. See Girouard, *Country House*, 150.
25. Poovey, *History of the Modern Fact*, 37, quoted in Chico, "Privacy," 41–42. See also Chico, *Designing Women*, 66–69.
26. Chico, "Privacy," 41–42.
27. Chico, *Designing Women*, 44 (original italics).
28. Ibid., 197.
29. Benedict, *Curiosity*, 142–43.
30. Richardson, *Pamela*, 77–82. J. W. Fisher, "'Closet-work'," 21–37, shows how the closet setting contributes to the implied sexual violence of Mr B's voyeurism.
31. Brown, "The Female *Philosophe*," 98.
32. McKeon, *Secret History of Domesticity*, 660–72.
33. Crary, *Techniques of the Observer*, 29.
34. Lyons, "Camera Obscura," 179–95.
35. Locke, *Human Understanding*, 2.11.17, 163.
36. Ibid., 1.2.15, 55.
37. Pasanek, "Rooms," *Metaphors of Mind*. A search of Pasanek's online database returns more than fifty instances of closet or cabinet as a metaphor for the mind from the long eighteenth century. See also Silver, "Case 1. Metaphor" and "Case 2. Design," in *Mind Is a Collection.*
38. Wright, *Clean and Decent*, 118.
39. Klein, "Gender and the Public/Private Distinction," 104.
40. Spacks, *Privacy*, 167.
41. Spacks, *Privacy*, 21, is summing up philosophies by Charles Fried, Robert Gerstein, Jeffrey Reiman, Ruth Gavison, and Julie Inness here.
42. Ibid., 24.
43. Perry, *Literature and Favoritism*, 18.
44. Girouard, *Country House*, 110.

45. Ibid., 128.
46. Ibid., 131.
47. Ibid., 128.
48. Ibid., 149.
49. King, *Gendering of Men*, 5.
50. Girouard, *Country House*, 146.
51. Pominan, *Collectors and Curiosities*, 9.
52. Loveman, *Books*, 258.
53. Ffolliott, *Women Patrons and Collectors*, xxvii.
54. Bleichmar, "Seeing the World in a Room," 30.
55. Brewer, *Pleasures*, 257, also remarks that not all such invitations were accepted: the author and publisher Horace Walpole, though an aristocrat and noted collector and connoisseur of antiques, refused to join the Society of Dilettanti, which had formed in 1734, commenting that "the nominal qualification for membership is having been in Italy, and the real one, being drunk." See also Redford, *Dilettanti*.
56. Recent studies of the rise of the museum by James Delbourgo, Peter Mancall, and others retrospectively detail the global human costs of seventeenth- and eighteenth-century collecting practices that led to the English appropriation and exhibition of not only of objects, plants, and animals but also people from around the world. As Barbara Benedict, "Collecting Trouble," observes of the British Museum, such display was intended to produce a positive, shared national identity in museumgoers and improve the standing of the museum's founder, in particular. See Purinton, "Pseudoscience of Curiosity Cabinets," for an account of how some smaller curiosity cabinets also transformed "from private, amateur collections into public, professional demonstrations" throughout this period (250).
57. Taylor, *Modern Social Imaginaries*, 25–26.
58. Locke, *Two Treatises*, 2.8.95, 330.
59. On pleasure gardens, see Ogborn, *Spaces of Modernity*, 116–57. On libraries, see Brewer, *Pleasures of the Imagination*, 148–56. On masquerades, see Castle, *Masquerade and Civilization*. On coffee houses, see Cowan, *Social Life of Coffee* and Ellis, *Coffee House*.
60. Love, "Early Modern Print Culture," 75–76.
61. Habermas, *Structural Transformation*.
62. Ibid., 47.
63. Ibid., 50. See also Anderson, *Imagined Communities*.
64. Habermas, *Structural Transformation*, 50–51.
65. Siskin and Warner, *This Is Enlightenment*, 23, 11.
66. Sterne, *Audible Past*, 8.
67. Siskin and Warner, *This Is Enlightenment*, 23.
68. Taylor, *Modern Social Imaginaries*, 13.
69. Habermas, *Structural Transformation*, 47.
70. For discussions of Habermas's implicit centering of white, cisgendered, straight masculinity, see Fraser, "Rethinking the Public Sphere"; Warner, *Publics and Counterpublics*, 65–124; and Berlant, *Cruel Optimism*, 33–34.

FAVOR

1. 7 October 1660 (1.260–61). *Diary* editors Latham and Matthews, 261, note that much of this rumor "is fabrication. Anne Hyde had secretly married the Duke at her father's house on 3 September; a son was born on 22 October. The Duke had entered a contract of marriage in November 1659." The public acknowledgement of the marriage is recorded in the *Diary* entry for 21 December 1660 (1.320).
2. 17 November 1667 (8.535). For a detailed account of Clarendon's downfall and the rise of the cabal, see Kenyon, *Stuarts*, 117. The term *cabal* derived from the Jewish mystical

interpretation of the Old Testament, the *Kabbalah*, but was also an acronym for its members: Clifford, Arlington, Buckingham, Ashley-Cooper, and Lauderdale. Political historians now view this cabal as an interim structure somewhere between a group of favorites and an officially appointed cabinet of ministers.

3. 26 March 1666 (7.83).
4. 31 December 1665 (6.342).
5. 26 April 1667 (8.181–87). Both Arlington and Clifford would soon become members of Charles's cabal.
6. 23 September 1667 (8.447).
7. 25 May 1660 (1.157).
8. 26 July 1665 (6.170)
9. 1 November 1665 (6.285).
10. 19 December 1665 (6.333).
11. 20 December 1665 (6.334–35).
12. 21 December 1665 (6.335–36).
13. 15 September 1668 (9.306–7).
14. 25 March 1668 (9.131–33).
15. 21 April 1660 (1.113) and 14 November 1660 (1.292).
16. 17 September 1664 (5.273).
17. 18 September 1664 (5.274).

CHAPTER 2: THE DUCHESS OF YORK'S BATHING CLOSET

1. Antoine Varillas, *Anekdota Herouiaka, or the Secret History of the House of Medicis*, trans. F. Spence (London: 1686), quoted in Rebecca Bullard, *Politics of Disclosure, 1674–1725* (London: Pickering & Chatto, 2009), 1. Reproduced with permission of Cambridge University Press through PLS Clear.
2. Northrup Frye wrote this comment in the margins of the bathing-closet scene in his copy of Anthony Hamilton's *Memoirs of the Court of Charles the Second*, ed. Walter Scott (London: Henry G. Bohn, 1859), Annotated no. 121, E.J. Pratt Library, Victoria University, University of Toronto, 230. Courtesy of Victory University Library (Toronto).
3. Bridget MacAuliffe (@bfrances15), Twitter, March 18, 2019. MacAuliffe refers to Yorgos Lanthimos's 2018 film *The Favourite*, about how Queen Anne came to prefer the Tory Abigail Hill, later Baroness of Masham, over her cousin, the Whig Sarah Churchill, the Duchess of Marlborough, who had long been her favorite.
4. Castle, *Lesbianism*, 36.
5. Like David Onnekink in "Re-emergence of the English Favourite," 693, this chapter emphasizes "the continuity of favouritism in English politics."
6. Elliott, "Introduction," *World of the Favourite*, 1.
7. Feros, "Royal Favourite and the Prime Minister," 206.
8. Bray, *Friend*, 8.
9. Wootton, "Francis Bacon," 189.
10. Bacon, "Of Followers and Friends," 6, quoted in Wootton, "Francis Bacon," 195.
11. Wootton, "Francis Bacon," 191.
12. Tadmor, *Family and Friends*, 236.
13. Perry, *Literature and Favoritism*, 10.
14. Elliott, *World of the Favourite*, 7.
15. Perry, *Literature of Favoritism*, 5.
16. Ibid., 3.
17. Bray, *Friend*, 218.
18. King, *Gendering of Men*, 5. For a discussion of the feelings in politicized friendships between men, see Haggerty, *Men in Love,* especially "Heroic Friendships," 23–43.

19. Cecil, *Secretorie of Estates Place*, quoted in Stewart, *Close Readers*, 176. Cecil further advises that an administrative confidant needs to have been "of his own making" rather than indebted to another master for his training.
20. Day, *English Secretorie*, quoted in Stewart, *Close Readers*, 171.
21. Stewart, *Close Readers*, 185.
22. For an account of the eighteenth-century invention of the secretary as a new type of desk, in which papers and the writing surface itself could be hidden, see Goodman, "The *Secrétaire*."
23. Rambuss, *Closet Devotions*, 135.
24. Brooks, *Privie Key of Heaven*, 70.
25. Ibid., 460.
26. See, for example, Bray, *Homosexuality in Renaissance England*, 13–32.
27. Marlowe, *Edward the Second*, 1.4.401, quoted in Perry, *Literature and Favoritism*, 197.
28. Perry, *Literature and Favoritism*, 133.
29. According to Ruth Clark, *Anthony Hamilton*, 202–3, Hamilton began composing his "Mémoires de Grammont" in 1704 or 1705, and finished the bulk of the manuscript before Grammont's death in 1707.
30. See Weil, *Political Passions*, 162–230.
31. Bucholz, *Augustan Court*, 247–48.
32. Ibid., 12.
33. Hamilton, *Memoirs of the Court of Charles the Second*, 36. Though all references to Hamilton's book are from Walter Scott's edition, the more common title, *Memoirs of Count Grammont*, is used here.
34. Hamilton, *Memoirs*, 100.
35. Ibid., 101.
36. Ibid., 102.
37. While Hamilton's portrait of the king as a self-indulgent maker of favorites is quite similar in substance to Pepys's, it leans in the opposite political direction, underscoring the need for a more rigorous embodiment of divine right.
38. Ibid., 106.
39. Ibid., 107.
40. Ibid., 105. Clark, *Anthony Hamilton*, 217, stresses that Hamilton attributes the positive assessment of James to the Court. He is doing due diligence in his portrait of the Duke of York, Clark suggests: Jacobite on principle, Hamilton is largely unimpressed by the man himself.
41. The identity of the protagonist of this episode is a bit of a mystery. In the original French edition of *Mémoires de la Vie du Comte de Grammont, contenant particulièrement l'Histoire Amoureuse de la Cour d'Angleterre sous le Regne du Roi Charles II* published in 1713, the Duchess of York's favorite is named Mademoiselle Hubert. The original 1714 English translation by Abel Boyer, a *roman à clef*, represents this character as "Miss H——t," and the key to this English edition, published in 1715, identifies her as "Mrs. Hobart" (8), while the 1719 English edition specifies "Mrs Hobart, sister to Sir John Hobart of Norfolk," who was a baronet and member of Parliament. Without naming them, Frederic Barlow in his *Complete English Peerage* (Vol. 2), 45, mentions that this Sir John Hobart had two sisters: "the eldest was married to Sir Charles Pye … ; but the other died unmarried." However, according to James William Johnson, *Profane Wit*, 87, the historical "Miss Hobart," who got between Rochester and Anne Temple, was in fact Dorothy Howard, later libeled in a verse of his "Signor Dildo." In the entry for 4 March 1669 of his *Diary* (9.468–69), Pepys enjoys dining with Dorothy Howard and two of the Duchess of York's other maids of honor, drinks excellent wine, "more then I have drank at once these seven years," and, like Hamilton, finds the Duchess of York "very witty."
42. Hamilton, *Memoirs*, 221.
43. Ibid., 226–27.

44. Ibid., 228.
45. Ibid., 233.
46. Ibid., 241.
47. Ibid., 243.
48. The literary historians of sexuality who have been most attentive to the Hobart-Temple episode are: Andreadis, *Sappho*, 167–70; Castle, *Lesbianism*, 219–20; Donoghue, *Passions between Women*, 53–54, 187–90; Robinson, *Closeted Writing*, 28, 136–38, 153–55, 159; and Wahl, *Invisible Relations*, 215–17, all of which are discussed further below. Other recent criticism of this memoir includes Gervey, "Un récit émancipé," 127–150; and Love, "Hamilton's *Memoirs*," 95–102. Other studies of intimacies between elite women of the eighteenth century include Herbert, *Female Alliances*; and Mills, "'To be both Patroness and Friend.'" Dealing with a later period, Marcus, *Between Women*, identifies and corrects a tendency among cultural historians to occlude or find troubling the mingling of female friendship with sexual and political interests.
49. Andreadis, *Sappho*, 169.
50. Wahl, *Invisible*, 215.
51. Donoghue, *Passions*, 25 and 54. Large genitals, whether fully functioning penises, prolapsed vaginas, or penis-like clitorises that grew erect when aroused, were represented as both primary cause and symptom of women's homoerotic passions.
52. Robinson, *Closeted*, 137.
53. Eve Sedgwick, *Epistemology of the Closet*, 5. Sedgwick is particularly important to Robinson, *Closeted*, whose book argues that the misleading oppositions now embodied in the figure of the closet, between knowledge and visibility, on the one hand, and ignorance, secrecy, and invisibility, on the other, have been continuous features of Western discourses of homoeroticism since the ancients.
54. Hamilton, *Memoirs*, 191.
55. Ibid., 192.
56. Ibid., 193.
57. Ibid., 167.
58. Ibid., 268.
59. Ibid., 147–48.
60. Ibid., 263.
61. Ibid., 110.
62. Stewart, *Close Readers*, 174.
63. Hamilton, *Memoirs*, 273.
64. Ibid., 274–75.
65. Ibid., 275. Astell, *Reflections upon Marriage*, 102. See Gallagher, "Embracing the Absolute"; and McKeon, *Secret History of Domesticity*, 147–55, for arguments about how Astell draws on absolutist sovereignty in her model of female autonomy in particular. For a different account of Astell's incipient feminism, see Helen Thompson, *Ingenuous Subjection*, and her penetrating review of *Secret History of Domesticity*, "The Personal Is Political."
66. While the original print publication gives "Roxelane" as the duped actress's role, Abel Boyer changed it to "Roxana," but subsequent translations used Roxolana, the English spelling of "Roxelane." In an article on the historical events leading to this scandal, John Harold Wilson, "Lord Oxford's 'Roxolana,'" 14, names Hester Davenport as the leading performer who "left the stage to live with Lord Oxford." Roxana, first wife of Alexander the Great, was best known to later Restoration audiences through Nathaniel Lee's 1677 tragedy *The Rival Queens*, whereas Roxolana, first wife of Solyman the Magnificent, is the heroine of *Siege of Rhodes*, William Davenant's two-part heroic drama (also credited as the first English operetta), whose first performances roughly coincide with the period chronicled in the *Memoirs*. A telling point of connection between both Eastern queens is their eroticized jealousy of female rivals. In the epilogue to *The Rival Queens*, Lee recalls the Roxolana episode, generalizing it to be the condition of all actresses to be "Charmed with the noise of sett'ling an estate." See especially lines 28–33.

67. Hamilton, *Memoirs*, 275–77.

68. Baine, "Roxana's Georgian Setting," 465, remarks that this anecdote about the Roxolana actress's sham marriage "was widely circulated in various versions." Before Hamilton's *Memoirs*, it appears in D'Aulnoy, *Memoirs of the Court of England*, 439–49. A roughly contemporaneous episode alluding to the Eastern queen appears in Manley, *New Atalantis* (Vol. 1), 65–103. This early modern tale of sexual bargaining almost certainly played a role in the development of the plots of *Roxana; or, the Fortunate Mistress* and perhaps also of *Pamela*. As Frye speculates in his marginalia in the *Memoirs*, 231: "source for Richardson?" "source for Defoe?"

69. See Nussbaum, *Torrid Zones*, 34, and notes. For an overview of the intricate connections between English and Eastern forms and themes through the long eighteenth century, see Ballaster, *Fabulous Orients*. For Ballaster's discussions of this composite figure in particular, see "Roxolana: The Loquacious Courtesan," 59–70, and her article "Performing *Roxane*."

70. Knolles, *Generall historie of the Turkes*, 719–67.

71. Croutier, *Harem*, 105, remarks that this new proximity of the harem and the sultan's quarters in the Ottoman capital "marked the beginning of the Sultanate, or the Reign of Women, which lasted a century and a half."

72. In the words of another seventeenth-century Eastern queen character, in Racine's tragedy *Bajazet*, 1.3, 11, sultans had "made themselves a vaunted law / Not to restrain their loves with marriage vows."

73. As seventeenth-century English historian and diplomat Paul Rycault, *Present State*, 155, understands it, sultans generally "take no feminine companion of their Empire in whom they may be more concerned than in Slaves" because, they believe, were the custom of marriage in use "the chief Revenue of the Empire would be expended in the Chambers of Women, and diverted from the true Channels in which the Treasure ought to run for nourishment of the Politick body of the Common-wealth."

74. Hamilton, *Memoirs*, 276.

75. Ibid., 278.

76. Dobie, "Orientalism, Colonialism, and Furniture," 16.

77. Girouard, *Country House*, 250, hails Royal Society engineer Samuel Morland as "the great maestro of water supply in the reign of Charles II."

78. Thurley, *Whitehall Palace Plan*, 43.

79. Ibid., 34.

80. 21 February 1665 (6.40) Also cited in Wright, *Clean and Decent*, 76, who notes that Pepys "only once mentions his wife having a bath."

81. Hamilton, *Memoirs*, 228.

82. Revel et al., "Forms of Privatization," 184 and 189.

83. Rycault, *Ottoman Empire*, 29; and Herbert, *Female Alliances*, 55–62.

84. Dobie, "Orientalism, Colonialism, and Furniture," 16.

85. Bon, *Seraglio*, 37–38.

86. Yeazel, *Harems of the Mind*, 1–2.

87. Rycault, *Present State*, 38.

88. For other accounts of Turkey and the Muslim East specifically as sites of queer projection, see Lanser, *Sexuality of History*, 88–93.

89. Bon, *Seraglio*, 32–33; Le Stourgeon, "Description of the Turkish Empire," 238; Rycault, *Present State*, 31.

90. Melman, *Women's Orients*, 89. In her first-hand account in her *Turkish Embassy Letters*, 58–59, Mary Wortley Montagu fights against the usual terminal point of the associative slide from Eastern interiors to unranked homosociality to queer promiscuity exemplified in Busbecq's *Embassy into Turkey*: "The first sofas were covered with cushions and rich carpets, on which sat the ladies, and on the second their slaves behind them, but without any distinction of rank by their dress, all being *in the state of nature*, that is, in plain English, stark naked, without any beauty or defect concealed. Yet there was not the least

wanton smile or immodest gesture amongst them." For a fuller sense of the range of European engagements with Eastern female sexuality, including feminist counternarratives to the exploitative patterns described here, see Lewis, *Gendering Orientalism,* especially 180–83.

91. Busbecq, *Embassy into Turkey,* quoted in Andreadis, *Sappho,* 4.

92. Sandys, *Desscription of the Turkish Empire,* 69, quoted in Yeazel, *Harems,* 19.

93. See, for instance, Bacon's warnings against hot water in *History of Life and Death,* 390, and *Uninterrupted health to extreme old age,* 149–59, 152.

94. Manley, *New Atalantis,* 102–4. For an account of the historical relationship this episode is meant to allegorize, see Sachse, *Lord Somers,* 68.

95. Hamilton, *Les Quatre Facardins,* 329–30.

96. Perry, *Literature of Favoritism,* 4.

97. As Wilson, *Absolutism in Central Europe,* 51, puts it, "under absolutism, the concept of secrecy had become morally neutral, far removed from its earlier association with deceit." Quoted in Bullard, *Politics of Disclosure,* 6.

98. Keating, "In the Bedroom," 59.

99. Bullard, *Politics of Disclosure,* 6–7. Bullard's introduction to *Secret History in Literature,* 1–16, also plays up the progressive orientation of the form in late seventeenth- and early eighteenth-century England: "Against the secrecy and silence of arbitrary power, secret history pits the publicity and populism of print" (4). However, she also explores the political lability of the secret history as the century draws on (*Politics of Disclosure,* 22–24; *Secret History in Literature,* 11). For a summary of the differences between historians' and literary scholars' recent approaches to the genre, see Cowan's review essay "History of Secret Histories."

100. Hamilton, *Memoirs,* 35.

101. See ibid., 104, 128, and 147–48.

102. Clark, *Anthony Hamilton,* 203.

103. Except for the *Memoirs,* none of Hamilton's writings, which included poetry and several *contes* (fairy tales and parodies of Oriental tales) appeared in print during his lifetime. For a list of the various English and European translations of *Memoirs,* see Clark, *Anthony Hamilton,* 313–36.

104. Clark, *Anthony Hamilton,* 206.

105. McKeon, *Secret History of Domesticity,* 472.

106. Hamilton, *Memoirs,* 137–38 and 124; 230–31; 139.

107. McKeon, *Secret History of Domesticity,* 472.

108. Habermas, *Structural Transformation,* 49–51; Armstrong, *Desire and Domestic Fiction,* 116–42; Warner, *Licensing Entertainment,* 176–231; McKeon, *Secret History of Domesticity,* 639–59.

109. See especially McKeon, *Secret History of Domesticity,* 658: "Richardson's novel labors to show … that if a wife continues to be in some sense a servant, her work may also be clearly distinguished from domestic service by the fact of its comparatively 'public' status as both an actual and a virtual mode of 'government.'"

110. See Lanser, *Sexuality of History,* 146–92, for an extensive argument about "how the struggle the novel enacts over the place of female agency in the social order turns out to be imbricated with the sapphic" (148).

HOUSES OF OFFICE

1. Annotations on the Diary of Samuel Pepys website refer to typical sizes of houses of office as estimated in the *Historical Gazetteer of London before the Great Fire Cheapside.*

2. 13 October 1663 (4.332–33).

3. 25 May 1663 (4.154–57).

4. 25 September 1662 (3.205).
5. 25 May 1660 (1.158).
6. 21 December 1664 (5.352).
7. 20 October 1660 (1.269).
8. 7 July 1663 (4.220).
9. 16 July 1663 (4.233).
10. 28 July 1663 (4.252).
11. 8 September 1662 (3.192).
12. 30 April 1666 (7.113).
13. 6 December 1667 (8.565–66).
14. 29 August 1660 (1.233).
15. 13 June 1667 (8.263).

CHAPTER 3: LADY ACHESON'S PRIVY FOR TWO

1. Dustin Griffin, *Literary Patronage in England, 1650–1800* (New York: Cambridge University Press, 1996), 30. Reproduced with permission of Cambridge University Press through PLS Clear.
2. Girouard, *A Country House Companion*, 167.
3. Douglas, *Purity and Danger*, 35. Douglas elaborates this principle, which informs her cultural anthropological study as a whole: "The only way in which pollution ideas make sense is in reference to a total structure of thought whose key-stone, boundaries, margins and internal lines are held in relation by rituals of separation" (41).
4. Swift visited Market Hill three times: from 1728–29, 1729, and 1730. Irvin Ehrenpreis, *Swift*, 669, casts some doubt on the assumption that the poem was written and the privies built in 1730: "In [line] 204 we are told that Swift built the privies in twenty weeks— the sort of fact he was not likely to invent. But he did not stay so long at Market Hill in 1730." Market Hill was destroyed by fire in around 1805 and rebuilt in a neo-Norman style as Gosford Castle later in the century.
5. The scatological poetry, as this group has come to be known, was preceded by a few striking prose treatments of this theme, including in *A Tale of a Tub* (1704) and *Gulliver's Travels* (1726). Of all Swift's works, "Panegyric" treats the excretory setting most extensively.
6. Brown's *Life against Death*, 179–201, renewed critical interest in Swift's "excremental vision," defending it in Freudian terms from those who, like John Middleton Murray, author of that lasting phrase, pathologized it and him.
7. Fabricant, *Swift's Landscape*, 36, does not consider the poem's engagement with material history of excremental privacy, however the book as a whole offers (and inspires) geographically attuned criticism, which Fabricant sees as particularly apt for studies of Swift's scatology: "Excrement ... was very much a fact of life for Swift; his landscape was literally as well as linguistically full of it" (30).
8. Zimmerman, "Swift's Scatological Poetry," 137.
9. Anspaugh, "Reading the Intertext," 27. Anspaugh's essay, which provides an overview of critical approaches to Swift's scatology and of the influence on Swift of England's original privy designer, John Harington, has significantly informed this chapter. Equally attentive to the importance to Swift of the material culture of excretion is Blackwell, "The Two Jonathans," who argues that the outhouse manifests Swift's ambivalent desire for poetic posterity.
10. Bogel, *Difference Satire Makes*, 115.
11. Gee, *Making Waste*, 103.
12. Smith, *Between Two Stools*, 198.
13. Wright, *Clean and Decent*, 24.

14. Alan Corbin, *The Foul and the Fragrant*, shows how scientists' surveys of city smells in the eighteenth century led to "the great dream of disinfection" (231) in the nineteenth.

15. Davies, *The Ancient Rites*, 134–35, quoted in Wright, *Clean and Decent*, 30.

16. Wright, *Clean and Decent*, 49.

17. Girouard, *Country House*, 247.

18. Cited without attribution in Wright, *Clean and Decent*, 32, whose acknowledgments, xi, list numerous primary and secondary sources from which his account of monastic sanitation has developed.

19. Girouard, *Country House*, 57–58.

20. Wright, *Clean and Decent*, 71; Palmer, *Water Closet*, 26; and Donno's introduction to the *Metamorphosis*, 18, concur on this point.

21. Harington, *Metamorphosis*, 30. Written during one of the many periods when Queen Elizabeth's "saucy Godson" fell out of her favor, the *Metamorphosis* is also considered a veiled attack on the monarchy.

22. In her introduction to *Metamorphosis*, 11–12, Donno argues that Thomas Combe, a translator in Harington's service, was responsible for the *Anatomie*, which consists in a preface, two pages of illustrations, and a short apology. Combe, *Anatomie*, in Harington, *Metamorphosis*, 192.

23. Combe, *Anatomie*, in Harington, *Metamorphosis*, 194, 196.

24. Donno's introduction points out that the "encomium on a trivial or unworthy subject" "had had a long vogue, dating back to the Greek rhetoricians, and it received a new infusion of vitality during the Renaissance through the efforts of the humanists" (18).

25. Donno represents this masquerade as more game-playing than anything else since "numerous biographical and personal allusions in the work and the rebus on his name [included in the text] proclaim his authorship" (11). See also Pastor, "Epistemology of the Water Closet."

26. Harington, *Metamorphosis*, 57.

27. Ibid., 113.

28. Palladio, *Four Books of Architecture*, 38.

29. Fiennes, *Through England*, 307; Swift, *Mechanical Operations*, 157.

30. Quoted in Palmer, *Water Closet*, 38.

31. Roy Palmer, *Water Closet*, 25, cites the 1907 Act of Parliament, in which *water closet* was first defined in law, pointing out that many people in Britain had to wait for many more decades to have one: "The expression 'water closet' means closet accommodation used or adapted or intended to be used in connection with the water carriage system, and comprising provision for the flushing of the receptacle by means of a fresh water supply, and having proper communication with a sewer."

32. Girouard, *Country House*, 255–56.

33. Wright, *Clean and Decent*, 103. All the following reactions to the novelty of indoor closets of ease come from Wright, 103–4.

34. Aubrey, *Natural History*, 160.

35. Walpole, Letter 18, 27 March 1760, *Letters of Horace Walpole* (Vol. 3).

36. Fabricant, *Landscape*, 41.

37. Bray, *Friendship*, 210.

38. Swift, *Directions to Servants*, 764–65.

39. Girouard, *Country House*, 256.

40. Ibid.

41. Here the chapter follows Swift's practice in referring to the poem's speaker as Lady Anne, while the historical figure, who married into her title, is called Lady Acheson.

42. Swift, "Panegyric on the Dean in the Person of a Lady of the North," 436–44, lines 1, 5–6. Line numbers will appear in parentheses directly following all further citations of this poem.

43. Wright, *Clean and Decent*, 103. For an extensive rebuttal to this history, see Carter, "Sexism in the 'Bathroom Debates.'"

44. Swift, *Mechanical Operations*, 153–54.
45. Harington, *Metamorphosis*, 94.
46. Ibid., 94. See ibid., 92, for a discussion about how "a good stoole" may be more moving than a "bad sermon."
47. Dawes, *Duties of the Closet*, 17.
48. Brooks, *Privie Key of Heaven*, 8.
49. Harington, *Metamorphosis*, 184.
50. Ibid., 186.
51. Brooks, *Privie Key of Heaven*, 6.
52. Edson, "'Closet or a Secret Field,'" 17–18. Closets and cabinets were also featured as sites of noble learning and collecting in conventional seventeenth-century country house poems. See Preston, "Counsel of Herbs," for a discussion of George Mackenzie's "Caelia's Country-House and Closet," for instance, in which "the entire Carnegie estate ... is depicted as an Edenic cabinet, where all the natural features in the grounds and gardens are displayed as 'curious.' ... The green garden cabinet ... gives way to Anna Lady Carnegie's own closet of natural and artificial collections, and this interior tour is the core of the poem" (122).
53. For a description of Harington's diligence in closet prayer, see Rambuss, *Closet Devotions*, 119–20. In his *Works of Jonathan Swift,* Walter Scott draws on Patrick Delaney's first-person account of the regularity and discretion of Swift's private spiritual practices: "The place which he occupied as an oratory was a small closet, in which, when his situation required to be in some degree watched, he was daily observed to pray with great devotion. When his faculties, and particularly his memory, began to fail, he used often to enquire whether he had been in this apartment in the day, and if answered in the affirmative, to be delivered from the apprehension that he had neglected the duties of devotion" (396).
54. Quoted in Scott, *Jonathan Swift*, 398.
55. The iron age depicted in "Panegyric" recalls Book 2 of Pope's *Dunciad*, 321–38, lines 83–94, where Jove, sprawled on a privy seat, wipes himself with pages torn from Grub Street books and hands them to Cloacina.
56. The *Oxford English Dictionary* explains that *botargo*, like *caveer* (caviar), is fish roe, while *catsup* was in the early eighteenth century a kind of fish sauce originating in China.
57. Harington, *Metamorphosis*, 92.
58. Lady Anne blames the privy for the discord between minds and bodies "in our degenerate days." When "nature prompts," we do not always do its bidding because we worry about finding a suitably secluded place to go. In *Some Thoughts Concerning Education*, 1.1.27, 24, by contrast, John Locke presents the privy as a place where nature may in fact be disciplined.
59. Swift, "Lady's Dressing-Room," *Complete Poems*, 448–52, line 118.
60. Swift, "Dressing-Room," lines 2, 76–78.
61. In his *Philosophical Dialogue* (discussed below), 43, Samuel Rolleston links the decline of ancient civilizations to the use of ostentatious vessels like the duchess's: "It would have been well both for the Greeks and Romans if they had but remain'd contented with these earthen *Jurdens*—We may date the commencement of the ruin of both from the introduction of gold and silver chamber-pots, and closestool pans."
62. The short final stanza of "Panegyric," in which "Sleek — claims [Cloacina] as his right" (343–44), has stumped critics. Pat Rogers, *Complete Poems*, endnote for line 344, 824, believes that "the blank is impossible to fill in." For a discussion of how the poem's conclusion contributes to Swift's battle in verse with Dean Jonathan Smedley, see Blackwell, "Two Jonathans."
63. According to Zimmerman, "Scatological," the poem's instability, like that of Erasmus's *Praise of Folly*, stems from the paradox upon which it is founded: the content (shit) continually undermines the form (encomium).

64. The full title page of Rolleston's treatise reads: *A Philosophical Dialogue Concerning Decency. To which is added, A Critical and Historical Dissertation on Places of Retirement for necessary Occasions, Together With an Account of the Vessels and Utensils in use amongst the Ancients, being a Lecture read before a Society of learned Antiquaries.*
65. Ibid., 25.
66. Ibid., 28.
67. Ibid., 3.
68. Ibid., 10.
69. Ibid., 11.
70. Ibid., 10.
71. Philoprepon may still be musing on the Mossynians, a people "from somewhere in Asia," as Eutrapelus recalls, who, in addition to defecating and urinating "were us'd to copulate in the publick streets without any manner of ceremony" (ibid., 5).
72. Fowler, "Country House Poetry," 5; Virgil, *Georgics* I.
73. See Karian, *Jonathan Swift*, 1–8.
74. See especially the introduction of Griffin, *Literary Patronage*, 1–12.
75. Griffin, *Literary Patronage*, 23.
76. Ibid., 19.
77. Griffin, *Literary Patronage*, suggests that "the period is characterized by overlapping 'economies' of patronage *and* marketplace" (10) and, moreover, that this bivalent system had always been "a site of contestation, as authors and patrons, later joined by booksellers and critical reviewers, jockeyed for position and for authority" (9).
78. Ibid., 99–122.
79. Swift, *Gulliver's Travels*, 33–34. Discussed in Griffin, *Literary Patronage*, 115–16.
80. Griffin, *Literary Patronage*, 116. See also Hammond and Seager, "Swift the (Tor)mentor," 63.
81. Swift, "Libel on Dr Delaney," lines 21–26, quoted in Griffin, *Literary Patronage*, 119. Griffin calls the "Panegyric" "a bizarre fantasy about the reciprocal benefits of patronage, and the patron's (rather than the client's) desire to 'make suitable Returns,' or to even the account" (118).
82. Schakel, "Swift's Voices," 313–16.
83. Rogers, *Complete Poems*, 822.
84. In *Literary Patronage*, Griffin also comments on the double inflection of this passage: "When she declares that 'the World shall know' of her 'Gratitude,' one hears the conventional accents of the grateful dependent, but also perhaps Swift's proud and embittered determination (projected onto innocent Lady Acheson) to publish the truth about an intimate patron-client relationship" (117–18).
85. Girouard, *Country House*, 23. See also Williams, *Country and the City*, especially chapters 3 through 10.
86. Hibbard, "Country House Poem," 160.
87. Though more recently Fowler, "Country House Poems," 11, cautions against exaggerating the importance of architectural space within this early modern form, he too stresses that "in its portrayal of eating arrangements, the estate poem's idealization is particularly evident."
88. Jonson, "To Penshurst," lines 67–70.
89. Herrick, "Panegyrick to Sir Lewis Pemberton," lines 59–70.
90. Fabricant, *Landscape*, 161.
91. Swift to Pope, 29 October 1729, *Correspondence of Pope*, iii, 65, quoted in Blackwell, "Two Jonathans," 131. Blackwell argues that Swift's ambivalence about Drapier's Hill mirrors his ambivalence about his own poetic authority: "On the one hand, Swift longed for the monumental distinction that would differentiate him from pretenders to poetry.... On the other hand, [he] heaped scorn upon writers too confident in the expectation that their works would [last]."
92. Fabricant, *Landscape,* 119.

93. Hamilton, *Memoirs*, 193.
94. Harington, *Metamorphosis*, 98.
95. Ibid., 90.
96. Harington concludes: "And for other good fellowships I doubt not, but from the beginning it hath often happened, that some of the Nymphes of this gentle goddesse [Cloacina], have met so luckily with some of her devout chaplens, in her chappels of ease, and payd their privie tithes so duly, and done their service together with such devotion; that for reward she hath preferred them with fortie weeks after to *Juno Lucina*" (92).
97. Ibid., 91.
98. In Rolleston's *Concerning Decency*, 5, Eutrapelus suggests that the conduct of Harington's French ambassador is typical for Venetians: "They esteem it a part of noble liberty to discharge where and before whom they please." Interestingly, in this later characterization, the act expresses aggressive indifference to inferiors rather than temporary social leveling.
99. Jaffe, "Swift," 131, calculates that Lady Acheson was likely about twenty-five years younger than Swift. Both Jaffe and Ehrenpreis, *Swift*, 685, concur that the fact that Swift met the Achesons around the time Stella died shaped his relationship to Lady Acheson: "The first, longest visit to Market Hill, which only ended a year after he lost Stella, allowed him to transfer many feelings to Lady Acheson." For other excellent accounts of their relationship and the poetry representing it, see Mueller, "Imperfect Enjoyment at Market Hill"; and Hammond and Seager, "Swift the (Tor)mentor."
100. Ehrenpreis, *Swift*, 604.
101. Ibid., 685.
102. See Schakel, "Swift's Voices," 311–25, 313–16.

Breaking and Entering

1. 27 December 1668 (9.401–3) and 19 March 1669 (9.487–89). Also discussed on page 24.
2. 9 April 1667 (8.159).
3. 21 May 1667 (8.226).
4. 27 July 1667 (8.355) and 7 August 1667 (8.376).
5. 10 July 1666 (7.200).
6. 21 June 1663 (4.190). In his *Diary*, 293, John Evelyn records a conversation with Pepys about an intenser experience of this sort in 1685. At start of his brief kingship, James II, the former Duke of York, had wanted to prove that Charles had also been Catholic all along. Evelyn records that James bid Pepys "follow him into his Closett, where opening a cabinet, he shew'd him two papers, containing about a quarter of a sheet on both sides, written in the late King's owne hand, several arguments opposite to the doctrine of the Church of England."
7. See page 22.
8. 11 February 1667 (8.39).
9. 1 January 1669 (9.405).
10. 18 May 1664 (5.152).
11. 14 September 1662 (3.197).
12. 3 May 1664 (5.141).

Chapter 4: Miss C——y's Cabinet of Curiosities

1. Amanda Vickery, *Behind Closed Doors: At Home in Georgian England* (New Haven, CT: Yale University Press, 2010), 28. Reproduced with permission of Yale Representation Limited through PLS Clear.

2. Tristram Shandy, *Miss C——y's Cabinet of Curiosities*, 19. As noted in the British Library Catalogue, the provenance given in the novella, "Utopia: printed for William Whirligig, at the Maiden's Head," is fictitious.

3. Lemi Baruh, "Mediated Voyeurism," 208, distinguishes between the compulsive and the "common" voyeur. Unlike the former, who pursues a fetish, the latter is merely opportunistic, "acting when sources of private moments, expressions or information become readily available for easy and safe consumption."

4. The appendix is an archive of over two hundred works of this kind that were published between 1550 and 1800. *Miscellany* is the designation for textual compilations that ultimately prevails, with over 2,750 returns on an Eighteenth Century Collections Online (ECCO) title keyword search. However, earlier on, as print culture was evolving, *closet* and *cabinet* were more relevant, returning 354 publication records on Early English Books Online (around fifty more than for *miscellany*) and more than 638 records on ECCO. The discrepancy between the number of electronic records and the number of discrete publications listed in the appendix reflects the many re-editions of these works.

5. Alan Stewart and Barbara Benedict have briefly considered closet and cabinet as textual categories. Stewart, *Close Readers*, views these designations as false advertising since "what these collections emphatically do *not* contain are details of the knowledge-processing technologies of the male study-closet" (179). For Benedict, *Curiosity*, by contrast, there is little tension between these volumes' elite and exclusive referents and the accessible print culture in which readers encountered them: "Like their material counterparts, these collections of literary objects, designed for both use and admiration, demonstrate the intellectual ambition of their readers" (135). Focused on how these new textual designations try to resolve existing social contradictions and produce new ones, this chapter's argument synthesizes both perspectives and particularly draws on Benedict's argument about the symbolic importance of the visual sense within them: "As literary analogues to the museums and repositories all over England, these cabinets celebrate the elite ownership of nature and culture enacted through observation: the extension of material possession to symbolic possession by means of the eyes" (162).

6. Price, *Anthology*, 11–12, remarks that paratextual apparatuses reveal eighteenth-century editors' "unspoken premises and institutional bases." The long titles, prefaces, dedications, and frontispieces—or what Price calls the "liminary moments"—in the anthologies known as closets and cabinets engage the shifting values of the book trade.

7. Kramnick, *Making the English Canon,* 6.

8. Warner and Siskin, *Enlightenment*, 10.

9. McKitterick, *Print*, 21. See also the introduction and chapter twelve, "Manuscript," in the Multigraph Collective, *Interacting with Print*.

10. Johns, *Nature of the Book*, 2–3.

11. Ibid., 28, 31–32.

12. Chartier, *Order of Books*, 61–88. In England, a text equivalent to or translated from a French textual *bibliothèque sans murs* might be known as a *library*, as in Henry Curzon's *Universal library: or, Compleat Summary of Science* (1712), or a *bibliotheca*, the Latin equivalent, as in James Woodman's *Bibliotheca Antiquaria & Politica* (1723).

13. See Chartier, *Order of Books*, 65.

14. Ibid., 88.

15. See also Pasenek and Wellmon, "Enlightenment Index," which describes the emergence of a new kind of indexical order "that was supposed to manage bibliographic excess by bibliographic means" (360).

16. Shevlin, "Warwick Lane Network," 166.

17. For discussions of the range of things kept in closets and the processes of cataloguing and displaying them, see *Origins of Museums* and Delbourgo, *Collecting the World*.

18. Stewart, *Close Readers*, 186–87.

19. See especially "Amateur Moment," Bruce Redford's introduction to his *Dilettanti*, 1–12.

20. Quoted in Eger, "Paper Trails," 131.
21. As Lisa Gittelman puts it in *Always Already New*, "Each new medium represents its predecessors, as Marshall McLuhan noted long ago" (4).
22. Defoe, *Robinson Crusoe*, 1.
23. Richardson, *Pamela*, 1.
24. *Cabinet Open'd*, iv–vi.
25. See the earlier discussion of the variable politics of disclosure on pages 90–95.
26. *The Queens closet opened*, A3, A4.
27. In subsequent editions of the book, the queen's secretary builds up the prefatory materials to highlight the recipes' elite origins and reception. See Knoppers, "Opening the Queen's Closet," especially 473.
28. *Modern Curiosities*, A3.
29. Haym, *British Treasury* (Vol. 1), vii.
30. Woolley, *Ladies Delight*, A2–A3. Wooley's recipe book, often reprinted throughout the Restoration, was better known as *The Queen-Like Closet* and was first published in London in 1670.
31. *Golden Cabinet of true Treasure*, A10–A11.
32. Auila, *Audi filia*; Brooks, *Cabinet of Choice Jevvels*; and Bradbury, *Cabinet of Jewels*.
33. White, *Rich Cabinet*, A1.
34. *Kings Cabinet opened*, A6.
35. Bacon, *Novum Organum*, 40.
36. Sprat, *History of the Royal Society*, 74–75.
37. Other prominent examples of museums that emerged from personal cabinets of curiosity include those that John Soane and Ashton Lever built in their own houses. See Mauriès, *Curiosity*, 198, 202; and Delbourgo, *Collecting the World*.
38. Dodsley, *General Contents of the British Museum*, xi–xii (original italics).
39. Shapin, *The Scientific Revolution*, 87.
40. Shapin, *A Social History of Truth*, 69.
41. Wadham, *England's Choice Cabinet of Rarities*, A2.
42. *Mother Bunch's closet newly broke open,* 15–19.
43. *Wit's Cabinet*, 1–2.
44. Basset, *Curiosities*, A5–A7.
45. Smyth, *Profit and Delight*, 143.
46. Hamilton, *Memoirs*, 262–63.
47. Chico, *Designing Women*, 30, cites Michel Delon's *L'Invention du boudoir*, noting that he "dates the boudoir's appearance as a variant of the cabinet in French literature to 1735."
48. de Crébillon, *Le Sopha*, 333; Brown, "Female *Philosophe*," 102.
49. *Rare Verities*, A7, A1, A5
50. Kendrick, *Secret Museum*, 244, points out that the modern collection of sexual books has been packaged as an erudite and antiquarian pursuit: "Like 'pornography,' 'erotica' is a modern coinage with a specious aura of antiquity."
51. Sedgwick, *Epistemology of the Closet*, 73.
52. Benedict, *Curiosity*, 118–57.
53. Mercier, *Tableau de Paris,* 193, quoted in Brown, "Female *Philosophe*," 96.
54. Brown, "Female *Philosophe*," 98.
55. H[arington], "Of a Ladyes Cabinet," quoted in Stewart, *Close Readers*, 168–69.
56. Wycherley, *Country Wife*, 5.2.84–85, 103.
57. Addison, no. 411, *Spectator* (Vol. 2), 535–36.
58. In *Excitable Imaginations*, Kathleen Lubey argues that erotic scenes in Restoration and eighteenth-century literature, "since they cause most readers to balance illicit curiosities with the social, moral, and aesthetic refinement they seek in books" (3), vigorously elicit and exercise all of "the virtual pleasures associated with reading."
59. Benedict, *Curiosity*, 143.

60. "The Discovery" appears on the first pages of the *Cabinet of Love*, a separate section of *The Works of the Earls of Rochester, Roscommon, Dorset, &c. In two volumes. Adorn'd with cuts*, published in London in 1714. Other editions had appeared in 1709 and 1711, and reprintings continued throughout the eighteenth century. Kearney, *History of Erotic Literature*, 40–41, notes the importance of this whole collection to the history of English pornography.

61. See Chico, *Designing Women*, 25–26; and Benedict, *Curiosity*, 142.

62. *Lovers Cabinet:*, 61–63.

63. Mr H——l, "Miss in her Teens," 61–63.

64. See Baruh, "Mediated Voyeurism"; and Calvert, *Voyeur Nation*.

65. See Miller, *Crisis of Presence in Contemporary Culture*, 1–30.

66. For legal perspectives on mediated voyeurism in the United States through the end of the twentieth century, see Calvert, "Free Press, Free Voyeurs?," *Voyeur Nation*, 133–72. Nonconsensual voyeurism was first recognized as a sex crime in the United Kingdom in 2004 and in Canada in 2005. As of 2019, twelve states in the United States also treat certain forms of voyeurism as criminal.

67. For a thorough account of the varieties of anonymity in print culture, see Vareschi, *Everywhere and Nowhere*.

68. In Jacques Lacan's theory of the gaze in *The Four Fundamental Concepts of Psycho-Analysis*, 67–122, insecurity and frustration are endemic to all visual relations because, though things seem to offer themselves to our sight, as they reflect light back to us, they remind us of the illusory nature of visual possession: "*You never look at me from the place from which I see you*" (103). The geometry of perspective functions to put each of us at the center of our own visual world, but the light on which our vision depends comes from beyond us—and typically above us—generating a conflicting impression that we are the objects of both a lateral gaze as well as all-seeing gaze from on high. Lacan notes that the illusion at heart of the visual sense echoes the castration complex, which structures a feeling of inadequacy in every psychic subject.

69. See Laqueur, *Solitary Sex*, especially 185–358, for a full account of the eighteenth-century condemnation of masturbation as "a false pleasure" and "a perversion of the real" (190).

70. Kristina Straub cites Robert Hitchcock's 1788 *Historical View*, 135, in *Sexual Suspects*, 128. Suggesting uncertainty, the British Library catalogue gives 1780? as the publication year for "A Brief Narrative of the Life, of the celebrated Miss C*tl*y." Either the catalogue misses the mark or "Tristram Shandy" refers to some other memoir of Anne Catley available fifteen years earlier.

71. Frank, *Origins of Criticism*, 150.

72. As Newbould, *Adaptations of Sterne's Fiction*, has shown, Laurence Sterne's original voice and style immediately spawned numerous imitators and spin-offs, of which *Miss C——y's Cabinet of Curiosities* is just one example.

73. Fawcett, *Spectacular Disappearances*, 119, observes in her study of Laurence Sterne's over-expressive (printed) performance that "throughout *Tristram Shandy* and his other works, Sterne plays with the ways that the meanings of his words change as his own reputation develops."

74. *Miss C——y's Cabinet*, 15.

75. Straub, *Sexual Suspects*, 10.

76. Ibid., 127, argues that though such roles represented a threat to increasingly polarized notions of gender and sexuality, on the whole, for eighteenth-century audiences, "the ambiguity ... was in fact part of the fun of seeing women in breeches."

77. Nussbaum, *Rival Queens*, 26.

78. Chico, *Designing Women*, 49, writes, "The Lord Chamberlain issued public protests and royal warrants to seal off the tiring-rooms from the audience on 25 February 1663/64 and again on 16 May 1668.... These edicts reflect an effort to construct the tiring-room as a space marked off from the public stage, but likewise highlight the fact that the Restoration tiring-room ... instituted a theater within the playhouse." Chico, 51–54, also writes

about Pepys's "sense of dislocation" in the tiring-room when the actress Elizabeth Knepp invited him there. Among other things, he "loathes" the women's thick make-up as well as the men's trashy manners and appearance, which are so different from what their performances have led him to expect: "What base company of men . . . , and how lewdly they talk! and how poor the men are in clothes, and yet what a shew they make on the stage by candle-light."

79. Chico, *Designing Women*, 50. Exchanging theater anecdotes was called "talking green room." See the first definition in the *Oxford English Dictionary*, s.v. "green room, *n.*"

80. *Miss C——y's Cabinet*, 20.

MOVING CLOSETS

1. 26 April 1667 (8.187).
2. 13 June 1665 (6.126–27). John Mennes had served as a naval officer under both James I and Charles I. According to an annotation at pepysdiary.com, the passages Mennes mentions are like those uncovered during a recent renovation at Apethorpe Palace in Northamptonshire.
3. 24 September 1664 (5.279).
4. 16 February 1666 (7.45).
5. 6 October 1665 (6.254).
6. 4 April 1666 (7.90).
7. 13 August 1666 (7.244).
8. 29 October 1665 (6.282).
9. 23 May 1666 (7.131) and 15 July 1665 (6.158–59).
10. 31 January 1668 (9.44).
11. 5 October 1665 (6.253).
12. 31 December 1660 (1.325).
13. 26 October 1664 (5.306–7)
14. 2 December 1666 (7.394) and 5 February 1667 (8.46).
15. 2 January 1666 (7.2) and 12 July 1666 (7.204–5).
16. 6 February 1668 (9.55).
17. 6 August 1668 (9.274) and 18 November 1668 (9.366).
18. 1 September 1668 (9.297).
19. 12 May 1666 (7.122).
20. 11 May 1667 (8.210).
21. 1 May 1669 (9.540).
22. 23 September 1667 (8.445) and 26 April 1663 (4.112).
23. 11 May 1669 (9.551). In English folklore, washing one's face in May-dew was thought to be good for the complexion.
24. 24 August 1667 (8.399).
25. 2 March 1662 (3.40).
26. 11 May 1667 (8.209). Similarly, on 21 April 1667 (8.174), he admits to being "almost ashamed to be seen in a hackney."
27. 26 April 1667 (9.186–87).
28. 1 May 1667 (8.196).
29. April 1663 (4.95).
30. 23 September 1667 (8.446).
31. 5 January 1666 (7.4).
32. 26 February 1666 (7.57).
33. 18 March 1669 (9.487).
34. 11 April 1669 (9.515).
35. 1 May 1667 (8.193).

36. 1 May 1669 (9.540).
37. 1 May 1667 (8.193).
38. 7 January 1664 (5.6) and 1 May 1667 (8.193).
39. 2 February 1667 (8.40).
40. 1 March 1668 (9.99)
41. 20 October 1668 (9.332)
42. 29 November 1668 (9.378–79).
43. 10 May 1669 (9.551).

CHAPTER 5: PARSON YORICK'S VIS-À-VIS

1. Tomkins, *Affect, Imagery, Consciousness* (Vol. 3–4), 373.
2. Berlant, "Intimacy," 284, argues for an approach to intimacy not as an experience fixed in particular locations, institutions, narratives, or relationships, but rather "as a drive that creates spaces around it through practices."
3. Sterne, *A Sentimental Journey*, 17. This and subsequent references are to the 2002 edition edited by Melvyn New and W. G. Day.
4. Sterne, *Continuation of the Bramine's Journal*, 18 April 1768, 173. New and Day point out in their introduction to this volume that the *Journal* and the *Journey* "were intertwined for many months in Sterne's own mind, and the reading of them should be similarly inter-wined in our own" (xlvi). See also Gardner Stout's considered reassessment of earlier criticism, which sharply contrasts the sensibility and style of the contemporaneous texts in appendix E of *A Sentimental Journey*, 322–26.
5. Sterne, *Bramine's Journal*, 7 June 1768, 197.
6. Ibid., 29 June 1768, 209, original emphasis.
7. Sterne, Letter 167, *Letters*, 281.
8. Sterne, *Bramine's Journal*, 18 April 1768, 173, and 9 June 1768, 198.
9. In the *Journal*, he tells Eliza, 206, "Ive been as far as York to day with no Soul with me in my Chase but yr Picture—" (22 June 1768). Later he decides to make a necklace of the little portrait, so, 220, "—it shall be nearer my heart—" (9 July 1768). Eliza has a cameo role in the novel too (3).
10. This argument is especially indebted to Dupas, *Sterne; Ou, Le vis-à-vis*; Dussinger, "'The Glory of Motion'"; Nagle, "Pleasures of Proximity"; and Lamb, "Hartlean Associationism."
11. See Ross, "Sterne's Life"; Fanning, "Sterne and Print Culture"; and Fawcett, "The Canon of Print," *Spectacular Disappearances*.
12. Griffin, *Literary Patronage*, 267. See also Greene, *Trouble with Ownership*, 195–218.
13. For a succinct account of Sterne's many efforts to ensure that *Tristram Shandy* would be read and talked about, see Ross, "Sterne's Life," 9–17.
14. Ross, "Sterne's Life," 18, points out that this number was "fewer than Sterne had hoped to attract, but still testimony to the entrepreneurial skills of the seriously ill writer, and to the deep affection he continued to inspire." Day, in "*Tristram Shandy*," 247, who gives the number of subscribers to the first edition of *A Sentimental Journey* as 281, provides evidence of Sterne's greater success with the sermons, whose first two volumes had 606 subscribers, and the second two, 693.
15. Sterne, *Life of Tristram Shandy*, 11. For more on Tristram's relationships to readers, see Anderson, "Reader's Imagination"; Benedict, "'Dear Madam'"; and Matuozzi, "Schoolhouse Follies." For more on eighteenth-century Sternean imitations and adaptations, see Newbould, *Adaptations*; and Oakley, *Culture of Mimicry*. For an argument about how Sterne appropriated the voices of his imitators, see Fawcett, *Spectacular Disappearances*, 131–33.
16. Swift, *Tale of a Tub*, 163–64.
17. Sterne took three long trips to France, from January 1762 to the spring of 1764, in the autumn of 1765, and again in spring 1766. See Battestin, "*Philosophes*"; and Asfour, *Lau-*

rence Sterne in France, for an account of the friends and acquaintances he made there, including Baron D'Holbach, Denis Diderot, Jean-Baptiste-Antoine Suard, Julien Offray de La Mettrie, and Voltaire. See Chandler, *Archaeology of Sympathy*, 164; and Ross, "Sterne's Life," 17–18, for discussions of the importance of these journeys to his fiction.

18. Smith, *Theory of Moral Sentiments*, 1.1.1.1, 13.
19. Lamb, *Evolution of Sympathy*, 2.
20. Smith, *Moral Sentiments*, 1.1.2.6.
21. See, for example, Barker-Benfield, *Culture of Sensibility*; Ellis, *Politics of Sensibility*; and Carey, *British Abolitionism*. For an account of how this same discourse also helped to justify colonial expansion and violence, see Festa, *Sentimental Figures of Empire*.
22. See Chandler, "Sentimental Journeys," 185 and 191.
23. 1 May 1665 (6.94).
24. Taylor, *Wheeles*, 11.
25. Ibid.
26. Taylor, *Wheeles*, 12.
27. Originally, the privilege of a hackney coach license was reserved for those who were willing to keep four good horses continually available for the king's use. After the number of hackney coaches rose rapidly, Charles I prohibited their use within three miles of the town. See Straus, *Carriages and Coaches*, 90; and Tarr, *The History of the Carriage*, 237.
28. Peachum, *Coach and Sedan*, 7.
29. Straus, *Carriages and Coaches*, 89, remarks on the persistence of these signs of the coach's stately origins: "Nearly every hansom and four-wheeled cab at the end of the nineteenth century bore some sort of coronet on its panels."
30. Peachum, *Coach and Sedan*, 17–18.
31. *A hue & cry after P[epys] and H[arbord] & Plain Truth*, quoted in Sanders, "Libel Upon Pepys," 369–71.
32. Rochester, "Tunbridge Wells," line 2, 73.
33. Ibid., lines 4–5, 10, and 8, respectively.
34. Ibid., lines 11–14 and 19–21.
35. Ibid., lines 125–6.
36. Taylor, *Wheeles*, 19.
37. Steele, no. 144, *Tatler*, 266. All citations of this essay are from this page.
38. Gay, *Trivia*, 2.574–90.
39. Steele, *Tatler*, 266.
40. Peachum, *Coach and Sedan*, 18.
41. Gay, *Trivia*, 2.272–73 and 2.276–77.
42. Ibid., 2.451–54.
43. Ibid., 2.251–53.
44. For discussions of motion, speed, and subjectivity in eighteenth-century literary carriages, particularly Sterne's, see Drury, *Novel Machines*, 108–42; Ewer, *Mobility*, 110–60; Landreth, "Vehicle of the Soul"; and Takanashi, "Yorick's Sentimental Vehicle."
45. Gay, *Trivia*, 1.113–14.
46. Ibid., 2.523–26.
47. Ibid., 2.530–34.
48. As Straus, *Carriages and Coaches*, 119, explains, glass coaches, coaches with windows made of glass, were first known in France in the early seventeenth century and introduced in London during the Restoration. See page 187.
49. Taylor, *Wheeles*, 14.
50. See Schivelbusch, *Railway Journey*, 74.
51. Ibid.
52. Ibid., 75. For other classic sociological research on the history of stranger relations, see Simmel, *Sociology of Georg Simmel*; Goffman, *Relations in Public*; and Giddens, *Consequence of Modernity*.
53. Manley, *Stagecoach Journey*, 5.

54. Ibid., 4.

55. Ibid., 1.

56. Ibid., 28.

57. Ibid., 11 and 25 (original spelling).

58. Ibid., 27.

59. Steele, no. 132, *Spectator* (Vol. 2), 25.

60. Fielding, *Joseph Andrews*, 52.

61. As Sandra Macpherson, *Harm's Way*, 110, argues, Fielding here makes it clear that, unlike the lawyer's concern with liability, the postillion's charity "requires compassion understood as a capacity to view strangers as friends."

62. Johnson, no. 84, *Adventurer*, 407.

63. Ibid.

64. Ibid., 84, 410.

65. Buzard, "Grand Tour and After," 37.

66. Colletta, introduction, *Legacy of the Grand Tour*, xv.

67. See "Vehicles," in Black, *British and the Grand Tour*.

68. In a reading that emphasizes the value of the preface in the desobligeant as a catalog of contemporary attitudes toward the Grand Tour, Stout, 78–85, and appendix E, 326–30, glosses its many allusions, including Sterne's own sermon on the Prodigal Son, which urges intellectual and emotional preparedness for travel.

69. *Oxford English Dictionary*, s.v. "solitaire, *n.*"

70. As Ewer, *Mobility*, 136, notes, "The Desobligeant rocks from side to side so quickly that two Englishmen wonder 'what could occasion its motion.' It is partly a lewd joke (what could a single man be doing inside a coach to make it rock?)."

71. Addison, no. 10, *Spectator* (Vol. 1), 44.

72. See Lyons, "*Camera Obscura*," 179–95.

73. See pages 36–37.

74. See Battesin "*Philosophes*"; and Chandler "Sentimental Journeys," for further accounts of Sterne's skeptical embrace of empiricism.

75. Locke, *Concerning Education*, 2.A.94, 68.

76. Hume, "Study of History," 568.

77. Pope, *Dunciad*, 3.185–86, 347.

78. Johnson, "Preface to Shakespeare, 1759," 86.

79. For a different reading of the spiraling temporality of the preface, see Nagle, "Proximity," 827–28.

80. For other critical treatments of the desobligeant and vis-à-vis, see Chandler in *The Age of Cultural Revolutions*, 137–70, especially 153; Dussinger, "'Glory of Motion,'" 212; Haggerty, "Amelia's Nose," 141; Keymer, "Readers," 210; and Lamb, "Associationism," 293.

81. Though, as transportation historians point out, seventeenth- and eighteenth-century carriage names were often used interchangeably, there is a factual basis for Sterne's fictional association of a vis-à-vis with the Calais coach yard. Straus, *Carriages and Coaches*, 172, includes an announcement from *The Gazeteer and New Daily Advertiser* for 21 July 1767, in which Monsieur Dessein, the real-life coach broker and hotelier on whom Sterne's character is based, advertises "a Travelling *Vis-à-Vis* ... varnished in the newest taste, and covered with an oiled case to preserve it from the weather in travelling, and [requiring] nothing but a new set of wheels to be in perfect repair."

82. Taylor, *Wheeles*, 8.

83. Farquhar and Motteux, *Stagecoach*, 19. First produced on the London stage in 1701 or 1702, the play is a translation of Jean de la Chapelle's *Les Carrosses d'Orléans* (1680).

84. Taylor, *Wheeles*, 13.

85. Ibid., 15.

86. 12 January 1669 (9.413). In the decades following the publication of *A Sentimental Journey*, the vis-à-vis was particularly associated with female promiscuity. See "The Vis-a-vis of Berkeley Square," 14; and Bleackley, *Ladies Fair and Frail*, 282.

87. Casanova, *History of My Life* (Vols. 3 and 4), 25.
88. Manley, *Stagecoach Journey*, 10.
89. Quoted in paraphrase in Tarr, *History*, 257.
90. As Sedgwick, *Between Men*, 67–82, 80, points out, "the lambency of Yorick's eros makes it especially difficult to isolate homosocial elements as distinct from heterosexual ones."
91. Ibid., 68.
92. For an account of the real life events on which this episode is based, see Battesin, "*Philosophes*," 19: "It was d'Holbach who was instrumental in securing a passport for Sterne—no simple matter for an Englishman in those hostile times."

CODA: COMING OUT

1. Nelson, "Coming Out Online."
2. Josh Thomas, *Please Like Me*, "Portuguese Custard Tarts," Episode 1.3.
3. Judith Butler, "Imitation and Gender Insubordination," in *The Lesbian and Gay Studies Reader*, eds. Henry Abelove, Michèle Aina Barale, and David M. Halperin (New York: Routledge, 1993), 307–20, 309. Reproduced by permission of Taylor and Francis Group, LLC, a division of Informa plc.
4. Foster, "Golden Globes Speech."
5. The GLAAD (formerly the Gay & Lesbian Alliance Against Defamation) Media Reference Guide (10th ed.) defines coming out as "A lifelong process of self-acceptance. People forge a LGBTQ identity first to themselves and then they may reveal it to others. Publicly sharing one's identity may or may not be part of coming out." https://www.glaad .org/reference.
6. "Jodie Foster's Moving Coming Out Speech."
7. Petrow, "Step Backward."
8. Comment on Fuller, "Golden Globes Best Moments."
9. Quoted in James, "Jodie Foster Coming Out."
10. Hansen, "History of Digital Desire," 583, 596.
11. Masten, *Queer Philologies*, 77–78.
12. See pages 218–19.
13. Chesterfield, Letter CXII, 4 October 1746, *Letters to His Son*, 141–43, 143.
14. Fraser, "Rethinking," especially page 67; and Warner, *Publics*, 60.
15. Habermas, *Structural Transformation*, 56 (original italics).
16. Cited in *Oxford English Dictionary*, s.v. "closet, *n.*" Unless otherwise noted, all citations in this section are from this entry.
17. Austen, *Pride and Prejudice*, 69.
18. Urbach, "Closets, Clothes, Disclosure," 64.
19. See especially Sedgwick, "Introduction: Axiomatic," *Epistemology*, 1–63.
20. Butler, "Imitation," 309.
21. Warner, *Publics*, 52.
22. An exception is Stewart, "Epistemologies of the Early Modern Closet," *Close Readers*, 169–88, an argument that has been formative for my own.
23. Joyrich, "Epistemology of the Console"; and Villarejo, "Ethereal Queer," 55.
24. See, for instance, Chasin, *Selling Out*.
25. Becker, *Gay TV and Straight America*, 109–10.
26. Sender, *Making of the Gay Market*, 200–226.
27. Hansen's "Digital Desire," 583, begins, "In or about 1996, sex changed ... it started going more or less digital."
28. Madianou and Miller, "Polymedia," 169–87, quoted in Renninger, "Networked Counterpublics," 1513–29. Hansen, "Digital Desire," 596, illustrates how thoroughly intertwined embodied and virtual sites of erotic connection have become.
29. Hansen, "Digital Desire," 595.

30. Fink and Miller, "Trans Media Moments"; and Renninger, "Networked Counterpublics." For a polemical critique of the political effects of the proliferation of hyperspecialized sexual identities and communities online, see Nagle, *Kill All Normies*.
31. Warner, *Publics*, 120.
32. Absolut Vodka, Advertisement, *New York Times Magazine* (October 11, 2003).
33. Chaikin, *L Word*, "L'Ennui."
34. Zakarin, *L Word*, "Listen Up."
35. Wilgus, "I Came Out."
36. Savage and Miller, *It Gets Better*, 3.

BIBLIOGRAPHY

Addison, Joseph and Richard Steele. *The Spectator* (Vols. 1 & 2), edited by Donald Bond, Oxford: Clarendon, 1965.

Anderson, Benedict. *Imagined Communities: Reflections of the Origins and Spread of Nationalism.* New York: Verso, 2016.

Anderson, Howard. "Tristram Shandy and the Reader's Imagination." *PMLA* 86, no. 5 (1971): 966–73.

Andreadis, Harriette. *Sappho in Early Modern England: Female Same-Sex Literary Erotics 1550–1714.* Chicago: University of Chicago Press, 2001.

Anspaugh, Kelly. "Reading the Intertext in Jonathan Swift's 'A Panegyrick on the Dean.'" *Essays in Literature* 22, no. 1 (Spring 1995): 17–30.

Armstrong, Nancy. *Desire and Domestic Fiction: A Political History of the Novel.* New York: Oxford University Press, 1987.

Asfour, Lana. *Laurence Sterne in France.* London: Continuum, 2008.

Astell, Mary. *Reflections Upon Marriage.* In *The First English Feminist*, edited by Bridget Hill. Aldershot, UK: Gower, 1986.

Aubrey, John. *Natural History and Antiquities of the County of Surrey.* London: 1718–19.

Austen, Jane. *Pride and Prejudice.* Bloomington, IN: Archway Publishing, 2012.

Avila, Jean de, Saint. *Audi filia, or a rich cabinet full of spirituall iewells.* Translated by Tobie Matthew. Saint-Omer: 1620.

Bacon, Francis. *The best and easiest method of preserving uninterrupted health to extreme old age.* London: 1748.

———. *The History of Life and Death, The philosophical works of Francis Bacon ... methodized, and made English* (Vol. 3). London: 1733.

———. *Novum Organum.* Edited and translated by Peter Urbach and John Gibson. Chicago: Open Court, 1994.

———. "Of Followers and Friends." In *Essayes.* London: 1597.

Baine, Rodney. "Roxana's Georgian Setting." *Studies in English Literature* 15, no. 3 (1975): 459–71. https://doi.org/10.2307/449991.

Ballaster, Ros. *Fabulous Orients: Fictions of the East in England 1662–1785.* New York: Oxford University Press, 2005.

———. "Performing *Roxane*: The Oriental Woman as the Sign of Luxury in Eighteenth-Century Fictions." In *Luxury in the Eighteenth Century: Debates, Desires and Delectable Goods*, edited by Maxine Berg and Elizabeth Eger, 165–77. New York: Palgrave MacMillan, 2003.

Barker-Benfield, G. J. *The Culture of Sensibility: Sex and Society in Eighteenth-Century Britain.* Chicago: University of Chicago Press, 1996.

Barlow, Frederic. *Complete English Peerage* (Vol. 2). London: 1772–73.

Baruh, Lemi. "Mediated Voyeurism and the Guilty Pleasure of Consuming Reality Television." *Media Psychology* 13, no. 3 (2010): 201–21. https://doi.org/10.1080/15213269.2010.5 02871.

Basset, Robert. *Curiosities: Or, The Cabinet of Nature. Contyning Phylosophicall Naturall and Morall Questions answered.* London: 1637.

Battestin, Martin. "Sterne among the *Philosophes*: Body and Soul in *A Sentimental Journey*." *Eighteenth-Century Fiction* 7 (1994): 17–36.

Becker, Ron. *Gay TV and Straight America.* New Brunswick, NJ: Rutgers University Press, 2006.

Benedict, Barbara. "Collecting Trouble: Sir Hans Sloane's Literary Reputation in Eighteenth-Century Britain." *Eighteenth-Century Life* 36, no. 2 (Spring 2012): 111–42. https://muse.jhu .edu/article/472276.

———. *Curiosity: A Cultural History of Early Modern Inquiry.* Chicago: University of Chicago Press, 2001.

———. "'Dear Madam': Rhetoric, Cultural Politics and the Female Reader in Sterne's *Tristram Shandy*." *Studies in Philology* 89, no. 4 (Fall 1992): 485–99.

Bennett, Tony. *The Birth of the Museum: History, Theory, Politics.* New York: Routledge, 1995.

Berlant, Lauren. *Cruel Optimism.* Durham, NC: Duke University Press, 2011.

———. "Intimacy: A Special Issue." *Critical Inquiry* 24 (Winter 1998): 281–88

Black, Jeremy. *The British and the Grand Tour.* London: Croom Helm, 1985.

Blackwell, Mark. "The Two Jonathans: Swift, Smedley and the Outhouse Ethos." In *Locating Swift*, edited by Aileen Douglas, Patrick Kelly, and Ian Campbell Ross, 129–49. Dublin: Four Courts Press, 1998.

Bleackley, Horace. *Ladies Fair and Frail: Sketches of the Demi-Monde during the Eighteenth-Century with Sixteen Illustrations.* London: John Lane, 1909.

Bleichmar, Daniela. "Seeing the World in a Room: Looking at Exotica in Early Modern Collections." In *Collecting across Cultures: Material Exchanges in the Early Modern Atlantic World*, edited by Daniela Bleichmar and Peter C. Mancall, 15–20. Philadelphia: University of Pennsylvania Press, 2013.

Bogel, Frederich. *The Difference Satire Makes: Rhetoric and Reading from Jonson to Byron.* Ithaca, NY: Cornell University Press, 2001.

Bon, Ottaviano. *A description of the Grand Signor's seraglio.* Translated by Robert Withers. Edited by John Greaves. London: 1650.

Bradbury, Charles. *Cabinet of Jewels Opened to the Curious, by a Key of Real Knowledge.* Berwick: 1785.

Bray, Alan. *The Friend.* Chicago: University of Chicago Press, 2003.

———. *Homosexuality in Renaissance England.* New York: Columbia University Press, 1995.

Brewer, John. *Pleasures of the Imagination: English Culture in the Eighteenth Century.* Chicago: University of Chicago Press, 1997.

Brooks, Thomas. *Cabinet of Choice Jewels Or, A Box of precious Ointment.* London: 1669.

———. *The Privie Key of Heaven, or, Twenty Arguments for Closet-Prayer.* London: 1665.

Brown, Diane Berrett. "The Female *Philosophe* in the Closet: The *Cabinet* and the Senses in French Erotic Novels, 1740–1800." *Journal for Early Modern Cultural Studies* 9, no. 2 (2009): 96–123. https://doi.org/10.1353/jem.0.0035.

Brown, Norman O. *Life against Death: The Psychoanalytical Meaning of History.* 1959. Middletown, CT: Wesleyan University Press, 1966.

Bucholz, R. O. *The Augustan Court: Queen Anne and the Decline of Court Culture.* Stanford, CA: Stanford University Press, 1993.

Bullard, Rebecca. *Politics of Disclosure, 1674–1725.* London: Pickering & Chatto, 2009.

Bullard, Rebecca, and Rachel Carnell, eds. *Secret History in Literature, 1660–1820.* New York: Cambridge University Press, 2017.

Burroughs, Catherine. "'Hymens's Monkey Love': The Concealed Fancies and Female Sexual Initiation." *Theatre Journal* 51, no. 1 (March 1999): 21–31. https://doi.org/10.1353/tj .1999.0009.

Busbecq, Ogier Ghislain. *The Four Epistles of A. G. Busbequius Concerning His Embassy into Turkey*. London: 1694.

Butler, Judith. "Imitation and Gender Insubordination." In *The Lesbian and Gay Studies Reader*, edited by Henry Abelove, Michèle Aina Barale, and David M. Halperin, 307–20. New York: Routledge, 1993.

Buzard, James. "The Grand Tour and After (1660–1840)." In *Cambridge Companion to Travel Writing*, edited by Peter Hulme and Tim Youngs, 37–52. New York: Cambridge University Press, 2002.

The Cabinet Open'd, Or the Secret History of the Amours of Madam de Maintenon, With the French King, translated from the French Copy. London: 1690.

Calvert, Clay. *Voyeur Nation: Media, Privacy, and Peering in Modern Culture*. Boulder, CO: Westview Press, 2000.

Carey, Brycchan. *British Abolitionism and the Rhetoric of Sensibility: Writing, Sentiment, and Slavery, 1760–1807*. Basingstoke, UK: Palgrave Macmillan, 2005.

Carter, W. Burlette. "'Sexism in the 'Bathroom Debates': How Bathrooms Really Became Separated by Sex." *Yale Policy & Law Review* 37 (2018): 227–97.

Casanova, Giacomo. *History of My Life (Vols. 3 and 4)*, translated by Willard Trask. New York: Harcourt, Brace and World, 1967.

Castle, Terry, ed. *The Literature of Lesbianism: A Historical Anthology from Ariosto to Stonewall*. New York: Columbia University Press, 2003.

Castle, Terry. *Masquerade and Civilization: The Carnivalesque in Eighteenth-Century Culture and Fiction*. Stanford, CA: Stanford University Press, 1986.

Cecil, Robert. *The State and Dignities of a Secretoire of Estates Place, With the care and perill thereof*. London: 1642.

Chaikin, Ilene. *The L Word*. Season 1, episode 7, "L'Ennui." Directed by Tony Goldwyn. Aired February 29, 2004. Showtime.

Chandler, James. *An Archaeology of Sympathy: The Sentimental Mode in Literature and Cinema*. Chicago: University of Chicago Press, 2013.

———. "Moving Accidents: The Emergence of Sentimental Probability." In *The Age of Cultural Revolutions: Britain and France, 1750–1820*, edited by Colin Jones and Dror Wahrman, 137–79. Berkeley: University of California Press, 2002.

Chartier, Roger. "Libraries without Walls." In *The Order of Books*, translated by Lydia Cochrane, 61–88. Stanford, CA: Stanford University Press, 1994.

Chasin, Alex. *Selling Out: The Gay and Lesbian Movement Goes to Market*. New York: Palgrave, 2004.

Chesterfield, Philip Dormer Stanhope. *Letters to His Son in The Works of Lord Chesterfield*. New York: Harper, 1856.

Chico, Tita. *Designing Women: The Dressing Room in Eighteenth-Century Literature and Culture*. Lewisburg, PA: Bucknell University Press, 2005.

———. "Privacy and Speculation in Early Eighteenth-Century Britain." *Cultural Critique* 52 (Fall 2002): 40–60. https://doi.org/10.1353/cul.2003.0004.

Clark, Ruth. *Anthony Hamilton: His Life, His Works, and His Family*. London: J. Lane, 1921.

Clery, E. J. *The Feminization Debate in Eighteenth-Century England: Literature, Commerce and Luxury*. New York: Palgrave MacMillan, 2004.

Colletta, Lisa. Introduction to *The Legacy of the Grand Tour: New Essays of Travel, Literature, and Culture*, ix–xx. Lanham, MD: Fairleigh Dickinson University Press, 2015.

Comment on Bonnie Fuller. "Golden Globes Best Moments." *Hollywood Life* (blog), January 13, 2013. http://hollywoodlife.com/pics/golden-globes-2013-highlights-70th-golden-globe-awards-best-moments/#!1/show-moments-lead/.

Congreve, William. *The Way of the World*. In *The Broadview Anthology of Restoration and Early Eighteenth-Century Drama*, edited by J. Douglas Canfield, 760–809. Peterborough, ON: Broadview Press, 2001.

Corbin, Alan. *The Foul and the Fragrant: Odor and the French Social Imagination*. Translated by

Miriam Kochan, Roy Porter, and Christopher Prendergast. Cambridge, MA: Harvard University Press, 1986.

Cowan, Brian. "The History of Secret Histories." *Huntington Library Quarterly* 81, no.1 (Spring 2018): 121–51.

——. *The Social Life of Coffee: The Emergence of British Coffeehouses*. New Haven, CT: Yale University Press, 2005.

Crary, Jonathan. *Techniques of the Observer: On Vision and Modernity in the Nineteenth Century*. Cambridge, MA: MIT Press, 1991.

Crébillon, Claude-Prosper Jolyot. *Le Sopha*. 1742. Editions Slatkine, 1996.

Croutier, Alev Lytle. *Harem: The World behind the Veil*. New York: Abbeville Press, 1989.

Curzon, Henry. *Universal library: or, Compleat Summary of Science*. London: 1712.

d'Aulnoy, Marie. *Memoirs of the Court of England*. London: B. Bragg, 1707.

Davies, John. *The Ancient Rites, and Monuments of the Monastical, & Cathedral Church of Durham, Collected out of Ancient Manuscripts*. London: W. Hensman, 1672.

Dawes, William. *Duties of the Closet*. London: 1732.

Day, Angel. *The English Secretoire*. London: 1592.

Day, W. G. "The Dissemination of *Tristram Shandy* in Northern Europe: A Preliminary Survey of the Subscription List in Bode's Translation." *Revue de la société d'études anglo-américaines des XVIIe et XVIIIe siècles* (2010): 247–56.

Defoe, Daniel. *Robinson Crusoe*. New York: Oxford University Press, 1998

Delbourgo, James. *Collecting the World: Hans Sloane and the Origins of the British Museum*. Cambridge, MA: Harvard University Press, 2017.

——. "Slavery in the Cabinet of Curiosities: Hans Sloane's Atlantic World." *The British Museum*. https://www.britishmuseum.org/research/news/hans_sloanes_atlantic_world .aspx.

Dobie, Madelaine. "Orientalism, Colonialism, and Furniture in Eighteenth-Century France." In *Furnishing the Eighteenth Century: What Furniture Can Tell Us about the European and American Past*, edited by Dena Goodman and Kathryn Norberg, 13–37. New York: Routledge, 2007.

Dodsley, Robert. *General Contents of the British Museum*. London: 1761.

Donno, Elizabeth Story. Introduction. *The Metamorphosis of Ajax* by John Harington. London: Routledge and Kegan Paul, 1960.

Donoghue, Emma. *Passions between Women: British Lesbian Culture 1668–1801*. London: Scarlet Press, 1993.

Douglas, Mary. *Purity and Danger: An Analysis of Concepts of Pollution and Taboo*. 1966. Boston: Routledge, 1979.

Drury, Joseph. *Novel Machines: Technology and Narrative Form in Enlightenment Britain*. New York: Oxford, 2018.

Dupas, Jean-Claude. *Sterne; Ou, Le vis-à-vis*. Lille, France: Presses-universitaires de Lille, 1984.

Dussinger, John. "'The Glory of Motion': Carriages and Consciousness in the Early Novel." In *The Country Myth: Motifs in the British Novel from Defoe to Smollett*, edited by H. George Hahn, 207–20. New York: Peter Lang, 1991.

Edson, Michael. "'A Closet or a Secret Field': Horace, Devotion and British Retirement Poetry." *Journal for Eighteenth-Century Studies* 35, no. 1 (March 2012): 17–41. https://doi .org/10.1111/j.1754-0208.2010.00347.x.

Eger, Elizabeth. "Paper Trails and Eloquent Objects: Bluestocking Friendship and Material Culture." *Parergon* 26, no. 2 (2009): 109–38. https://doi.org/10.1353/pgn.0.0181.

Ehrenpreis, Irvin. *Swift: The Man, His Works, and the Age, Volume Three: Dean Swift*. Cambridge, MA: Harvard University Press, 1983.

Elliott, J. H. Introduction. *The World of the Favourite*, edited by J. H. Elliott and L. W. B. Brockliss, 1–10. New Haven, CT: Yale University Press, 1999.

Ellis, Markman. *The Coffee House: A Cultural History*. London: Phoenix, 2005.

———. *The Politics of Sensibility: Race, Gender and Commerce in the Sentimental Novel.* New York: Cambridge University Press, 1996.

Evelyn, John. *Diary.* Edited by Guy de la Bedoyère. London: Boydell Press, 2004.

Ewer, Chris. *Mobility in the English Novel from Defoe to Austen.* Rochester, NY: Boydell & Brewer, 2018.

Fabricant, Carole. *Swift's Landscape.* Baltimore, MD: Johns Hopkins University Press, 1982.

Fanning, Christopher. "Sterne and Print Culture." In *The Cambridge Companion to Laurence Sterne*, edited by Thomas Keymer, 125–41. New York: Cambridge University Press, 2009.

Farquhar, George, and Peter Anthony Motteux. *The Stagecoach.* London: Benjamin Bragg, 1705.

Fawcett, Julia. "Creating Character in '*Chiaro Oscuro*': Sterne's Celebrity, Cibber's Apology, and the *Life of Tristram Shandy.*" *The Eighteenth Century* 53, no. 2 (2012): 141–61.

———. *Spectacular Disappearances: Celebrity and Privacy, 1696–1801.* Ann Arbor: University of Michigan Press, 2016.

Feros, Antonio. "Images of Evil, Images of Kings: The Constrasting Faces of the Royal Favourite and the Prime Minister in Early Modern European Political Literature, c.1580–c.1650." In *World of the Favourite*, edited by J. H. Elliott and L. W. B. Brockliss, 205–22. New Haven, CT: Yale University Press, 1999.

Festa, Lynn. *Sentimental Figures of Empire in Eighteenth-Century Britain and France.* Baltimore, MD: Johns Hopkins University Press, 2006.

Ffolliott, Sheila. Introduction to *Women Patrons and Collectors*, edited by Susan Bracken, Andrea M. Gáldy, and Adriana Turpin, xix–xxiv. Cambridge: Cambridge Scholars Publishing, 2011.

Fielding, Henry. *Joseph Andrews.* 1742. Edited by Martin Battestin. Middletown, CT: Wesleyan University Press, 1967.

Fiennes, Celia. *Through England on a Side Saddle in the Time of William and Mary.* London: Field and Tuer, The Leadenhall Press, 1888.

Fink, Marty, and Quinn Miller. "Trans Media Moments: Tumblr, 2011–2013." *Television & New Media* 15, no. 7 (2014): 611–26.

Fisher, J. W. "'Closet-work': The Relationship between Physical and Psychological Spaces in *Pamela.*" In *Samuel Richardson: Passion and Prudence*, edited by Valerie Grosvenor Myer, 21–37. London: Vision Press, 1986.

Folkenflik, Robert. "A Room of Pamela's Own." *English Literary History* 39, no. 4 (1972): 585–96.

Fowler, Alastair. "Country House Poetry: The Politics of a Genre." *The Seventeenth Century* 1, no. 1 (1986): 1–14.

Frank, Marcie. *Gender, Theatre, and the Origins of Criticism: From Dryden to Manley.* New York: Cambridge University Press, 2003.

Fraser, Nancy. "Rethinking the Public Sphere: A Contribution to the Critique of Actually Existing Democracy." *Social Text* 25/26 (1990): 56–80. http:doi.org/10.2307/466240.

Gallagher, Catherine. "Embracing the Absolute: The Politics of the Female Subject in Seventeenth-Century England." *Genders* 1, no. 1 (1988): 24–39.

Gay, John. *Trivia; Or, The Art of Walking the Streets of London.* 1716. In *The Poetical Works of John Gay*, edited by G. C. Faber, 57–87. London: Oxford University Press, 1926.

Gee, Sophie. *Making Waste: Leftovers and the Eighteenth-Century Imagination.* Princeton, NJ: Princeton University Press, 2010.

Gervey, F. "Un récit émancipé: les *Mémoires de la vie du comte de Grammont.*" *Cahiers de Littérature du 17 Siècle* 3 (1981): 127–50.

Giddens, Anthony. *The Consequence of Modernity.* Stanford, CA: Stanford University Press, 1990.

Girouard, Mark. *A Country House Companion.* New Haven, CT: Yale University Press, 1987.

———. *Life in the English Country House: A Social and Architectural History.* New Haven, CT: Yale University Press, 1994.

Gittelman, Lisa. *Always Already New: Media, History, and the Data of Culture*. Cambridge, MA: MIT Press, 2006.

Goffman, Erving. *Relations in Public: Microstudies of the Public Order*. New York: Harper & Row, 1972.

The Golden Cabinet of true Treasure: Containing the summe of Morall Philosophie. Translated by William Jewell. London: 1612.

Goodman, Dena. "The *Secrétaire* and the Integration of the Eighteenth-Century Self." In *Furnishing the Eighteenth Century: What Furniture Can Tell Us about the European and American Past*, edited by Dena Goodman and Kathryn Norberg, 183–204. New York: Routledge, 2007.

Greene, Jody. *The Trouble with Ownership: Literary Property and Authorial Liaibility in England, 1660–1730*. Philadelphia: University of Pennsylvania Press, 2011.

Griffin, Dustin. *Literary Patronage in England, 1650–1800*. New York: Cambridge University Press, 1996.

Gyford, Phil, ed. *The Diary of Samuel Pepys* (website). https://www.pepysdiary.com.

Mr. H——l. "Miss in her Teens." *The Cabinet of Love, or a collection of the most affecting Anecdotes of people renowned for their virtues or their vices by persons eminent in the world of literature*. London: 1792.

Habermas, Jürgen. *The Structural Transformation of the Public Sphere: An Inquiry into a Category of Bourgeois Society*. Translated by Thomas Burger. Cambridge, MA: MIT Press, 1995.

Hackel, Heidi Brayman. "The Countess of Bridgewater's London Library." In *Books and Readers in Early Modern England: Material Studies*, edited by Jennifer Anderson and Elizabeth Sauer, 138–59. Philadelphia: University of Pennsylvania Press, 2002.

Haggerty, George. "Amelia's Nose; Or, Sensibility and Its Symptoms." *The Eighteenth Century* 36, no. 2 (1995): 139–56.

——. *Men in Love: Masculinity and Sexuality in the Eighteenth Century*. New York: Columbia University Press, 1999.

Halfpenny, William. *Useful Architecture*. London: 1760.

Hall, Donald, and Annemarie Jagose, with Andrea Bebell and Susan Potter, eds. *The Routledge Queer Studies Reader*. New York: Routledge, 2013.

Hamilton, Anthony. *Memoirs of the Court of Charles the Second*. Edited by Walter Scott. London: Henry G. Bohn, 1859.

——. *Memoirs of the Court of Charles the Second*. Edited by Walter Scott. London: Henry G. Bohn, 1864.

——. *Les quatre Facardins, Oeuvres* (Tome Second). Paris: Antoine-Augustin Renouard, 1812.

Hammond, Brean, and Nicholas Seager. "'I will have you spell right, let the world go how it will': Swift the (Tor)mentor." In *Mentoring in Eighteenth-Century British Literature and Culture*, edited by Anthony W. Lee, 63–84. Burlington, VT: Ashgate Press, 2010.

Hansen, Ellis. "The History of Digital Desire, Vol. 1: Introduction." *South Atlantic Quarterly* 110, no. 3 (Summer 2011): 583–99.

Harington, John. *The Metamorphosis of Ajax*. 1596. Edited by Elizabeth Story Donno. London: Routledge and Kegan Paul, 1960.

H[arington], I[ohn]. "Of a Ladyes Cabinet" in "Epigrammes by Sir I.H. and others." *Alicia. Philparthens louing Folly etc*. London: 1613.

Haym, Nicholas. *The British Treasury; being cabinet the first of our Greek and Roman antiquities of all sorts. Never before printed* (Vol. 1). London: 1719.

Herbert, Amanda E. *Female Alliances: Gender, Identity, and Friendship in Early Modern Britain*. New Haven, CT: Yale University Press, 2014.

Herrick, Robert. "Panegyrick to Sir Lewis Pemberton." In *The Complete Poetry of Robert Herrick*, Vol. 2, 138–41. New York: Oxford University Press, 2013.

Hibbard, G. R. "The Country House Poem of the Seventeenth Century." *Journal of the Warburg and Courtauld Institutes* 19, no. 1/2 (1956): 159–74.

Historical Gazetteer of London Before the Great Fire Cheapside; Parishes of All Hallows Honey Lane,

St Martin Pomary, St Mary Le Bow, St Mary Colechurch and St Pancras Soper Lane. Originally published by Centre for Metropolitan History, London, 1987.

A hue & cry after P[epys] and H[arbord] & Plain Truth. London: 1679.

Hume, David. "Of the Study of History." In *Essays: Moral, Political, and Literary,* edited by Eugene F. Miller, 563–68. Indianapolis, IN: Liberty Classics, 1985.

Hyde, Edward, Earl of Clarendon. *History of the Rebellion and Civil Wars in England begun in the Year 1641.* Edited by W. Dunn Macray. Oxford: Oxford University Press, 1888.

Jaffe, Nora Crow. "Swift and the Agreeable Young Lady, but Extremely Lean." *Papers on Literature and Language* 14 (1978): 129–37.

James, Susan Donaldson. "LGBT Activists Cringe and Praise Jodie Foster Coming Out." *ABC News,* January 14, 2013. http://abcnews.go.com/Entertainment/lgbt-advocates-applaud-cringe-jodie-foster-coming/story?id=18211672.

"Jodie Foster's Golden Globes Speech: Full Transcript." *ABC News* (blog), January 14, 2013. http://abcnews.go.com/blogs/entertainment/2013/01/full-transcript-jodie-fosters-golden-globes-speech/.

"Jodie Foster's Moving Coming Out Speech." *The Independent,* January 14, 2013. http://www.independent.co.uk/voices/iv-drip/watch-jodie-fosters-moving-coming-out-speech-at-the-golden-globes-8450459.html.

Johns, Adrian. *The Nature of the Book: Print and Knowledge in the Making.* Chicago: University of Chicago Press, 1998.

Johnson, James William. *A Profane Wit: The Life of John Wilmot, Earl of Rochester.* Rochester, NY: University of Rochester Press, 2004.

Johnson, Samuel. no. 84, *Adventurer.* In *The Idler and The Adventurer,* edited by. W. J. Bate, John M. Bullitt, and L. F. Powell, 406–10. New Haven, CT: Yale University Press, 1963.

———. "Preface to Shakespeare, 1765." In *Johnson on Shakespeare,* edited by Arthur Sherbo, 59–113. New Haven, CT: Yale University Press, 1968.

Jonson, Ben. "To Penshurst." In *Norton Anthology of British Literature,* Vol. 1B, edited by George M. Logan, Stephen Greenblatt, and Barbara Lewalski, 1399–401. New York: Norton, 2000.

Joyrich, Lynne. "Epistemology of the Console." In *Queer TV: Theories, Histories, Politics,* edited by Glyn Davis and Gary Needham, 15–47. New York: Routledge, 2009.

Karian, Stephen. *Jonathan Swift in Manuscript and Print.* New York: Cambridge University Press, 2010.

Kearney, Patrick. *A History of Erotic Literature.* London: MacMillian, 1982.

Keating, Erin. "In the Bedroom of the King: Affective Politics in the Restoration Secret History." *Journal for Early Modern Cultural Studies* 15, no. 2 (Spring 2015): 58–82. https://doi.org/10.1353/jem.2015.0013.

Kendrick, Walter. *The Secret Museum: Pornography in Modern Culture.* New York: Viking, 1987.

Kenyon, J. P. *The Stuarts: A Study in English Kingship.* London: Fontana, 1970.

King, Thomas. *The Gendering of Men, 1600–1750: The English Phallus.* Madison: University of Wisconsin Press, 2003.

The Kings Cabinet opened: Or, Certain Packets of Secret Letters & Papers; Written with the Kings own Hand, and taken in his Cabinet at Nasby-Field. London: 1645.

Knolles, Richard. *The generall historie of the Turkes from the first beginning of that nation to the rising of the Othoman familie . . .* London: 1603.

Knoppers, Laura Lunger. "Opening the Queen's Closet: Henrietta Maria, Elizabeth Cromwell, and the Politics of Cookery." *Renaissance Quarterly* 60, no. 2 (2007): 464–99.

Kramnick, Jonathan. *Making the English Canon: Print-Capitalism and the Cultural Past, 1700–1770.* New York: Cambridge University Press, 1998.

Lacan, Jacques. "Of the Gaze as *Objet Petit a.*" In *The Four Fundamental Concepts of Psycho-Analysis,* translated by Alan Sheridan, 67–122. New York: Norton, 1992.

Lamb, Jonathan. *The Evolution of Sympathy in the Long Eighteenth Century.* London: Pickering and Chatto, 2009.

———. "The Language of Hartlean Associationism in *A Sentimental Journey*." *Eighteenth-Century Studies* 13 (1980): 285–312.

Landreth, Sara. "The Vehicle of the Soul." *Eighteenth-Century Fiction* 26, no. 1 (2013): 93–120.

Lanser, Susan. *The Sexuality of History: Modernity and the Sapphic, 1565–1830.* Chicago: University of Chicago Press, 2014.

Lanthimos, Yorgos, dir. *The Favourite*. Los Angeles: Fox Searchlight Pictures, 2018.

Laqueur, Thomas. *Solitary Sex: A Cultural History of Masturbation.* New York: Zone Books, 2004.

Lee, Nathaniel. *The Rival Queens.* Edited by P. F. Vernon. Lincoln: University of Nebraska Press, 1970.

Le Stourgeon, B. "Descripiton of the Turkish Empire." In *A compleat universal history, of the several empires, kingdoms, states &c. throughout the known world,* 236–41. London: 1732–38.

Lewis, Reina. *Gendering Orientalism: Race, Femininity, and Representation.* New York: Routledge, 1996.

Limpey, Oliver, and Arthur McGregor, eds. *The Origins of Museums: The Cabinet of Curiosities in Sixteenth- and Seventeenth-Century Europe.* Oxford: Clarendon Press, 1985.

Locke, John. *Essay Concerning Human Understanding.* Edited by Peter Nidditch. Oxford: Clarendon Press, 1989.

———. *Some Thoughts Concerning Education.* Edited by Ruth Grant and Nathan Tarcov. New York: Hackett, 1996.

———. *Two Treatises of Government.* Edited by Peter Laslett. Cambridge: Cambridge University Press, 2000.

Love, Harold. "Early Modern Print Culture: Assessing the Models." In *The Book History Reader,* edited by David Finkelstein and Alistair McCleery, 74–86. New York: Routledge, 2006.

Loveman, Kate. *Samuel Pepys and His Books: Reading, Newsgathering, and Sociability, 1660–1703.* New York: Oxford University Press, 2015.

Lovers Cabinet: A Collection of Poems. Dublin: 1755

Lubey, Kathleen. *Excitable Imaginations: Eroticism and Reading in Britain, 1660–1760.* Lewisburg, PA: Bucknell University Press, 2012

Lyons, John. "Camera Obscura: Image and Imagination in Descartes's *Méditations*." In *Convergences: Rhetoric and Poetic in Seventeenth-Century France,* edited by David Lee Rubin and Mary B. McKinley, 179–95. Columbus: Ohio State University Press, 1989.

Macpherson, Sandra. *Harm's Way: Tragic Responsibility and Novel Form.* Baltimore, MD: Johns Hopkins University Press, 2010.

Madianou, M., and D. Miller, "Polymedia: Towards a New Theory of Digital Media in Interpersonal Communication." *International Journal of Cultural Studies* 16 (2013): 169–87.

Mancall, Peter. "'Collecting Americans': The Anglo-American Experience from Cabot to NAGPRA." In *Collecting across Cultures: Material Exchanges in the Early Modern Atlantic World,* edited by Daniela Bleichmar and Peter C. Mancall, 192–216. Philadelphia: University of Pennsylvania Press, 2013.

Manley, Delarivier. *Secret Memoirs and Manners of several Persons of Quality of Both Sexes, from the New Atalantis, an Island in the Mediterranian* (Vols. 1 and 4). London: 1720.

———. *Stagecoach Journey to Exeter.* London: 1696.

Marcus, Sharon. *Between Women: Friendship, Desire, and Marriage in Victorian England.* Princeton, NJ: Princeton University Press, 2007.

Marlowe, Christopher. *Edward the Second.* Edited by Charles R. Forker. Manchester: Manchester University Press, 1995.

Masten, Jeffrey. *Queer Philologies: Sex, Language, and Affect in Shakespeare's Time.* Philadelphia: University of Pennsylvania Press, 2016.

Matuozzi, Jessica. "Schoolhouse Follies: *Tristram Shandy* and the Male Reader's Tutelage" *English Literary History* 80, no. 2 (2013): 489–518.

Mauriès, Patrick. *Cabinets of Curiosities.* London: Thames and Hudson, 2002.

McKeon, Michael. *The Secret History of Domesticity: Public, Private, and the Division of Knowledge*. Baltimore, MD: Johns Hopkins University Press, 2005.

McKitterick, David. *Print, Manuscript and the Search for Order, 1450–1830*. New York: Cambridge University Press, 2003.

Mercier, Louis-Sébastien. *Tableau de Paris, Volume II*. Paris: 1783.

Melman, Billie. *Women's Orients: English Women and the Middle East, 1718–1918*. London: MacMillan, 1995.

Miller, Vincent. *The Crisis of Presence in Contemporary Culture: Ethics, Privacy and Speech in Mediated Social Life*. Los Angeles: Sage Press, 2016.

Mills, Rebecca. " 'To be both Patroness and Friend': Patronage, Friendship, and Protofeminism in the Life of Elizabeth Thomas (1675–1731)." *Studies in Eighteenth-Century Culture* 38 (2009): 69–89. https://doi.org/10.1353/sec.0.0049.

Modern Curiosities of Art & Nature Extracted out of the Cabinets of the most Eminent Personages of the French Court. London: 1685.

Montagu, Mary Wortley. *Turkish Embassy Letters*. Edited by Malcolm Jack. Athens: University of Georgia Press, 1993.

Mother Bunch's closet newly broke open, containing rare secrets of art and nature, tried and experienced by learned philosophers, ... Second part. London: 1760.

Mueller, Judith C. "Imperfect Enjoyment at Market Hill: Impotence, Desire, and Reform in Swift's Poems to Lady Acheson." *English Literary History* 66, no. 1 (1999): 51–70.

The Multigraph Collective. *Interacting with Print: Elements of Reading in the Era of Print Saturation*. Chicago: Chicago University Press, 2018.

Nagle, Angela. *Kill All Normies: Online Culture Wars From 4Chan & Tumblr to Trump & the Alt-Right*. Washington, DC: Zero Books, 2017.

Nagle, Christopher. "Sterne, Shelley, and Sensibility's Pleasures of Proximity." *English Literary History* 70, no. 3 (2003): 813–45.

Nelson, Carrie. "Coming Out Online Is a New First Step before Coming Out IRL." *Daily Dot* (October 11, 2015, updated December 11, 2015). https://www.dailydot.com/irl/coming-out-online/.

Newbould, Marie-Céline. *Adaptations of Laurence Sterne's Fiction: Sterneana, 1760–1840*. Farnham, UK: Ashgate, 2013.

Nicholson, Sue. "At Home with Mr. and Mrs Pepys." *The Diary of Samuel Pepys*. September 23, 2011. https://www.pepysdiary.com/indepth/2011/09/23/at-home/.

Nussbaum, Felicity. *Rival Queens: Actresses, Performance, and the Eighteenth-Century British Theater*. Philadelphia: University of Pennsylvania Press, 2010.

———. *Torrid Zones: Maternity, Sexuality, and Empire in Eighteenth-Century English Narratives*. Baltimore, MD: Johns Hopkins University Press, 1995.

Oakley, Warren. *A Culture of Mimicry: Laurence Sterne, His Readers and the Art of Bodysnatching*. Leeds: MHRA Texts and Dissertations, 2010.

Ogborn, Miles. *Spaces of Modernity: London's Geographies, 1680–1780*. London: Guilford Press, 1998.

Onnekink, David. " 'Mynheer Benting now rules over us': The 1st Earl of Portland and the Re-emergence of the English Favourite, 1689–99." *English Historical Review* 121, no. 492 (June 2006): 693–713. https://doi.org/10.1093/ehr/cel103.

Palladio, Andrea. *Four Books of Architecture*. 1570. Translated by Isaac Ware. London: 1738.

Palmer, Roy. *The Water Closet: A New History*. Newton Abbot, UK: David and Charles, 1973.

Pasanek, Brad. *Metaphors of Mind: An Eighteenth-Century Dictionary*. Baltimore, MD: Johns Hopkins University Press, 2014.

Pasanek, Brad, and Chad Wellmon. "The Enlightenment Index." *The Eighteenth Century* 56, no. 3 (2015): 357–80.

Pastor, Gail Kern. "The Epistemology of the Water Closet: John Harrington's *Metamorphosis of Ajax* and Elizabethan Technologies of Shame." In *Material Culture and Cultural Materialisms*, edited by Curtis Perry," 139–58. Turnhout, Belgium: Brepols, 2001.

Peachum, Henry. *Coach and Sedan Pleasantly Disputing for Place and Precedence*. London: 1636.

Pepys, Samuel. *The Diary of Samuel Pepys* (Vols. 1–11). Edited by Robert Latham and William Matthews. Berkeley: University of California Press, 1970.

Perry, Curtis. *Literature and Favoritism in Early Modern England*. New York: Cambridge University Press, 2006.

Petrow, Stephen. "Was Jodie Foster's 'Coming Out' a Step Backward for Gays and Lesbians?" *New York Times*, January 22, 2013. http://www.nytimes.com/2013/01/22/booming /was-jodie-fosters-coming-out-a-step-backward-for-gays-and-lesbians.html?_r=0.

Pominan, Krystof. *Collectors and Curiosities: Paris and Venice, 1500–1800*. Translated by Elizabeth Wiles-Portier. Cambridge, MA: Polity Press, 1990.

Poovey, Mary. *A History of the Modern Fact: Problems of Knowledge in the Sciences of Wealth and Society*. Chicago: University of Chicago Press, 1999.

Pope, Alexander. *The Dunciad, Poetry and Prose of Alexander Pope*. Edited by Aubrey Williams. New York: Houghton Mifflin, 1969.

Preston, Claire. "The Counsel of Herbs: Scientific Georgic." In *The Poetics of Scientific Investigation in Seventeenth-Century England*, 196–240. New York: Oxford University Press, 2015.

Price, Leah. *The Anthology and the Rise of the Novel*. New York: Cambridge University Press, 2000.

Purinton, Marjean D. "George Colman's *The Iron Chest* and *Blue-Beard* and the Pseudoscience of Curiosity Cabinets." *Victorian Studies* 49, no. 2 (Winter 2007): 250–57. https:// muse.jhu.edu/article/218885.

The Queens closet opened. Incomparable secrets in physick, chirurgery, preserving, candying, and cookery; as they were presented to the Queen by the most experienced persons of our times / Transcribed from the true copies of her Majesties own receipt books, by W.M. one of her late servants. London: 1655.

Raber, Karen. *Dramatic Difference: Gender, Class, and Genre in the Early Modern Closet Drama*. Newark: University of Delaware Press, 2001.

Racine, Jean. *Bajazet*. Translated by Alan Hollinghurst. London: Chatto and Windus, 1991.

Rambuss, Richard. *Closet Devotions*. Durham, NC: Duke University Press, 1998.

Rare Verities. The Cabinet of Venus Unlocked, and Her Secrets laid open. Being a Translation of part of Sinibaldus, his Geneanthropeia, and a collection of some things out of other Latin Authors, never before in English. London: 1658.

Redford, Bruce. *Dilettani: The Antic and the Antique in Eighteenth-Century England*. Los Angeles: J. Paul Getty Museum, 2008.

Renninger, Bruce. "'Where I can be myself ... where I can speak my mind': Networked Counterpublics in a Polymedia Environment." *new media & society* 17, no. 9 (2015): 1513–29.

Revel, Jacques, Orest Ranum, Jean-Louis Flandrin, Jacques Gélis, Madeline Foisil, and Jean Marie Goulernot. *A History of Private Life: III. The Passions of the Renaissance*, edited by Roger Chartier and translated by Arthur Goldhammer. Cambridge, MA: Belknap Press of Harvard University Press, 1989.

Richardson, Samuel. *Pamela; or, Virtue Rewarded*. Edited by Thomas Keymer and Alice Wakely. New York: Oxford University Press, 2001.

Robinson, David M. *Closeted Writing and Lesbian and Gay Literature: Classical, Early Modern, Eighteenth Century*. Burlington, VT: Ashgate Press, 2006.

Rochester. "Tunbridge Wells." In *Complete Poems of John Wilmot, Earl of Rochester*, edited by David Vieth, 73–80. New Haven, CT: Yale University Press, 2002.

Rolleston, Samuel. *Philosophical Dialogue Concerning Decency*. London: 1751.

Ross, Ian Campbell. "Sterne's Life, Milieu, and Literary Career." In *The Cambridge Companion to Laurence Sterne,* edited by Thomas Keymer, 5–20. New York: Cambridge University Press, 2009.

Rycault, Paul. *The Present State of the Ottoman Empire*. New York: Arno Press and the New York Times, 1971.

Sachse, William Lewis. *Lord Somers: A Political Portrait*. Manchester, UK: University of Manchester Press, 1975.

Saggini, Francesca. "Memories beyond the Pale: The Eighteenth-Century Actress between Stage and Closet." *Restoration and 18th Century Theatre Research* 19, no. 1 (Summer 2004): 43–63.

Sanders, Harry. "A Libel Upon Pepys," *Notes and Queries* 5, no. 7 (May 12, 1877): 369–71.

Sandys, George. *A Relation of a Journey begun An: Dom: 1610 ... Cointaining a desscription of the Turkish Empire, of Aegypt, of the Holy Land, of the Remote parts of Italy, and Iland adjoining*. London: 1615.

Savage, Dan, and Terry Miller. *It Gets Better: Coming Out, Overcoming Bullying, and Creating a Life Worth Living*. New York: Dutton, 2011.

Schakel, Peter. "Swift's Voices: Innovation and Complication in the Poems Written at Market Hill." In *Reading Swift: Papers from the Fourth Münster Symposium on Jonathan Swift*, edited by Hermann J. Real and Helgard Stüver-Leidig, 311–25. Munich: Fink, 2003.

Schivelbusch, Wolfgang. *The Railway Journey: The Industrialization of Time and Space in the 19th Century*. 1977. Reprint, Berkeley: University of California Press, 1986.

Scott, Walter. *Works of Jonathan Swift, with Notes and a Life of the Author*. Edinburgh: 1814.

Sedgwick, Eve Kosofsky. *Between Men: English Literature and Male Homosocial Desire*. New York: Columbia University Press, 1985.

———. *Epistemology of the Closet*. Berkeley: University of California Press, 2008.

Sender, Katherine. *Business, Not Politics: The Making of the Gay Market*. New York: Columbia University Press, 2004.

Shandy, Tristram. *Miss C——y's Cabinet of Curiosities; or, the Green-Room Broke Open*. London: 1765.

Shapin, Simon. *The Scientific Revolution*. Chicago: University of Chicago Press, 1998.

———. *A Social History of Truth: Civility and Science in Seventeenth-Century England*. Chicago: University of Chicago Press, 1995.

Shevlin, Eleanor F. "The Warwick Lane Network and the Refashioning of 'Atalantis' as a Titular Keyword: Print and Politics in the Age of Queen Anne." In *Producing the Eighteenth-Century Book*, edited by Laura Runge and Pat Rogers, 163–92. Newark: University of Delaware Press, 2009.

Silver, Sean. *The Mind Is a Collection: Case Studies in Eighteenth-Century Thought*. Philadelphia: University of Pennsylvania Press, 2015.

Simmel, Georg. *The Sociology of Georg Simmel*. New York: Free Press, 1976.

Siskin, Clifford, and William Warner. "This Is Enlightenment: An Invitation in the Form of an Argument." In *This Is Enlightenment*, 1–33. Chicago: University of Chicago Press, 2010.

Smith, Adam. *Theory of Moral Sentiments*. Edited by Knud Haakonssen. New York: Cambridge University Press, 2002.

Smith, Peter. *Between Two Stools: Scatology and Its Representations in English Literature from Chaucer to Swift*. Manchester, UK: Manchester University Press, 2012.

Smyth, Adam. *"Profit and Delight": Printed Miscellanies in England, 1640–1682*. Detroit: Wayne State University Press, 2004.

Sprat, Thomas. *History of the Royal Society*. London: 1667.

Steele, Richard. no. 144. *The Tatler*. 1709–11. Philadelphia, PA: Woodward, 1831.

Sterne, Jonathan. *The Audible Past: Cultural Origins of Sound Reproduction*. Durham, NC: Duke University Press, 2003.

Sterne, Laurence. *Continuation of the Bramine's Journal*. In *Works* (Vol. 6), edited by Melvyn New and W. G. Day. Gainesville: University of Florida Press, 2002.

———. Letter 167. In *Letters of Laurence Sterne*, edited by Lewis Perry Curtis. New York: Oxford University Press, 1965.

———. *The Life and Opinions of Tristram Shandy, Gentleman*. New York: Penguin, 2003.

Sterne, Laurence. *A Sentimental Journey through France and Italy by Mr. Yorick*. In *Works* (Vol. 6), edited by Melvyn New and W. G. Day. Gainesville: University of Florida Press, 2002.

Stewart, Alan. *Close Readers: Humanism and Sodomy in Early Modern England*. Princeton, NJ: Princeton University Press, 1997.

Stewart, Susan. *On Longing: Narratives of the Miniature, the Gigantic, the Souvenir, the Collection*. Baltimore, MD: Johns Hopkins University Press, 1984.

Stone, Lawrence. *Family, Sex, and Marriage in England, 1500–1800*. New York: Harper & Row, 1977.

Straub, Kristina. *Sexual Suspects: Eighteenth-Century Players and Sexual Ideology*. Princeton, NJ: Princeton University Press, 1992.

Straus, Ralph. *Carriages and Coaches: Their History and Evolution*. London: Martin Secker, 1912.

Straznicky, Marta. *Privacy, Playreading, and Women's Closet Drama, 1550–1700*. Cambridge: Cambridge University Press, 2004.

Swift, Jonathan. *Directions to Servants*. In *Basic Writings*, edited by Claude Rawson and Ian Higgins, 717–69. New York: Modern Library, 2002.

———. *Gulliver's Travels*. New York: Oxford World Classics, 2005.

———. "The Lady's Dressing Room." In *Complete Poems*, edited by Pat Rogers, 448–52. New Haven, CT: Yale University Press, 1983.

———. *Mechanical Operations of the Spirit*. In *Basic Writings of Jonathan Swift*, edited by Claude Rawson and Ian Higgins, 141–60. New York: Modern Library, 2002.

———. "Panegyric on the Dean in the Person of a Lady of the North." In *Complete Poems*, edited by Pat Rogers, 436–44. New Haven, CT: Yale University Press, 1983.

———. *A Tale of a Tub*. In *Major Works*, edited by Angus Ross and David Woolley, 62–164. New York: Oxford University Press, 2008.

Tadmor, Naomi. *Family and Friends in Eighteenth-Century England: Household, Kinship, and Patronage*. Cambridge: Cambridge University Press, 2001.

Takanashi, Kyoko. "Mediation, Reading, and Yorick's Sentimental Vehicle." *Novel* 49, no. 3 (2016): 486–503.

Tarr, Lazlo. *The History of the Carriage*. Translated by Elizabeth Hoch. Budapest: Corvina Press, 1969.

Taylor, Charles. *Modern Social Imaginaries*. Durham, NC: Duke University Press, 2004.

Taylor, John. *The World Runnes on Wheeles; Or, Odds between Carts and Coaches*. London: 1623.

Thomas, Josh. *Please Like Me*. Season 1, episode 3, "Portuguese Custard Tarts." Directed by Matthew Saville. Aired March 7, 2013. Australian Broadcasting Company.

Thompson, Helen. *Ingenuous Subjection: Compliance and Power in the Eighteenth-Century Domestic Novel*. Philadelphia: University of Pennsylvania Press, 2005.

———. "The Personal Is Political: Domesticity's Domestic Discontents." *The Eighteenth Century* 50, no. 4 (Winter 2009): 355–70.

Thurley, Simon. *The Whitehall Palace Plan of 1670*. London: London Topographical Society, 1998.

Tomalin, Claire. *Samuel Pepys: The Unequalled Self*. Toronto: Penguin, 2003.

Tomkins, Silvan. *Affect, Imagery, Consciousness* (Vol. 3–4). New York: Springer, 2008.

Tout, T. F. *A First Book of British History*. London: Longmans, 1903.

Traub, Valerie. "The New Unhistoricism in Queer Studies." *PMLA* 128, no. 1 (January 2013): 21–39. https://doi.org/10.1632/pmla.2013.128.1.21.

Urbach, Henry. "Closets, Clothes, Disclosure." *Assemblage* 30 (August 1996): 62–73.

Vareschi, Mark. *Everywhere and Nowhere: Anonymity and Mediation in Eighteenth-Century Britain*. Minneapolis: University of Minnesota Press, 2018.

Varillas, Antoine. *Anekdota Herouiaka, or the Secret History of the House of Medicis*, translated by F. Spence. London: 1686.

Vickery, Amanda. *Behind Closed Doors: At Home in Georgian England*. New Haven, CT: Yale University Press, 2010.

Villarejo, Amy. "Ethereal Queer." In *Queer TV: Theories, Histories, Politics*, edited by Glyn Davis and Gary Needham, 48–62. New York: Routledge, 2009.

"The Vis-à-vis of Berkeley Square; Or, A Wheel off Mrs. W*t*n's Carriage." London: 1783.

Wadham, William. *England's Choice Cabinet of Rarities; Or, the Famous Mr. Wadhams Last Golden Legacy*. London: 1700.

Wahl, Elizabeth. *Invisible Relations: Representations of Female Intimacy in the Enlightenment*. Stanford, CA: Stanford University Press, 2001.

Wall, Cynthia. *The Prose of Things: Transformations of Description in the Eighteenth Century*. Chicago: University of Chicago Press, 2006.

Walpole, Horace. Letter 18 to George Montagu, 27 March 1760. In *Letters of Horace Walpole* (Vol. 3). Project Gutenberg EBook. http://www.gutenberg.org/ebooks/4773.

Ware, Issac. *A Complete Body of Architecture*. London: T. Osborne and J. Shipton, 1756.

Warner, Michael. *Publics and Counterpublics*. New York: Zone Books, 2002.

Warner, William B. *Licensing Entertainment: The Elevation of Novel Reading in Britain, 1684–1750*. Berkeley: University of California Press, 1998.

Weil, Rachel. "Part III: Women and Political Life in the Age of Anne." In *Political Passions: Gender, the Family and Political Argument in England, 1680–1714*, 162–230. Manchester, UK: University of Manchester Press, 1999.

White, John. *Rich Cabinet with Variety of Inventions in several Arts and Siences*. London: 1658.

Williams, Raymond. *The Country and the City*. New York: Oxford University Press, 1973.

Wilson, John Harold. "Lord Oxford's 'Roxolana,'" *Theatre Notebook* 12, no. 1 (Autumn 1957): 14.

Wilson, P. H. *Absolutism in Central Europe*. London: Routledge, 2000.

Wilgus, Alison. "I Came Out Late in Life and That's Okay." In *The Nib*, April 26, 2019. https://thenib.com/i-came-out-late-and-that-s-okay.

Wit's Cabinet: A Companion for Gentlemen and Ladies. London: 1715

Woodman, James. *Bibliotheca Antiquaria & Politica*. London: 1723.

Woolley, Hannah. *The Ladies Delight: Or, A Rich Closet of Choice Experiments & Curiosities, Containing the Art of Preserving & Candying....* London: 1672.

Wootton, David. "Francis Bacon: Your Flexible Friend." In *World of the Favourite*, edited by J. H. Elliott and L. W. B. Brockliss, 184–204. New Haven, CT: Yale University Press, 1999.

The Works of the Earls of Rochester, Roscommon, Dorset, &c. In two volumes. Adorn'd with cuts. London: 1714.

Wright, Lawrence. *Clean and Decent: The Fascinating History of the Bathroom and the Water Closet*. New York: Penguin, 1960.

Wycherley, William. *The Country Wife*. In *The Broadview Anthology of Restoration and Early Eighteenth-Century Drama*, edited by J. Douglas Canfield, 1038–100. Peterborough, ON: Broadview Press, 2001.

Yeazel, Ruth. *Harems of the Mind: Passages of Western Art and Literature*. New Haven, CT: Yale University Press, 2000.

Zakarin, Mark. *The L Word*. Season 1, episode 8, "Listen Up." Directed by Kari Skogland. Aired March 7, 2004. Showtime.

Zimmerman, Everett. "Swift's Scatological Poetry: A Praise of Folly." *Modern Language Quarterly* 48, no. 2 (June 1987): 124–44. https://doi.org/10.1215/00267929-48-2-124.

INDEX

Note: Figures are indicated by italicized page numbers.

absolutism: court architecture and king's two bodies, 28–29; decline of, xii, 46, 71; and divine right of kings, 48; in the family, 62; and favoritism, 46–47, 48; and female agency, 70; philosophical rejection of, 34; secrecy under, 230n97; Whitehall as symbol of, 52. *See also* favoritism

Absolut Out campaign, 200, *201*

Acheson, Lady Anne, xii, 79–80, 103, 232n41, 235n99. *See also* "Panegyric on the Dean" (Swift)

Acheson, Lord Arthur, 79, 108–9

Addison, Joseph, *Spectator* no.138, 193; *Spectator* no.10, 177

Andreadis, Harriette, 58, 59

Anne (queen of England), 46, 52, 102, 226n3

anonymity: in author/reader relationships, xi, 40; of booksellers, 122; celebration of, 167; in libel against Pepys, 163; of printed texts, 101, 143; of readers, 123, 147; and social rank, 187; in stranger sociability, 174

Anspaugh, Kelly, 80

anthologies: textual closets and cabinets as, 121; changing frequency of use of term, 115. *See also* textual closets

the Ark, 16, 18, *18*

Astell, Mary, *Reflections on Marriage*, 62

Aubrey, John, 86–87

The audi filia (Doctour Auila, 1620), 127

Austen, Jane: on changing meanings of closet, 195; *Pride and Prejudice*, 195

author-reader relationship: patrons and, 102; shifts in, x–xi; and social difference, 40, 147; Sterne and, xii, 157–58, 159, 189; Swift and, 157–58; as virtual favoritism, xii, 58, 71, 73–74; and voyeurism, 67, 142. *See also* virtuality

authors: closets' appeal to, x–xi; relationships with nobility of, xii, 36, 59, 125–26; and support from subscriptions, 157, 240–41n14. *See also* patrons and patronage

authorship: and copyright, 35, 73; professionalization of, 35, 101

Bacon, Francis, 47, 48, 133, 230n93; *Novum Organum*, 130

Barlow, Frederic, 227n41

Baruh, Lemi, 114, 236n3

bathing closets: associations with courtliness, xi–xii; and cleanliness, 66, 229n80; compared to water closets, xiv; and favor, 61; improvements in, 65–66; and orientalism, 66–68, 70; and sexual subservience, 68, 70. See also *Memoirs of Count Grammont* (Hamilton)

Becker, Ron, 198

Behn, Aphra: "Golden Age," 94; *Oroonoko*, 68

Benedict, Barbara, 20, 25, 138, 139, 225n56, 236n5

Bentinck, Hans William (Earl of Portland), 46

Berkeley, Lord, 102

Berlant, Lauren, 155, 240n2

privies and water closets: chamber pots, 87, 95–96, 233n61; compared to bathing closets, xiv; and domestic service, 82–83, 87–88; first citation of water closet, 97; in house design, 82; men's and women's, 91; in monasteries and castles, 81–82; as parodies of country house architecture, 106; as prayer closets, xiv, 91–93, *92*; privacy in, 89, 91–92, 93, 97–98, 231n7, 233n58; privy intimacy, 82–83, 106–10; technological changes to, 83–86; terminology for, 82. *See also* earth closets; excretory practices; "Panegyric on the Dean" (Swift); privacy; water closets: use of term

Procopius, *Anecdota* or *Secret History*, 71

Prosser, Samuel, 83–86

The Queen-Like Closet (1670), 115

The Queens closet opened (1655), 124, 128, 237n27

queerness: Absolut Out's representation of, 200; broad definition of, 9, 221n2 (preface); and closeted/out binary, 197–200; identity and mass mediation of, xvi; and intimacy, ix; market appeal of, 198; as new normal, 192; precursors to, 49 (*see also* same-sex relationships); and queer liberation, 191, 196; queer pride and visibility, 202. *See also* coming out; heteronormativity; homophobia; same-sex relationships

Rambuss, Richard, 22, 49, 50

Rare Verities (1658), 136

reality television, 114, 143

Richardson, Samuel, 25, 74–75. *See also* *Clarissa*; *Pamela*

Robinson, David, 58, 59

Rochester (Earl of): "The Discovery" (falsely attributed to), 138, 238n60; in Hobart-Temple affair, 54, 55, 58, 64, 65, 70; "Tunbridge Wells," 163–64. *See also* Hobart-Temple affair

Rolleston, Samuel, *A Philosophical Dialogue Concerning Decency* (1751), 97–99, 233n61, 234n71, 235n98

Ross, Ian Campbell, 240–41n14

Roxolana scandal, 62–64, 145, 228n66, 229n68

Royal Society of London for Improving Natural Knowledge, 18, 26, 86, 120, 130, 160, 229n77

Rycault, Paul, 63–64, 66, 67

same-sex relationships: and bodily intimacy, 49; closets and, 193; and friendship, 47–48, 49; and male privilege, 59–60; as political relationships, 47–50, 59

sanitation, 81–82, 232n14. *See also* excretory practices

satire. *See* "Panegyric on the Dean" (Swift)

Savage, Dan, 202

Schakel, Peter, 103, 109

Schivelbusch, Wolfgang, 169–70

science and scientific knowledge: advancement of, 130–31; and closet collections, 14, 16, *17*, 118–19; and curiosity, 16, 18, 25, 119–21; and elitism, 131; emerging discourse of, 25–26, 130; and inventions, 86–87 (*see also* water closets); in textual closets and cabinets, 125–26, 127, *129*, 132–33. *See also* empiricism; Royal Society of London for Improving Natural Knowledge; Shapin, Simon

secretaries, 6, 29–30, 50, 72, 119, 227n19, 227n22, 237n18

secret history: *Anecdota*, 71; *The Cabinet Open'd* (1690), 123–24, 128; country house poetry compared to, 104; *Diary of Samuel Pepys* as, xv; genre of, xiii, 71–75, 230n99; *The New Atalantis*, xv, 68, 229n68; publication of, 118, 123–25; and rise of domestic novel, 74; *A Sentimental Journey* as, 187. *See also* *Memoirs of Count Grammont* (Hamilton); *Miss C——y's Cabinet of Curiosities*; Pepys, Samuel; *A Sentimental Journey*

sedan chairs, 161–62, 168

Sedgwick, Eve: *Epistemology of the Closet*, 59, 136–37, 187, 197, 198, 228n53; *Between Men*, 243n90

Sender, Katherine, 198

sentimentalism. *See* sympathy, nature and philosophy of

A Sentimental Journey (Sterne): coach intimacy in, 156; encounters with strangers in, 157, 158, 185–86; and sentimentalism, 158; and social inequities, 194; and Sterne's *Bramine's Journal*, 240n4; success of, 241n14; sympathy in, 186–87; writing of, 155; Yorick's learned privacy in, 175–76, 179, 181, 184; Yorick's motives for traveling in, 175–76, 184–85; Yorick's sexual desire in, 181, 183–84

Shapin, Simon, 131

Shevlin, Eleanor, 117